Roland Kumagai
10448 Vista Knoll Blvd
Cupertino, Cal
732-357X

Roland Kumagai
10448 Vista Knoll Blvd
Cupertino, Cal

Mastering The Art
Of Fly-tying

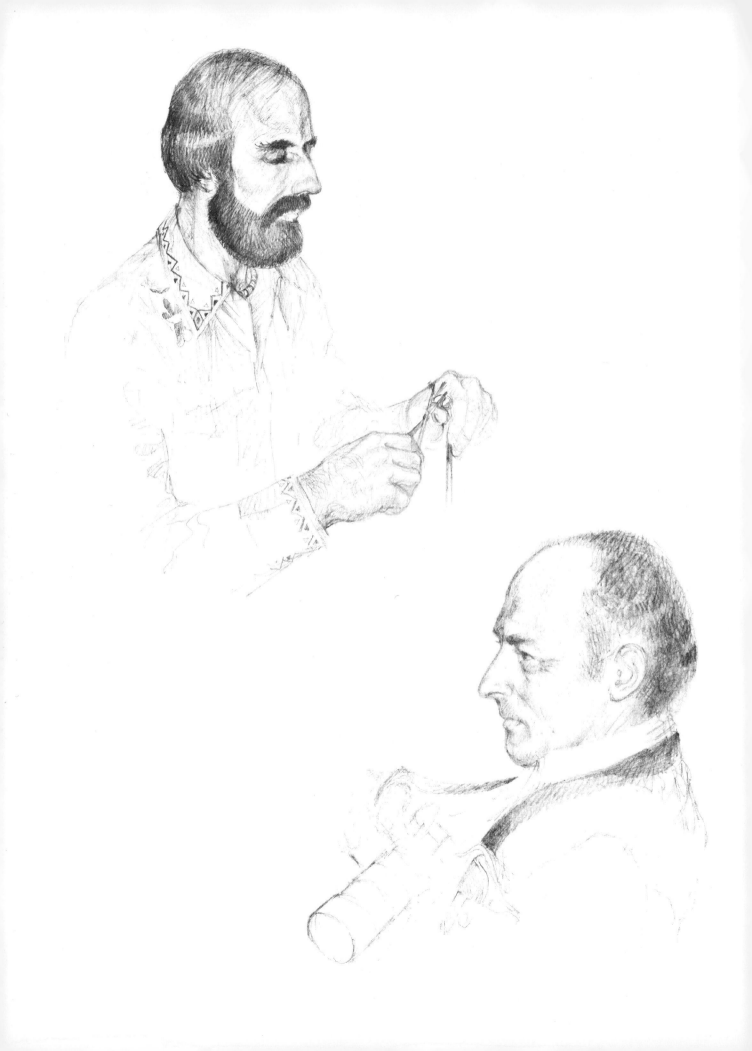

Mastering The Art Of Fly-tying

by

Richard W. Talleur

Photography by Matthew Vinciguerra

Drawings by Ernest W. Lussier

Stackpole Books

MASTERING THE ART OF FLY-TYING
Copyright © 1979 by Richard W. Talleur

Published by
STACKPOLE BOOKS
Cameron and Kelker Streets
P.O. Box 1831
Harrisburg, Pa. 17105

Published simultaneously in Don Mills, Ontario, Canada
by Thomas Nelson & Sons, Ltd.

Printed in the U.S.A.

Library of Congress Cataloging in Publication Data

Talleur, Richard W
   Mastering the art of fly-tying.

   Bibliography: p.
   Includes index.
   1. Fly tying. I. Title.
SH451.T29   1979   799.1′2   78-32041
ISBN 0-8117-0907-8

To the memory of

Howard Lemasurier

and

Ray Smith

Contents

Foreword

Dick Talleur has been a good friend for several years, and we first met at the meetings of the Theodore Gordon Flyfishers in New York. Our actual fishing was limited in those early years to laughter and good talk and theory, leavened with the catalyst of fine pot-still whisky. Perhaps the most surprising thing about Talleur, for those who know him only through his writings, is his irrepressible skill at free association and whimsy. The technical disciplines of the communications engineer are mixed with a healthy shot-glass dollop of fun and wild humor.

His readers perhaps know him best through his first book *Fly-Fishing for Trout,* which Talleur intended as a guide for adult beginners. It is clearly the best book of that type. Such books are often the most difficult to write, since they must assume no prior knowledge of fishing, no streamside experience or wisdom, and no understanding of fishing talk itself. *Fly-Fishing for Trout* did not talk down to its readers, while providing a solid foundation of tactics and fishing tackle and technique. Talleur also included an extensive analysis of flies in his *Fly-Fishing for Trout,* intended to help a beginning angler select flies in the tackle shops, and understand the fundamentals of matching the hatch.

His new book *Mastering the Art of Fly-Tying* evolved naturally from those beginnings, and from the steady flow of magazine pieces devoted to fly-dressing in journals like *Fly Fisherman.*

Talleur is a unique talent who understands that virtually all fishing writers (and it seems only honest to include myself) are guilty of writing only for a readership that already possesses considerable skill and knowledge. There are many techniques in fly-making, particularly in the simple manipulation of tools and working nylon and feathers, which are seldom discussed. Experts too often perform these basic techniques without thinking about them, and simply ignore discussing them in books.

This book is an obvious exception. Talleur has the ability to cope with the circuitry and signal systems and miracles of communications technology in his daily work, and such mental disciplines are translated into the detailed instructions of his books. *Mastering the Art of Fly-Tying* examines each step so thoroughly that no basic techniques have been ignored—everything is here for the beginner and intermediate tier, and many who believe themselves experts should study this book.

These pages provide several important contributions, including handling tools and basic skills, with an equilibrium of rich details and fresh insights. They translate these specific techniques into a full spectrum of major fly-patterns, and finally introduce a few original dressings and fresh concepts that Talleur believes will develop into whole families of easily tied patterns.

Talleur also introduces a few fishing friends in this book. His list includes people like Frank Mele, who combines the poetic skills of writing and chamber music and fishing from his home in the Catskills. Hoagy Carmichael and Matthew Vinciguerra are superb fly-tiers and rodmakers from the lower Hudson Valley. Art Flick is probably the most famous, and is widely known through his *Streamside Guide to Naturals and Their Imitations* as the

Dean of the Schoharie. Francis Betters is the wizard of the Ausable. Gardner Grant has served as president of both the Theodore Gordon Flyfishers and the Federation of Fly Fishermen, and is one of the regulars on the Beaverkill. Perhaps his closest fishing friend is Dudley Soper, the friend of the late Everett Garrison and poet laureate of the Battenkill.

We have never fished together on the eastern rivers we both know after so many years, rivers like the Ausable and Battenkill and Brodheads, but we both hope to change that in the future.

Our fishing has been confined to explorations in Wyoming, Idaho, and Montana. We have fished rivers like the winding Green in the October barrens of the Bridger Basin, and smaller rivers like the Gibbon, Firehole, and Madison in the Yellowstone. Other travels included a trip behind the Teton Range to sample the cut-throat fishing at Henry's Lake, and the remarkable fly-hatches on the Henry's Fork in Idaho. There was a beautiful autumn float-trip on the Snake at Jackson Hole, and if you ever get the chance to share a river with Talleur, you will discover his best skills—a wry perspective on life mixed with a rich ability to laugh and enjoy its equally rich currents.

ERNEST SCHWIEBERT

 # Acknowledgments

The author wishes to thank the following persons for their generous and significant contributions to his development as a fly-dresser: Del Bedinotti, Bill Dorato, Marv Goodfriend, Jim Hopkins, and Dud Soper. Howard Lemasurier and Ray Smith, two outstanding fly-dressers, were instrumental in getting me started and keeping me going through those difficult early days in my fly-dressing career; my debt to them is great. Invaluable technical assistance in evaluating hooks was given by Lee Thomas; thanks also to Buck Metz for input to and evaluation of the hackle section.

Special thanks for service above and beyond the call of duty in connection with the production of this book to Ernest W. Lussier, for outstanding artist's renditions; Dick Mrstik, for superb photo-processing, technical assistance, and a large measure of patience; and Matt Vinciguerra, for great photography and fly-dressing advice.

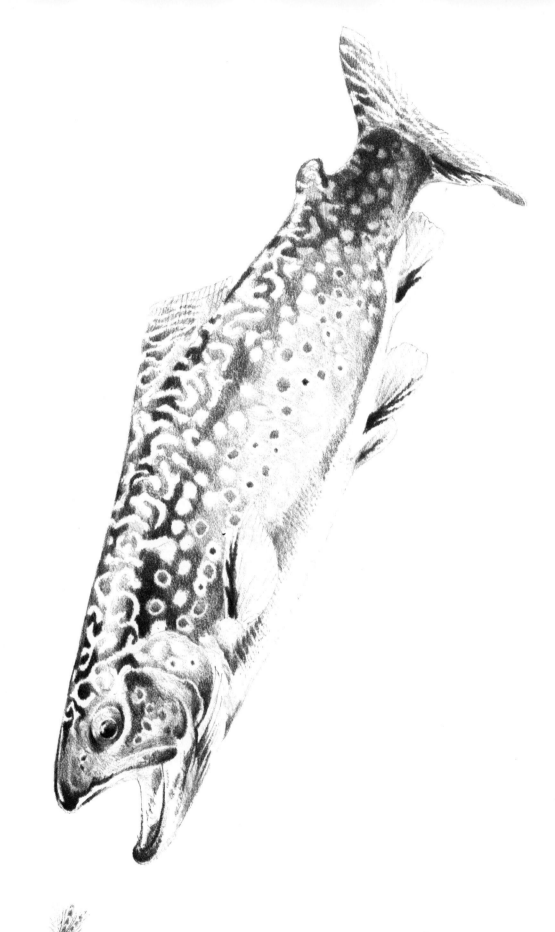

Brook Trout

Introduction

The purpose of this book is to solve fly-tying problems. Every time a hook goes into a vise, a particular set of problems is set up, the difficulty and complexity of which depend on what fly is about to be tied. A fly pattern is a miniature obstacle course which must be successfully negotiated if the desired result is to be obtained.

As if that were not challenge enough in itself, fly-fishers and tiers today face a new very serious problem: how to deal with the technology that has come to pervade angling. I'm not speaking of the dam builders, road builders, and polluters; that's another set of problems. I refer to the avalanche of technical information, new products, new fly patterns, and, of course, new books. No area of fly-fishing is excluded, least of all fly-tying, which has always been fraught with a great deal of esoteric and confusing information.

I am not against technology per se, in fact, I am most interested in new advances that can benefit the tier's art by making flies easier to tie and more effective. The trick is to be able to recognize a true improvement when it comes along and to actually be able to use it for your benefit. That requires sound technique, which is something apart from mere technology. In part it is the ability to evaluate fly-tying tools and materials from the point of view of practicality and cost. And it assumes the development of a broad set of manual skills and good tying habits, for while some advances make the beginning tier's life easier, others benefit only the highly skilled. Developing skills is also part of what this book is about. If there are two essential ingredients to mastering fly-tying today they are the ability to evaluate patterns, tools, and materials and the skills required to use them all.

The final answer to all of this is, I feel, entirely personal. I think that each angler and tier must decide how much technology he requires to optimize his enjoyment. Some of us care about Latin taxonomy and precise hatchmatching; others prefer to fish an Adams and be done with it. If you are getting what you want from your fishing and tying, don't let anyone intimidate you.

Of course, if you're looking to improve, that's another matter entirely—and one which does not necessarily imply adding more tools to your bench. There are virtually limitless opportunities to improve physical skills and eye-hand coordination. Not only is this in itself a hedge against technology, it often allows us to take advantage of legitimate advances when they occur. For example, a fly-tier who is really competent at handling dubbed body materials will have little difficulty working with new synthetics, some of which can be challenging.

Chapters 1 through 4 form the orientation section of the book. They provide specific information and criteria for making assessments in such areas as essential tools, hooks, capes, and hackles. Many vital, little-known facets of the art of fly-tying are covered here, such as scissors sharpening and adjustment, hook sharpening and debarbing, and essential thread-handling techniques.

Chapters 5 through 28 use fly-tying sequences to teach certain important skills which all fly-dressers use constantly. While all the flies are excellent fish-takers, the patterns were chosen primarily for their instructional value.

Each teaches at least one particular procedure or material-handling technique; some teach several. In many cases the tying sequence is followed by notes which further explore the peculiarities of the techniques and materials used in the exercise. Often there are alternatives and variations which are also important and worthy of consideration.

Some of the patterns, dressings, and techniques are actually new, having been created by myself or an angling acquaintance. The flies are realistic, yet simply constructed, and made of inexpensive, easily obtained materials. They catch fish like crazy. Examples are my Alternative, Dud Soper's Gangly-Legs, Bill Dorato's Dry Hare's Ear, and Francis Betters' Haystack. I hope you will very much enjoy dressing and fishing these rather unconventional patterns. You will also find some refined techniques for familiar patterns including a method for protecting the deer-hair collar of the Muddler and one for putting the hackle collar on the Grouse and Green.

The text and illustrations are quite detailed and extremely precise. I feel it can't be otherwise. It isn't easy to teach this sort of thing with words and still pictures, and the only way to do so effectively is to use plenty of illustrations and very circumspect terminology. Each step which is illustrated is marked in parenthetical form. Steps which carry no crossreferences are not illustrated.

I have been teaching fly-dressing to beginners and to advanced tiers for many years and have great confidence in my methods. However, I definitely want to avoid creating the impression that the methods I advocate are invariably the best or the only correct ones. I myself inherited a tendency toward inflexibility from my early instructors, and if Marv Goodfriend hadn't come into my life when he did, I might still be rolling dubbing on my leg and tying half-hitches all over the place.

Now let's dress a few flies and enjoy ourselves.

Assessing the Essential Tools

A basic fly-tying treatise might be expected to begin its discussion of tools with a series of pictures captioned "This is a vise" and "This is a bobbin." This will be dispensed with here, as this book assumes a modicum of orientation and competence with fly-tying instruments, materials, and procedures. The purpose of this chapter is rather to create a *functional* appreciation and a set of criteria which will assist the reader in evaluating the three vital tools we all use constantly: vise, hackle pliers, and scissors.

There is a tremendous variety of tools available today, much more so than when I began tying. Some are rather gimmicky; others suffer from deficiencies in design and quality. Many are well-conceived, well-made, and quite useful. Technology pervades fly-tying, for better or for worse, and it behooves all of us to ensure, as much as we can, that the impact is positive. To do this, we must evaluate the technological influence rather than let it manipulate us.

There is no way any book today can remain current even for a brief period if it relies on cataloging the various items a fly-tier can acquire; developments are coming far too thick and fast for that. My approach is to examine new items on a functional level—that is, how well the particular item does its intended task. The first question to ask is, "Does the existence of this tool make any real sense, or is it just another case of technological overkill?"

If a new item passes the "reasonableness" test, the next questions should be: Is it a problem-solving device? Is it a labor-saving device? Are the quality and technology acceptable? Are the benefits commensurate with the cost?

You may think of others. For me personally, the ultimate question is, "Do *I* really want to automate or mechanize this procedure?" For example, I still prefer to execute the whip finish with my fingers, which is not to imply that I have anything against whip-finishing tools.

On that note, let's get on with the specifics.

Vises

We are at long last beginning to see improvements in the field of fly-tying vise design. A great many makes and models are available today, ranging from not-so-hot to superb.

The primary task of the vise is, of course, to hold the hook with absolute security while the tier does his thing. Beyond that, certain fine attributes make a vise more or less desirable: ease of operation of the grip and release mechanism; ease of adjustment for various hook sizes; a jaw or chuck design which maximizes ease of access to the working section of the hook; and compatibility with various attachments, such as the materials clip and hackle guard.

For general purpose fly-tying the Thompson Model A is still a great favorite. It is a widely imitated vise, an indication that the Thompson people must have done something right when designing the Model A many years ago. For this reason, the Thompson will be used to demonstrate the workings of a typical fly-tiers' vise.

This vise operates on a basic lever-cam principle. A cam

Typical Thompson-Type Vise

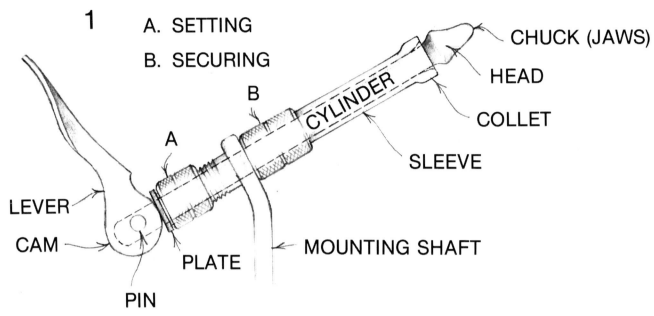

JAW WIDTH ADJUSTMENTS

1

A. SETTING

B. SECURING

CHUCK (JAWS)

HEAD

B

CYLINDER

COLLET

A

SLEEVE

LEVER

CAM

MOUNTING SHAFT

PLATE

PIN

Jaws Open, Side View

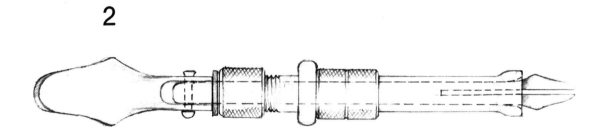

2

Jaws Open, Top View

3

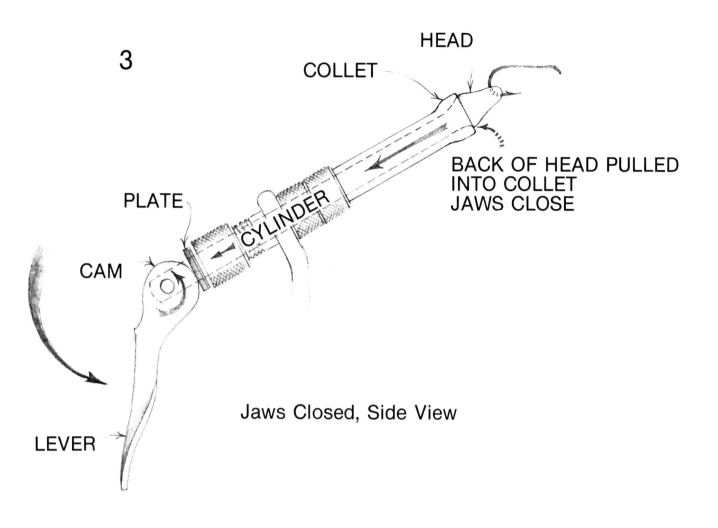

HEAD

COLLET

BACK OF HEAD PULLED
INTO COLLET
JAWS CLOSE

PLATE

CYLINDER

CAM

Jaws Closed, Side View

LEVER

4

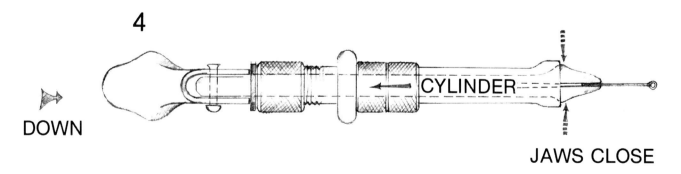

DOWN

CYLINDER

JAWS CLOSE

Jaws Closed, Top View

is simply an out-of-round or off-set disc or cylinder mounted on a spindle or axle. When rotated, the cam produces a reciprocating action in a part or parts of a mechanism which interact with it. In machinists' jargon, the type of cam employed here is known as a wiper cam or increasing-radius cam.

The illustrations show how the Thompson Model A vise operates. The machined steel cylinder which forms the head and chuck is inserted into the sleeve or collet, which screws into the vise mount. At the rear, the cylinder protrudes slightly from the sleeve. Here, the lever is affixed to the cylinder with a pin, on older models, with a nut and bolt.

The front of the lever is actually a cam. When the lever is pressed downward, cam action takes place which draws the tapered rear of the head into the collet. This causes the chuck, or jaws, to close.

The jaw setting can—and very definitely should—be adjusted to accommodate various hook diameters. Fully opened, the jaw gap of a Model A measures .050 inch (about 1 mm). Properly adjusted, the vise will accommodate a hook diameter of .050, which allows the tier to operate on some very substantial hooks. For instance, a Mustad #34007 saltwater hook in size 1/0 measures .050 on a micrometer. A Mustad #36890 black japanned salmon hook in size 1/0 mikes at .045, a Mustad #3665A streamer hook in size 2 mikes .040. These diameters may vary slightly from box to box.

On this particular model, the tier need have no qualms about mounting hooks having the same diameter as the maximum jaw gap. However, the vise *must* be properly adjusted, for if it is set a bit too tight, the pressure applied to the lever can spring or chip the jaws, a permanent impairment. Under no circumstances do I advocate the use of a hook diameter greater than the maximum jaw spread, even though one may be able to force the jaws apart and wedge in the hook.

The vise is correctly adjusted when it grips the hook securely with the lever in the positional range indicated in the illustration. Adjustment is accomplished primarily by turning the cylindrical mechanism immediately in front of the cam, which is thread-mounted into the top of the shaft, or stem. Then to secure the adjustment, tighten the sleeve, which is also threaded on the inside. Sometimes it is necessary to fine tune by repeating the adjust-and-secure procedure several times. When properly adjusted, the vise will grip the hook securely with the handle in approximately the eight o'clock position, as shown.

Like most vises, the Thompson Model A has two other adjustments. Height may be varied by loosening the set screw in the mounting base, sliding the shaft up or down, and retightening the screw. Selection of proper height is a matter of personal preference. I like mine set fairly high, to minimize the downward angle at which the fly is viewed, thus decreasing visual distortion.

The other adjustment is in the mounting base, and allows the vise to be affixed to tabletops of various thicknesses. Here, the Thompson could stand a little improvement. The maximum gap of the modified **C**-clamp which constitutes its mounting is 1½ inches (38 mm), minus about ¹/₁₆ inch for the felt protector. Consequently, the thickest tabletop which will accommodate the clamp is about 1⅜ inches (35 mm). In my travels, I have encountered many tables in excess of 1⅜ inches, and this can be extremely vexing.

I have used the Thompson Model A for illustrative purposes because it was the industry standard for so many years, and almost all tiers are conversant with it. This is not to say there aren't other good vises in the moderate price range. One I might mention is the Crest, which is operationally similar to the Thompson. It is a well-made tool, and a bargain at three or four dollars below the price of the Thompson.

New vises are coming onto the market at a truly remarkable rate. Some are redos of trusty old models, others are more innovative, sophisticated, and complex, offering extremely enticing features and designs. However, these advanced features would mean little if the vise didn't satisfy the basic evaluative criteria.

Most of these new vises carry price tags considerably higher than the Thompson and similar models. Of course, I would certainly want to try such an instrument before making an investment. This may often present a problem, because many of the new vises are sold primarily or exclusively by mail order, and are not readily available for inspection in retail stores.

The fly-fishing gatherings which are becoming so popular offer excellent opportunities for hands-on experience with vises and other new products. Trout Unlimited, the Theodore Gordon Flyfishers, and the Federation of Fly-Fishermen sponsor excellent events, as do many local and regional groups. If you are a member (shame on those who aren't), you will receive notifications of events in your area. If you aren't, contact someone who is, for very few of these functions are limited to members.

One of the new manufacturers—as a matter of fact, the one whose product I was most skeptical of—sold me on his vise in a most convincing manner. Bill Hunter of New Boston, New Hampshire, who produces the HMH vise, gave me a call, at the instigation of Dr. Fred Horvath, who puts out the excellent Andra Spectrum line of fly-body material. I told him I had only seen it in pictures, and while the tool looked impressive, I found it difficult to believe *any* vise could be worth the kind of money he was asking. He had only one comment: "I'm sending you an HMH. Try it and let me know your reaction." So try it I

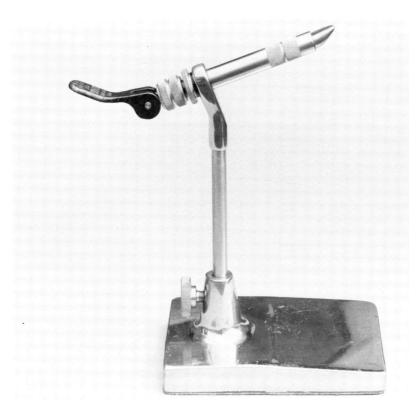

1-1 Assessing the essential tools: the HMH vise.

1-2 Three sets of jaws for the HMH.

did, and my reaction was to send him a check. What a tool! All components are superbly engineered, and the machine work is of a quality one would expect in a high-grade side-by-side shotgun.

The HMH is currently available with either a C-clamp mount or pedestal base, the latter being an added cost option. Three interchangeable heads are standard equipment, facilitating the use of hooks from size 32 to 6/0. Adjustments can be made extremely positively and smoothly; as a bonus, the instrument is devastatingly handsome. (photos 1-1, 1-2)

In summary, no matter what a vise costs, the criteria it should meet are essentially the same.

DESIGN POINTS

1. Simple, positive, convenient opening-and-closing mechanism.
2. Adequate mounting clamp or base.
3. Simple height adjustment.
4. Adequate jaw opening.
5. A jaw shape which allows the fingers uninhibited access to the entire working area of the hook.
6. Easy attachability or adaptation to any devices the tier intends to use, such as material clips, hackle guards, and gallows tools.
7. Stable adjustment of jaw spread.
8. Special features as desired, such as capability of inverting the jaws, interchangeable jaws, and auxiliary jaws for tiny hooks.
9. Adaptability and range of the table-mounting mechanism.

QUALITY POINTS

1. Jaws should meet precisely.
2. Jaws should be of sufficient temper to resist being sprung, yet not so hard as to be slippery.
3. Adjustment mechanism should be functional over entire range, as established by jaw design.

Special-purpose vises designed for extremely large or small hooks may, of course, be exempted from any criteria having to do with a wide range of adjustment.

Hackle Pliers

Without excellent pliers, winding hackle onto a fly becomes a frustrating task. When I started tying, pliers were generally poor, manufacturers' claims notwithstanding. For several years I struggled with pliers that slipped,

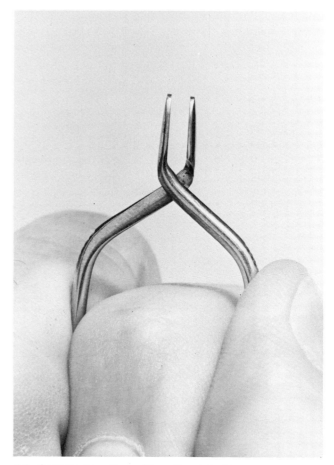

1-3 Open hackle pliers with well-matched jaws.

pliers that cut or crushed, and pliers that didn't fit my fingers. Fortunately, a number of well-made pliers are now available at modest cost.

Hackle pliers must be capable of holding a hackle securely enough to permit winding under moderate tension, yet not so tightly as to cut, crush, or break the delicate stem of the feather. Further, they should fit the tier's hands and fingers and should be compatible with his winding technique.

The gripping qualities are primarily a matter of the design of the jaws and the precision with which the two gripping surfaces match up. (photos 1-3, 1-4) Several gimmicks have been employed over the years to enhance the gripping qualities of hackle pliers. Notable among these are the addition of rubber pads to one or both of the jaws and the use of serrations on one or both of the gripping surfaces.

There is really no substitute for precision when it comes to hackle pliers, and hence, no need for embellishments, given a quality tool. I have no great problem with slight serrations of the jaws, provided they are *very* slight. Deep serrations can cut hackle stems. It is the manner in which the jaws meet, rather than the serrations, which governs how well the pliers hold. Rubber pads I have very low regard for. They add bulk and don't grip as well as precisely tooled metal jaws.

Spring pressure is also secondary to precision as a factor in gripping properties. In fact, too much pressure can be deleterious indeed. Hackle stems are, at best, not particularly tough, especially in the case of older capes, some of which have been off the bird since before World War II. The miniature hackles on size 22's and smaller are also very prone to breakage, and it is annoying to see these little beauties fall victim to excess pressure from hackle pliers.

The hackle pliers one encounters today are generally very good as to appropriate gripping pressure. The guidelines are:

1. The pliers should grip firmly enough to allow the application of a fair amount of tension, on the order of 75 percent of the breaking strength of a typical hackle. A feather should always break before the pliers slip off, otherwise, inferior gripping qualities are indicated.

2. The pliers should open with moderate finger pressure. If your hackle pliers are so difficult to open that you feel as though you're doing isometrics, they are too stiff.

Another matter deserving attention is the sharpness of the edges of the jaws. A slight rounding is preferable, for edges which are absolutely sharp can cut hackle stems. This varies somewhat among makes, and it is worth the time to inspect before purchasing.

Presently all commercially available hackle pliers worthy of serious consideration are quite similar in design. It is a matter of selecting the model which fits your fingers and suits your style best, and inspecting for precision. Although my hands are only average in size, I operate best with a good-sized tool with a large loop.

Scissors

Scissors are an extremely critical factor in the relative success of your fly-tying efforts. Poorly functioning scissors rank with insecure vises and slipping hackle pliers as the archenemies of efficient, effortless fly-tying.

Even the beginning tier definitely should have at least two pairs of scissors. One pair should be fairly substantial and capable of cutting tougher materials without suffering impairment. The other should be a high-quality, super-sharp instrument with delicate, precise points, to facilitate the intricate, near-surgical procedures required on fine dry

flies, nymphs, and midges. *They should be used solely for this type of work.* (photo 1-5)

The most important considerations when selecting a premier pair of scissors are the design, sharpness, and precision of the points and blades. Here are the criteria:

1. The points should come together perfectly, and should appear almost as a single piece of metal when viewed from any angle. (photos 1-6, 1-7)

2. The tips should be delicate and elongated, and should be very fine and free of bulk when viewed from the top. (photos 1-8, 1-9)

3. The cutting surfaces should meet perfectly and be extremely sharp. One should be able to snip a hair from a wrist with the tips of the blades.

4. There should be very little play at the axial point, where the screw joins the two limbs. The parts should be held together by a screw, rather than a pin or rivet which cannot be adjusted. (photo 1-10)

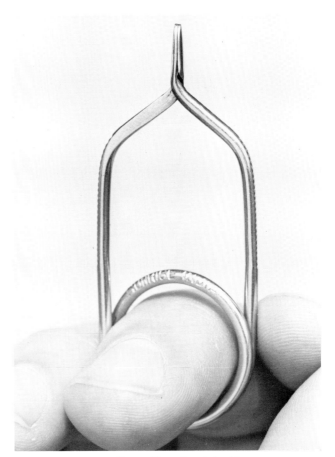

1-4 Closed hackle pliers with well-matched jaws.

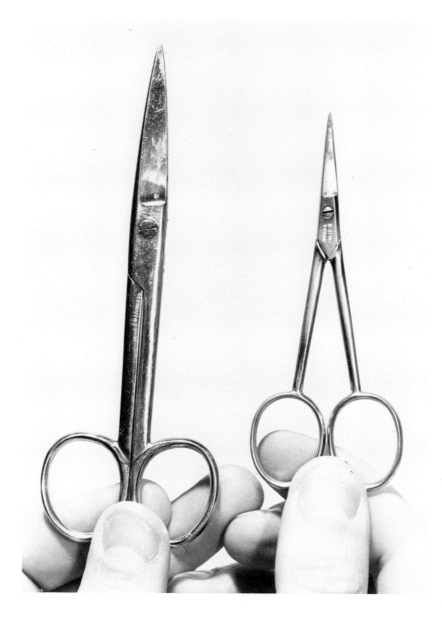

1-5 Typical scissors for heavy and fine work.

Ranking a close second in importance is the matter of a fit. This, of course, will vary with the physical characteristics of the tier, and also with his preferences.

1. The finger loops must fit properly, meaning they should accommodate the thumb and middle finger comfortably and without too much play. Most good fly-tiers hold their scissors with the thumb and middle finger, using the index finger for stability. If necessary, the loops may be cut and adjusted to the individual's fingers.

2. The scissors should be long enough to allow some clearance between the hand and the fly, mainly to allow the tier to see what he's doing. (photos 1-11–1-13)

A rugged, well-made pair of scissors will stay tight and sharp for a long while. Of course, a certain amount of durability must be sacrificed for delicacy in scissors used for fine work. Even so, there are models available today which are surprisingly tough, for all their refinement. These have been adapted from the medical profession, the field of optical surgery in particular.

Never compromise when purchasing scissors, particularly the high-precision pair. A truly excellent instrument presently costs well under ten dollars, and will last a great many years, given proper maintenance and avoidance of abuse.

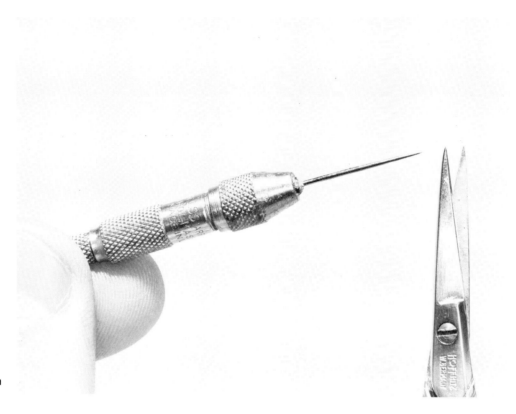

1·6 These points match
perfectly.

1·7 These points do not
match and will
cause trouble.

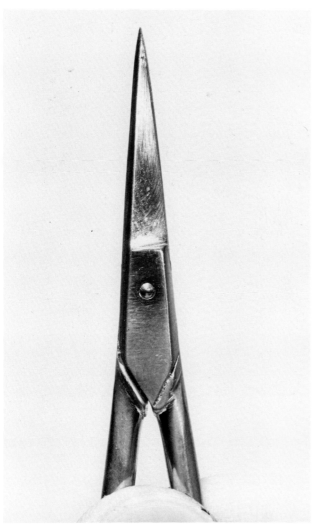

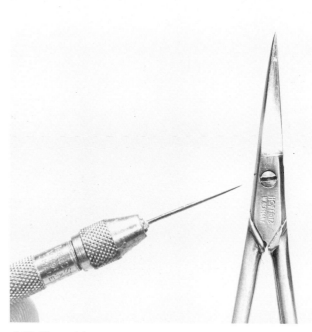

1-10 The axial screw.

1-8 Delicate tips free from bulk.

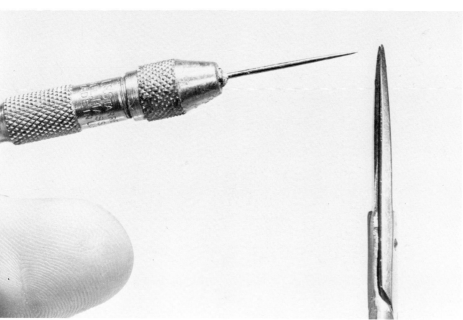

1-9 Delicate tips suited for intricate work.

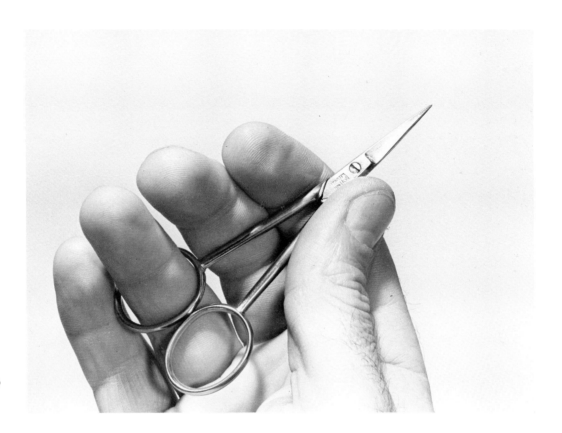

1-11 Good finger loop
fit and adequate
length.

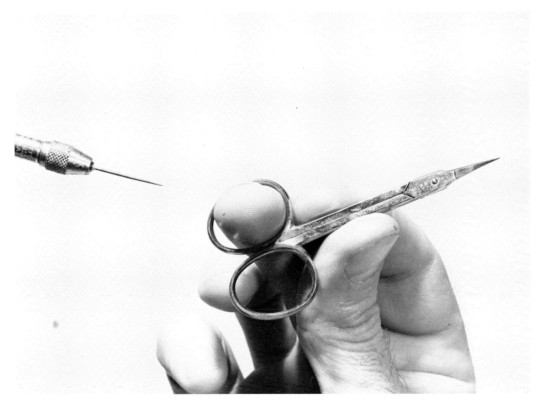

1-12 Poor finger loop fit,
possibly inade-
quate length.

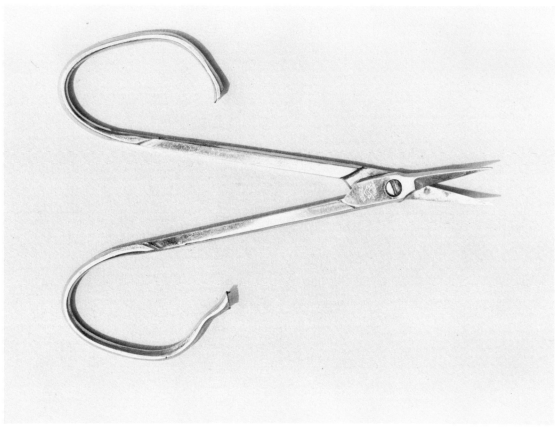

1-13 Loops cut and expanded to accommodate larger fingers.

SHARPENING SCISSORS

Even the best scissors will eventually become dull, however careful the user may be. It's not easy to find a commercial sharpening service capable of restoring small, high-precision scissors. It is best to learn this skill yourself. George Renner of the Beaverkill Sportsman has developed a simple, effective method for sharpening scissors which anyone can employ with very little practice.

1. Obtain a fine-grit stone of the highest quality, 6 to 8 inches in length and perfectly flat. Set it on the edge of a table.

2. Hold the scissors blades wide open. (photo 1-14)

3. Look directly down the blade from the tip and note the angle or bevel at which the blade is cut.

4. Place the blade on the stone with the bevel perfectly aligned with the stone's surface. Hold the blade in the attitude shown in the photograph. (photo 1-15)

5. Draw the blade along the stone in the direction indicated, maintaining a firm, even stroke. Pressure should be moderate, just heavy enough to permit the stone to do its work. *Make sure the blade and bevel are held in the proper attitude at all times.*

6. Check progress frequently. Do only the absolute minimum required to produce the desired results. Take your time.

7. Repeat with the other blade.

Selecting a proper stone is of the highest importance. Do not use an old stone which has been gouged by years of heavy use. A fine grit is required, but not so fine it won't cut. For example, an Arkansas stone wouldn't be appropriate, as this is an extremely fine, hard stone which is used for putting the finishing touches on blades.

Be absolutely certain the blade lies flat throughout the process, also that the integrity of the bevel is maintained. Do not allow the blade to rock, roll, or chatter. *Under no circumstances should you turn the blades on their sides and hone the flats.* The "feathers" which result from the sharpening process are immediately disposed of by working the scissors a few times with a normal cutting motion. This simulates the honing of a knifeblade against a sharpening steel.

Sharpening Scissors Blades

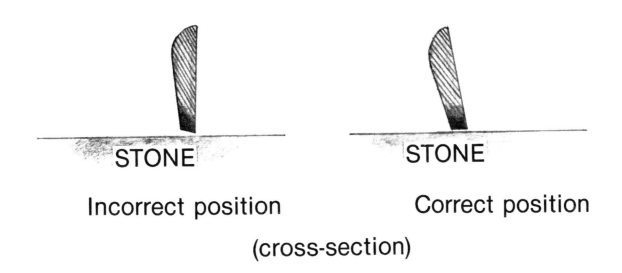

Incorrect position   Correct position

(cross-section)

Poorly Matched Scissors Points

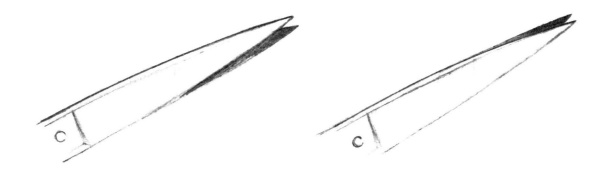

Points don't close entirely   Points over-close

1-14   Grip scissors thus when sharpening.

1-15   Attitude of blade on stone. Draw toward yourself.

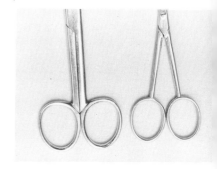

1-16   Scissors with tangent limbs and loops.

1-17   Honing loops to align points that do not close.

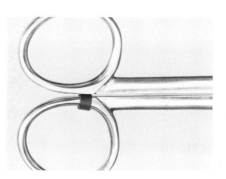

1-18   Supplementing loops to align points which overclose.

The stone may also be used to correct maladjusted points which do not close completely. There is more than one method, and the choice of which to apply may depend as much on the design of the scissors as on the amount of realignment the points require. Examine the two pairs of scissors in photograph 1-16. The limbs of the pair on the left lie against each other along their entire length, all the way from the axial screw to the loops. The points of these scissors can only be aligned by honing. However, the pair on the right is of different design; only the loops touch. So if the points don't quite close all the way, the finger loops may be reduced or flattened slightly with a stone at their point of tangency, which will correct the misalignment. (photo 1-17) I much prefer this method to honing the delicate points, however refined one's technique.

If the opposite situation exists—that is, the points overclose, like the beak of a scissor-billed bird—it is quite simple to supplement or build up the finger loops at the point of tangency. The result is exactly the opposite of that obtained from reducing the loops. A narrow strip of thin tape, such as plastic electrical tape, is ideal. Avoid using softer, thicker tapes, as a single layer may be too much, and the softness may cause the adjustment to vary with use. Incidentally, this technique will work on scissors with limbs which touch all the way down. (photo 1-18)

In some instances it is feasible to reduce the thickness of a pair of scissor points, making the instrument more suitable for fine work. One cannot use enough caution here. A slight error in judgment or execution can cause the quick ruin of an expensive tool. It is reasonable to assume the manufacturer had something in mind when he built the scissors, and quite possibly an alteration of this type won't be tolerated.

The most important factor to consider is the quality of the metal. Making this determination is generally not a simple matter; price alone certainly isn't a fool-proof indicator. The most dependable method is to take a practice stroke or two under minimal pressure and observe how readily the stone cuts the metal. If softness is apparent, leave that particular pair of scissors as is, because the thinned-down points will bend, even if used with discretion.

Hackle

The purpose of this chapter is to orient the reader in the evaluation of hackle for both wet and dry flies. Particular emphasis will be placed on the latter, since these feathers are expensive and the most difficult to assess.

Dry-Fly Hackle

Let me open this topic with a statement that may raise some eyebrows, though it's the truth: there is much more premier-grade dry fly hackle available today than there was ten years ago. All you have to do is pay for it! Of the many factors that have influenced the hackle boom, the prime one is economics. There now exists a fairly large, lucrative market for fly-tying materials, and in our culture, when a demand for something develops and profit potential exists, the supply is usually not far behind.

I am partial to superior-grade capes, and know very few tiers who aren't. In some cases, however, great flies can be tied from quite reasonably priced hackle at significant savings. Given basic adequacy of quality, the next two most important criteria in judging a cape are the color and the amount of hackle in desired sizes. I will frequently buy a cape which has great color but is so-so in other respects, provided the intended application will tolerate such a compromise. I also buy high-quality capes of poor coloration, because today's techniques for dyeing feathers —especially the photo-dyeing process for dun—enable one to take a poorly shaded cape with good-quality hackle

and transform it into a valued treasure. So, one can win both ways.

It is important to know how to recognize superior hackle, both to capture the occasional bargain and to avoid just plain being ripped off. While the cost of premium-quality hackle is usually justified, it is not always necessary to drain the bank account in order to obtain satisfactory material. What's essential is to be able to assess the price/value ratio, *keeping in mind the hackle's intended use.*

The first thing which attracts one to a cape is its eye appeal, but one must look deeper for true quality and value. One of the biggest problems in buying capes today is that so often the scene is a room crowded with hackle-junkies who at the very least are peering over one's shoulder, ready to snap up any good-looking cape which isn't purchased immediately.

Let us first examine the quality of a single hackle feather. Then we can proceed to the more practical aspects of cape selection. Forget color for the moment, just consider quality. Here's what to look for, not necessarily in the order listed:

1. *Aliveness, springiness, or vibrancy of the feather.* This is usually, but not always, accompanied by a nice sheen. It refers to the overall stiffness and springiness of the stem and barbules. It may be tested merely by flexing the feather and observing the response. Look for a feather that reassumes its normal position in quick sprightly fashion, with low damping action of the center quill. A

2-1 Hackle: feather on left has minimal
web and extensive useful portion.
Feather on right has excessive web
and is poorly shaped toward the
bottom. Only the tip is suitable for
dry fly work.

word of caution: hackles with overly thick or heavy centered quills usually exhibit aliveness, but tend to have
undesirable winding qualities.

2. *Hackle density, the number and closeness of barbules on the usable portion of the feather, from the tip to
where the softness starts.* This important consideration is
often overlooked. It is easy to judge; the denser and closer
the barbules, the fewer turns needed to hackle a fly. This
reduces the amount of center quill which must be wound
around the hook, making a neater, less cluttered winding
job. Also—and this relates closely with points 3, 4, and
5—high barbule density reduces the requirements for
feather length and continuity of shape.

3. *Length of usable portion of the feather.* This refers to
how far down the center quill the barbules remain of ade-

quate quality to hackle a dry fly. (photo 2-1)

4. *Trueness to size.* This simply means: does the hackle
which appears to be a size 14 when in repose actually turn
out to be a size 10 when flexed into the winding position?
Very small hackles are particularly deceptive. A further
point of quality is the consistency of this size throughout
the length of the feather. (photos 2-2–2-5)

5. *Feather shape, or the uniformity of barbule spread
throughout the usable length of the feather.* This relates
closely to point 4. A feather that is overly triangular or
wedge-shaped may have only a very short usable portion
near the tip in the size desired. (illus. 2-1)

6. *Fineness of the hackle stem.* An overly thick stem can
create winding problems.

7. *Relative lack of webbiness in the usable portion.* The

importance of web-free hackle for dry fly work is a very traditional consideration and somewhat overemphasized. True, one doesn't want a lot of webbiness here, but the presence of a moderate amount of web detracts little if at all from hackle quality, and is a secondary consideration. This is fortunate, for very few capes offer truly web-free hackles. Photograph 2-1 shows relatively webby and web-free feathers.

8. *Straightness of barbules, or freedom from hooking.* Excessive curvature at the tips of the barbules is undesirable. (photo 2-6)

9. *Adaptability of the feather to winding.* It is not always easy to detect a feather which will twist, roll, and otherwise resist being wound around a hook shank. Sometimes one can tell by flexing a feather into the winding position and looking at it edgewise. A feather with good winding properties will appear straight and flat. One apt to roll or twist may show barbules which tend to hook sideways. In more pronounced cases, the feather will resist being flexed into the winding position, and the center quill will turn over onto its side. (photos 2-7, 2-8)

Points 2 through 5 become very important when selecting capes for purchase. If a typical feather from a cape scores highly in these categories, the tier may very well be able to hackle a fly with only one feather, instead of the traditional two. This doubles the value of the cape, as it is worth twice as much—in terms of quantity alone—as a cape which is similar in other respects but which requires the use of two feathers. Important benefits also accrue in the neatness and ease of hackling with one feather.

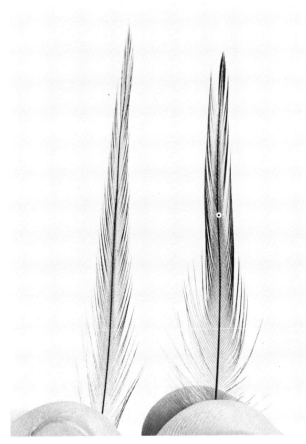

2-2 Unflexed, these feathers appear to be similar in size.

2-3 Flexed, the feather on the right manifests overly long barbules, and is at least one hook size larger.

Let's pretend you are in that rare and blissful situation where you have a great array of capes before you, of which you wish to select a half-dozen or so. You are alone, you have plenty of time, there is no pressure. How do you proceed? Here is my method:

1. Go through the entire batch and pick out the capes having the colors you are looking for, rejecting those which are so obviously of poor quality as not to justify consideration. Group the capes by color. If, during this process, you chance upon a cape of superior quality in a color you really aren't actively seeking, buy it anyway, especially if it is light enough to be eminently dyeable.

2-5 The short feather on the right appears to be suitable for a much smaller fly until flexed, when the barbule length proves to be the same as the larger feather.

2. Go through a color group and give each neck the squeeze test. Simply seize the cape as you would a sandwich and squeeze it gently a few times. You are looking for two things: thickness or bulk, which indicates a heavily feathered cape; and springiness, a first indicator of hackle quality. Capes with an unacceptable amount of webbiness tend to feel thick, so temper this test with other observations. Barred Rock capes can be particularly deceptive. (photo 2-9)

3. Carefully test the cape to see if the skin may be flexed without danger of breaking. If it passes, bend the cape so that the feathers in the prime hackle area—probably where the size 12–16 hackles are located—stick out from the skin. See if your visual observation of feather quantity agrees with the results of the squeeze test. Then, riffle the feathers with your fingers and observe the aliveness characteristics. (photo 2-10)

You will probably not be able to flex a dyed cape, photo-dyed excepted, because the heat of the dye bath usually renders the skin stiff and brittle. As an alternative, merely lift some hackles with the forefinger and do your testing in this manner. If you do break a cape, and value your relationship with the dealer, you should offer to buy it, whether you want the cape or not. A broken cape is devalued, even though its feathers are in no way impaired.

4. While you have the cape in the flexed position, evaluate the hackles, using the criteria described in points 2 through 5 for judging hackle quality.

2-4 Small hackles can be deceptive.

2-6 Excessive curvature or "hooking" of the barbules.

5. Consider what size flies you wish to tie from the cape, and determine whether or not these hackle sizes are present in good quantity. Be careful not to assume that because the feathers in the center of a cape are size 14's in a given area, the ones on either side will also be 14's in that area. When one examines the center of a cape, one is looking at the feathers from the back of the chicken's neck. Those on the edges are from the throat. These are usually of different configuration, running at least one size larger than the feathers located in the center.

At this point, you will have culled out of the various stacks those capes that you want to consider seriously. Proceed to test for points 6, 7, and 8 as previously described. After completing the entire procedure, you will probably have the selection narrowed down to some "definitely-will-buys" and perhaps a few "nice-but-can't decides." If you have time, run them through the entire process again and make your selections. Then pay your bill and leave promptly, before you start second-guessing yourself.

Of course, there are many subtleties and fine points in the evaluative process, and it is difficult to keep all of them in mind. This is especially true when pressed for time, an argument for leisurely feather-shopping. Remember that many of the criteria are relative, at least in part. For instance, diverse types and sizes of necks will vary in response to the squeeze test. You should keep in mind that a small cape with fine center quills won't have the bulk of a larger cape with thicker quills, yet it may have a generous amount of hackle.

There are several considerations having to do with color, over and above the basic visual observation. One should examine the backs of the feathers to see how closely the color matches that of the front. It will never be exactly the same, except on dyed capes, and some variance may occur even there. However, the shade should be reasonably true.

2-7 A good-quality hackle
feather winds with the
barbules straight and true.

2-8 A poorly formed feather
may tend to twist, roll, and
hook during the winding
process.

2-9 The squeeze test.

2-10 Don't bend a cape this much to test for aliveness, hackle quality and barbule length; the extreme is for illustrative purposes.

2-11 Unflexed, only the base looks white.

2-12 Discoloration of barbules is often not apparent until the feather is flexed.

The greatest disparity seems to occur in ginger and brown capes. Natural dun capes also frequently manifest this property.

Incidentally, it is always best to evaluate capes for color under natural daylight, particularly duns and dyed capes. When this is not possible, incandescent light is much preferred over fluorescent.

Sometimes, back-front shade disparity can work to one's advantage, particularly in the case of natural dun. Many capes that at first glance seem too dark come out significantly lighter when wound because of the lighter shade of the back side.

Often capes are not fully colored—that is, the feathers whiten towards the base. Don't discard such capes arbi-

trarily; they may be perfectly okay for tying. The important considerations are whether or not the whiteness extends into the usable portion of the feather and whether or not the ends of the barbules are whitened.

This latter point is a real sticky wicket, and can evade the notice of even a practiced eye. To the casual observer, a cape may appear to be white only at the base of the hackles. However, close scrutiny may reveal whiteness at the ends of the barbules well into the usable part of the feather. When examining a cape of this sort, be sure to closely examine individual feathers flexed into the winding position. You may even wish to use a magnifying glass or loupe. (photos 2-11, 2-12)

Another troublesome and misleading phenomenon is

the presence of pinfeathers, that is, feathers not yet fully grown out. When present in quantity, they can make a cape seem more desirable during the squeeze test than it actually is. The most apparent evidence of pinfeathers is usually around the rear perimeter of the cape, where the largest feathers are located. Most capes have some pinfeathers here but may have few or none in the "money" portion, where the desirable hackles are found. The presence of a few pinfeathers is of no consequence, but watch out for those capes which have them in quantity. (photo 2-13)

An easy way to determine the existence and location of pinfeathers on a properly dried cape is to look on the skin side for the presence of black dots showing through the skin. Each dot will have a true pinfeather on the reverse side. Feathers that are essentially mature but still have some chaff around them will not cause this dot. The chaff may be stripped away to reveal a fully mature feather, completely formed and suitable for tying.

Some capes have multiple uses which may enhance their value. Certain capes—particularly dun, badger, and grizzly—have a great many large feathers which make excellent wings for streamers and hackles for bass bugs, saltwater flies, and salmon flies. After the dry-fly portion of a cape has been used up, the remainder can be dyed for other applications, *providing* it is of dyeable color and not already dyed to begin with.

And then there is the matter of tail fibers for dry flies. The very finest-quality tails come from the shoulder or spade hackles, which are found around the edges of a cape. (photo 2-14) Not all capes have spade hackles. Often these valuable feathers are lost to unskilled or indiscriminate skinning. Also, many roosters are killed at too early an age, before the spade hackles have developed. Some birds simply don't have them. Spade hackles are also excellent for extralarge dry flies, such as Edward R. Hewitt's fabulous Neversink Skater, and the oversized patterns used for Atlantic salmon. The presence of good spade hackles is

2-13 Obvious and excessive pinfeathers.

considered by many as a point of quality in evaluating capes.

A word of caution: if one is fortunate enough to find good spade hackles on one edge of a cape, don't assume they are present in equal quantity on the other edge. Very often the distribution is uneven, and all of the spade hackles end up on one side.

As mentioned, many capes have no spade hackles. Fibers from large neck and saddle feathers may be substituted, if the barbules are sufficiently stiff and straight. A truly superb feather for tails is found on the "elbow" of a rooster's wing. I have never seen these listed in a catalog, however. Next best: spade hackles from saddles.

Special care should be exercised in evaluating capes which have been dyed, for the process can exact its toll. Today, most feather dealers understand the use of modern dyes and control the heat very carefully, so that the deleterious effect on the feathers is minimized. Now and then, however, capes are encountered which have been cooked at boiling or near-boiling temperatures. In addition to giving the skin of the cape the consistency of a potato chip, the excess heat causes a brittle center quill, a most undesirable property.

Eric Leiser, in his superb book *Fly Tying Material*, describes the use of glycerin to soften the skin of a dyed cape. Soak the cape in warm water until it softens, then rub in a little glycerin with the fingers. Let it set overnight, and the next day the cape will flex without breakage.

Eric's book is of great value to all fly-tiers, regardless of the stage of their fly-tying ability. There are sections dealing with the procurement, processing, storage, and dyeing of many types of fur, feathers, and other materials, plus

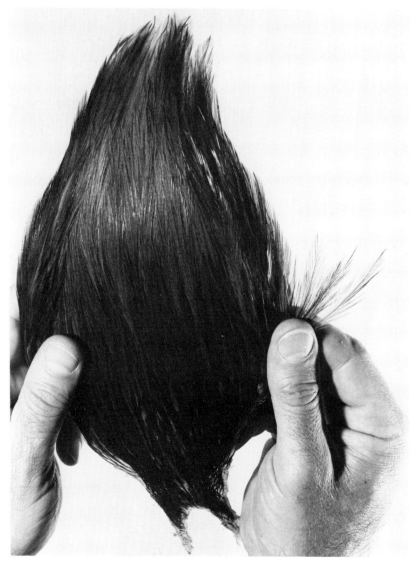

2-14 Location of spade hackles.

helpful tying hints. I recommend this volume without reservation.

A few comments on the feather-purchasing market, as it exists today: It is common knowledge that fly-fishing is now big business, which is a natural outgrowth of the immense and well-deserved popularity the sport has attained. To those who lament this popularity—and no one denies it is a mixed blessing—I can only say that if it hadn't gotten big, fly-fishing and, in fact, stream-fishing of any sort would no longer exist, except on a very limited basis in large state and national parks. The polluters, developers, dam builders, and channelizers would have annihilated virtually the entire resource.

The concommitant boom in fly-tying has had both good and bad effects on the supply of capes. Really great capes bring premium prices. Shades which were once relatively inexpensive—such as cream, ginger, and Barred Rock—are now on a price level with natural dun. If it weren't for photo-dyeing, I'd hate to guess what a top-quality dun might bring today. A hundred dollars, perhaps.

What must be kept in mind, however, is the fact that *at least we can get capes of this quality*. The reason, of course, is that it has become worthwhile to competent chicken-growers with a strong background in genetics to enter the fly-tying market. Just a few years ago, there was no Buck Metz, no Harry Hoffman, no Bill Tobin. It is extremely encouraging that such knowledgeable people are getting into the hackle-growing business.

In most respects the rises in cost are justified. The price of feed grain alone is enough to make one blanch. Pedigrees and the related genetic work and record-keeping are major costs. It is hardly a contrived shortage, for even with today's advanced methods, premier-quality capes cannot be mass-produced. I don't approve of market manipulation, but charging what the consumer is willing to pay is only good business. So when someone asks me if these beautiful domestic capes are worth the money, I answer with a qualified yes—if the individual capes score highly in the various categories, and the price-value comparisons are favorable.

The other major source of capes is the import trade, mainly from India, China, and the Philippines. These capes range widely in quality. Most of the capes don't run very large, although the Chinese birds are bigger than the others. It's good to see these capes back on the market again, after a long absence caused by the trade embargo with mainland China. This is a real shot in the arm for the feather dealers and the fly-tying public.

The major problem with the imports is the low incidence of excellent capes in critical shades. It looks like very little selective breeding or scientific methodology is applied to the raising of birds in the Orient. Colors are various shades of brown, with a lot of crosses and freak capes. Sometimes nice cream and light gingers come through, but about half of the capes are some shade of brown. A dun is a rare accident of nature.

Barred Rock is virtually unavailable in the import market. This breed was developed in America years ago as a dual-purpose bird for both meat and egg production, and is not common in the Orient. In this country, current economic pressures have resulted in specialized breeds for these purposes. Rhode Island Reds and New Hampshire Reds are also victims of this situation.

Although exports to the fly-tying market have grown significantly in importance overseas, feathers are still a by-product. There are a lot of hungry people in Asia, and the chickens are badly needed for food. Thus the birds are often killed too young, and it is infrequent that mature capes come through. In some areas, the birds still carry a pronounced strain of the Asian wild jungle fowl, which bolsters feather quality. Unfortunately, this strain is becoming more diluted as time goes on.

Incidentally, most birds are fully mature and prime for harvesting at nine to ten months of age. Contrary to popular belief, it is not necessary to keep roosters into their old age to optimize their hackle value. In fact, most birds are on the decline after their first year, especially if they've had a full complement of hens to service. As they grow older they eat more, are themselves edible only in fricasses and stews, and have plumage of declining quality. Also, the feathers of large old birds often have thick center quills, a detriment to neat hackling.

And so, the consumer of hackle is presented two alternatives: to opt for the higher priced but consistently superb domestic capes, or to paw through bales of relatively inexpensive imports, searching for the desired colors and quality. Assuming there is a practical limit to what one is willing and able to spend on capes, it pays to formulate a plan to optimize one's purchasing dollars.

While writing this chapter, I made an attempt to develop a ratio or formula which could be used to quantify various classes of capes on a feather-for-feather, dollar-for-dollar basis. What I wanted to do was compare, say, a very good Indian ginger to a very good domestic ginger so as to determine which was the better buy. Alas, the singularities and subtleties encountered in examining approximately a gross of domestic and imported capes representing virtually a complete span of price, quality, and size convinced me there is no slide-rule shortcut to cape selection.

If two capes are very similar in all respects, except that one has feathers long enough to supply the hackling of a fly with a single feather and the other does not, the first cape is worth twice as much as the second. That may sound elementary, but I am amazed at the number of experienced fly-tiers who don't seem to appreciate this fact, or fail to take it into consideration when selecting capes.

Even this simple axiom is subject to qualification, however. For one thing, just because single-feather hackling is possible with, let us say, the size 12's on a cape, don't assume the same is true of the 18's. Tiny hackles tend to be of markedly different configurations, especially those found around the edges of the neck area.

Years ago, George Leonard Herter put out a book on fly-tying and tackle-making. It is a fairly informative volume, despite the author's penchant for overstatement. In the chapter on hackles, there is a sketch of a cape, along with the number of hackles in each size one might expect to find. Mr. Herter mentions that these quantities will vary considerably, which is possibly the only understatement in the entire book.

Mr. Herter indicates there are from 500 to 700 feathers on a cock's cape. I did a rough count on some of my prime domestic capes and found this figure to be reasonably accurate. Some particularly well-feathered domestic capes have around 700 feathers, in a full range of hackle sizes. The distribution is approximately 100 of size 20–22, 100 of size 16–18, 150 of size 12–14, 100 of size 8–10, and the rest larger. These are exceptional capes, about as good as one might find anywhere.

The Indian capes are smaller and have a total feather count of 450 to 500. Although the neck portions of these capes are well-feathered, there are very few size 22 hackles, because the barbules are disproportionately long for the length of the center quill. On the best feathered of the Indian capes, the distribution is approximately 75 of size 20–22 with very few 22's, 75 of size 16–18, 100 of size 12–14, 75 of size 8–10, and the rest larger.

With the premier-quality domestics one can usually hackle a dry fly with one feather, but not so with the Indian. Comparing two capes of similar color—straw, let us say—I can tie approximately three times as many Light Cahills in sizes 12 to 18 with the domestic as with the Indian. The domestic cost $20.00, the Indian $6.00; so the cost-benefit ratios were a virtual tie in that regard, with perhaps a slight economic edge to the Indian, if all I was going to tie is Light Cahills in the more commonly used sizes. However, the generous quantity of very small hackles and the presence of spade hackles, which the Indian was lacking, swung the balance towards the domestic.

This is not to say that imported capes *never* have extra-small hackles, or are *never* of such quality as to enable one-feather hackling. Occasionally, such capes are encountered. They are very uncommon, however, at least from general sources of supply.

When sorting through runs of imported capes, one usually sees a great many crosses, variants, and exotics of various markings and colorations. Very often, these are the best-quality capes in the bunch. The fiery variant is perhaps the most common. This cape has barred Rock-type markings in light and dark ginger. Occasionally, one has mixed barrings of black or dark gray, ginger, and white or light gray. These are called multivariants, and are highly prized. One can tie a beautiful Adams from these hackles alone, with no mixing-in of grizzly.

I am very partial to variant-type capes, or in fact, any hackle which is mottled or other than a flat color. I feel that flies tied from multicolored hackles are very "fishy," and have enjoyed great success using them. Two of the best fishermen I know—Gardner Grant of Scarsdale, New York and Ed Van Put of Livingston Manor, New York—use the Adams in a wide range of sizes most of the time, and do very well indeed. Gardner is color-blind, and to him, *all* mayflies look like an Adams.

So one is well advised to look for bargains in the crossed-strain category. A good multivariant might help one avoid the purchase of a costly, hard-to-find barred Rock. Also, the more common crosses take photo-dye beautifully.

The true creams and straw-creams present a problem. I usually opt for the more costly domestic capes in these shades, for while they are imported in fair quantity, quality seems to be lacking. The capes are generally soft and often have overly long barbules. Use particular caution when selecting true cream capes, for the color is very seductive. Be sure to flex several feathers in the desired size range, as they may "grow" one or two sizes in the process.

Over the years there have been a number of attempts to lighten brown and dark ginger capes by bleaching, so as to produce the straw-creams and golden gingers for which a high demand exists. The process usually involved the use of beauty-parlor bleaches. After observing what these compounds did to capes I'm amazed there aren't more bald women in the world; I actually saw one cape reduced to nothing but stems!

Technology has apparently triumphed, however, for recently I was shown some bleached capes which survived the process in good condition. The shades were very attractive, and feather quality seemed to have suffered little if any impairment. Undoubtedly someone will publish the details eventually. Meanwhile, for those who might wish to experiment, I suggest the use of the cheapest feathers available.

By now, the reader may be wondering what happens to all of the capes no one wants. Actually, most capes which make it into the sales room or catalog of a reputable dealer will find a home with someone. A cape which didn't suit you, for one reason or another, may be just what the next guy is looking for. The tier of very small flies will turn up his nose at Chinese capes, which seldom have hackles smaller than size 16, while the lover of skaters and variants will take all of these capes he can get.

Another factor which aids the distribution of capes varying in quality is the grading system. Almost without exception, today's feather dealer is quite competent at grading capes into various price categories. Usually, several grades are offered, with most of the top suppliers listing capes as "prime," "select," and "wet." Prime capes are described as having stiffness of hackle, natural sheen, and a full range of hackle sizes. Select capes are described as being of excellent dry fly quality but either too small or limited in range of hackle sizes to be graded prime. Wet capes are described as being softer and appropriate for use on underwater flies. Price levels reflect quality.

Most dealers offer capes in assortments and selections of various descriptions. In the vast majority of cases, this is an honest attempt by the dealer to offer a bargain and coincidentally to sell capes in quantity and/or dispose of capes which are somewhat nonstandard in color or slightly off the mark in other respects. The purchaser can get some really good buys by purchasing assortments of five, six, or a dozen capes in a bunch. Occasionally he can also be ripped off, so be selective.

A recent offer in a major supplier's catalog read: "All of dry fly quality in natural colors only. Purchased individually, this selection would cost over $14.00. Natural colors of necks will be mixed, our selection only. Your price, $8.95." This attractive proposition offers a substantial discount in exchange for a volume purchase and acceptance of the dealer's color selection, not a bad deal at all, especially if one is looking for capes to photo-dye.

Now let us consider certain aspects of a very unique and coveted shade—or rather pattern—of hackle. I refer to Barred Rock, commonly called grizzly.

Time was when this was an easily obtained commodity. Several variations of the Plymouth Rock strain were raised in great quantity in the United States for eggs and meat, both of which these birds produce in superior quality and quantity. Several factors brought an end to this. A major one was the adaptability of the White Leghorn breed, which will tolerate and thrive in mass-production better than any other chicken. Another very important factor is the American consumer's demand for white-shelled eggs. I have raised many breeds of chickens, and for my money, the brown-shelled eggs from the Rocks were the best. Most Americans, however, simply won't buy them in the market. Today, barred Rocks are almost exclusively show birds, except for those raised for the fly-tying market.

Grizzly capes are once again available in fair quantity, and in qualities ranging from awful to fantastic. Price is the problem. Even mediocre grizzlies aren't cheap, and really superb ones run to thirty dollars and over. Very nice capes used to cost only three to six dollars in the early 1960s. A generation earlier paid a dollar or two.

Fortunately, there are several factors which tend to ameliorate the grizzly situation. The capes tend to be large and well-feathered, so one gets a lot of hackle for the money. Grizzly is seldom used alone, but is usually mixed with brown, ginger, or dun. The quality lent by these stiffer feather allows one to compromise on the barred Rock. This is fortunate, as Rocks tend to run soft. Also because of mixing, one can trim a Rock hackle and still tie a totally beautiful fly.

Because of their unique markings, grizzly capes are subject to several additional criteria. Distinct, finely barred markings produce a nice mottling when wound. Also, the tips of larger feathers with fine barrings can be used for hackle-tip wings, even on rather small flies. This extends the use of the cape. (photos 2-15, 2-16)

Some grizzly capes are so darkly marked that the black barring dominates the white. Flies tied with such hackle tend to have poor contrast and coloration. The lighter shades of grizzly mix nicely with cream and ginger in such patterns as the Gray Fox Variant. Also, they respond well to tint and dyeing, when special shades are wanted. Recently, I photo-dyed one of Henry Hoffman's miniature supergrizzlies, in order to create dun hackles in very small sizes. It came out beautifully.

As an additional ray of light, Buck Metz informs me that a natural grizzly-dun is now available from his hatchery in limited quantities. (photo 2-17)

Trimming is a controversial method for creating hackle in smaller sizes, thus getting more mileage out of capes. (photo 2-18) Opinions on trimming run the gamut. Some claim a trimmed hackle is actually superior to a natural one, primarily because the ends of the barbules are not as pointed and therefore float the fly better. Be that as it may, one thing I can tell you is that aesthetic appearance definitely suffers. Also, a feather which is to be trimmed must be quite web-free. Otherwise, you'll have little remaining after the trim job except soft web.

I have, for various reasons, trimmed hackles, but not drastically. I will do it to obtain a size I'm short of or to extend the use of a superior cape. I may also trim to correct the shape of overly triangular hackles, so as to effect continuity in size throughout the usable length of the feather. Usually, all I do is clip off the very ends of the barbules, reducing the spread no more than one hook size. This holds the adverse visual effect to tolerable proportions. (photo 2-19)

Since the procedure can extend the usability of hackles which are excellent in all respects except length of barbules, I advocate trimming, when skillfully and discretely done. Here are several suggestions which should prove helpful:

1. Spread the barbules so they stick out at a right angle from the center quill. Do not attempt to trim a feather with the barbules in the natural attitude.

2. Use very sharp scissors or a razor blade on cardboard.

2-15 Top: closely barred grizzly hackle feather.
Bottom: widely barred grizzly hackle feather.

3. Make sure the barbules on each side are trimmed to the same length from the center quill.

4. Make your cuts straight and parallel to the center quill.

No treatment of dry-fly hackle would be complete without some comments on saddle hackle. Saddle feathers vary tremendously in adaptability to fly-tying, and can be very deceptive. Expensive saddles can look super but be extremely difficult to work with and next to impossible to tie neat hackles out of. Saddles can cost next to nothing and produce beautiful hackles, but they are rare indeed.

Saddle hackles are evaluated by the same criteria as cape hackles. They are usually unsatisfactory in the following respects:

1. Trueness to size. Saddle hackles look very long, slender, and enticing in repose. When flexed into the winding position, they "grow" tremendously. (photos 2-20–23)

2. Consistency of size throughout usable portion of hackle.

3. Windability. Saddles tend to flare and spread, rather than wind into a neat, compact hackle.

4. Straightness of barbules. Saddles exhibit a marked tendency towards curvature of the barbules.

2-16 Markedly different effects when close- and wide-barred feathers are flexed into the winding position.

2-17 Top: Hoffman miniature supergrizzly.
    Bottom: large Metz grizzly. Both are superb when used for appropriate applications.

There are other undesirable traits which seem to occur more in saddles than capes. Front and back color differences are often great. Center quills can be brittle and weak. Web frequently runs to the very tip of the feather, and is not easily perceived.

On the positive side, top-quality saddles are generally quite satisfactory for very large dry flies in the size 4 to 10 category. They are particularly good for huge, densely packed dry flies used in night fishing, where five or six hackles are wound bivisible-style onto a hook. Neatness is hardly a factor here. Also—and this is possibly the highest use to which a saddle hackle can be put—the barbules, if reasonably straight, make excellent tailing material for dry flies which is not readily come by.

Money can be saved through the judicious purchase and use of saddle hackles, but caution is advised. Saddle feathers are usually sold either strung or on a saddle patch.

One gets a lot more feathers for the money with strung hackle, but certain problems are presented. Often it is bothersome and time-consuming to match up sizes. Also, many poor-quality feathers are frequently found among the good ones on a string.

Usually strung saddle feathers run very large, and if you want the smaller ones, it is necessary to buy saddle patches. Avoid being overly hasty and emotional when selecting saddle patches. The most common problem, especially for the uninitiated, is that saddle patches are often extremely beautiful in appearance, when actually there aren't that many usable feathers on them. One quick count on a very good Indian saddle patch revealed approximately eighty usable feathers in sizes 8, 10, and 12. On an Indian cape of comparable quality one would expect to find at least the same number of hackles in that size range, plus perhaps a couple of hundred smaller hackles, a hundred larger

2-18 Trimming a hackle.

2-19 Before and after trimming.

2-20 Typically, saddle hackles appear slender and short-barbuled in repose.

2-21 Tremendous growth of saddle hackle when flexed.

2-22 A prime Henry Hoffman saddle hackle.

2-23 The short barbules and beautiful contrasting markings of this Hoffman saddle hackle are also present in the flexed position.

feathers, and with luck, a few spades. So if the saddle patch cost $3.00 and the cape $6.00, the cape would be a far better value.

Incidentally, neck hackles are sometimes offered strung or in bulk, ostensibly at great savings. Be advised that much tedious work is involved in sorting these hackles for size, particularly with bulk-packaged feathers. Often, one will encounter considerable disparity in color and quality, with a high percentage of waste. I much prefer to buy my neck hackles on the cape.

Wet-Fly Hackle

An entirely different set of criteria apply to "hackle" materials used on sinking flies. In the case of the conventional dry fly, hackle is the major contributor to flotation, but in this case we want the fly to sink, or at least to ride low in the surface film. Also, we are not concerned with the wing silhouette, which dry-fly hackle represents, at least in part. On wet flies and nymphs the hackle suggests an insect's legs, and should be true in size, color, and form.

Tiers of the old school often wind their wet fly hackles in a manner similar to the dry-fly method, except that the hackle is folded so that it lies back around the body. This technique calls for a soft rooster hackle feather. If one is selective, beautiful folded hackles can also be made from hen capes. Most of the contemporary tiers employ other methods, such as simple bearding, that is, the tying-on of soft materials at the throat and sides of the fly. I favor bearding in most instances, except when tying the very beautiful and strictly traditional speckled trout and salmon fly patterns, which often call for folded hackle tied palmer-style, or as ribbing.

At this juncture it should be mentioned that the classic salmon flies of the British Isles have their own set of criteria as regards hackle. One of the most noteworthy is the shape of the feather. A gradual taper, or elongated wedge, shape is a positive attribute because it suits the design of these flies. This refers, of course to the ribbing or palmered hackle, which is tied in by the tip and should become a bit longer with each progressive wind.

For folded-and-wound hackle, a feather which is similar in shape to, but much softer than, a dry-fly hackle is called for. The problem is that most hackle feathers that have a nice, elongated shape are also fairly stiff. The softer, webbier capes generally produce feathers with very long barbules. When such feathers are folded and wound, the hackle is out of proportion to the rest of the fly. And when one attempts to compensate for this by going further towards the front of the cape for a smaller feather, one is liable to find it of insufficient length to do the job. Nowhere is this more apparent than in the case of hackle-wound palmer over the body.

If great difficulty is encountered finding capes for folded-and-wound hackling, try saddles. Some saddles have narrow, elongated, but rather soft feathers. These are ideal, especially for palmered hackle. Such feathers in pure white are a find, as they can be dyed to produce the bright hues called for in many salmon and speckled trout patterns.

The use of bearded hackle and its variations opens up a vast array of possibilities, for there are many soft, fibrous feathers which are ideally suited to this method. Probably the most common is hen hackle. Hen capes used to be a throwaway item, but those days are gone forever. Now they are available, at a price, from most feather dealers. Buck Metz feels they are vastly superior to cock capes for wet fly work, and I thoroughly agree, given good quality.

When selecting hen capes for bearded hackle, look for maximum softness, webbiness, and barbule density. Some hen hackle is composed almost entirely of web, which is desirable because such hackle produces a realistic simulation of an insect's legs. An additional, very important benefit is that the soft fibers tend to be active and life-suggesting in the water.

While the criteria for judging hen capes are not as stringent and sophisticated as with rooster capes, some important ones do exist. A good hen cape does not simply look like a poor cock cape, with soft, scraggly barbules. Hen feathers of that type do not produce good-looking wet-fly hackles.

When evaluating capes to be used strictly for bearded hackle, with no extra value assigned for other uses, apply three judgments, aside from color: quantity of large feathers on the cape; thick, webby texture, the more so, the better; price.

Item one may require some clarification. For wet-fly hackle, the tier wants larger feathers, because the barbules must be long enough to manipulate and also because he will get more than one bearded hackle per feather, thereby enhancing the value of the cape.

In recent years hen feathers have become popular for making hackle-tip wings on dry flies. This has driven up the price of hen capes having popular wing colorations, dun in particular. Time was when a chicken-grower raising dun birds for the fly-tying market was delighted to dispose of hen capes for fifty cents to a dollar. Last spring a dun hen cape was offered to me by the grower for seven dollars. It was a lovely cape, indeed—but seven dollars for a hen! I changed the subject.

The main consideration in the selection of hen feathers for wings is similar to but somewhat more critical than for hackle. Look for a feather that is virtually all web, and that is shaped like a wing. The feathers on certain capes are shaped so well they require little or no trimming, which is ideal. (photos 2-24, 2-25)

Quality natural dun hen capes are getting especially expensive and difficult to obtain. Plenty of white capes are available, however, and these may be dyed to the desired shades of gray. Hen capes take the regular hot dyes very well, making it a simple task to produce nice shades of dun. They also respond well to photo-dyeing, and can be run through with a batch of cock necks. Good as today's dye jobs are, however, the shade and quality of the natural are unmatched.

Hen cape feathers are only one of a great many materials suitable for hackle on underwater flies. Practically any feather having soft, webby fibers may be used with good effect. (photo 2-26) The more common ones are grouse

2-24 Left: hen hackle with poor attributes for cut wings. Right: hen hackle ideally suited for cut wings.

(partridge) neck and body feathers; hen pheasant neck and body feathers; chicken body feathers, both cock and hen; guinea fowl; turkey body feathers; duck flank and body feathers; and goose and swan body feathers. There are many others, so let your eyes be your guide.

As previously mentioned, some wet-fly hackles are wrapped in dry-fly fashion, either folded or as-is, while some are applied in one or another variation of the bearding method. Many types of feathers do not readily lend themselves to being wound onto the hook, notably grouse feathers, which are terrific in all other respects. There is a method for simulating wrapped wet-fly hackle with a bearding technique which distributes the barbules around the hook. This will be demonstrated in the chapter on thread-handling techniques and applied in the hands-on section.

The application of hackle to nymph patterns has opened up a vast area for innovation. Nymphs are being hackled with nearly every conceivable material and method, including fur. The object is to represent the legs of an aquatic insect in its larval stage, and the methods for doing this are many and diverse. It's a case of doing whatever works; so experiment to your heart's content.

2-25 Cut wing usually follows the web line quite closely.

2-26 Assorted wet fly hackle feathers, from left: tipped wood duck with unmarked side, hen pheasant body feather, hen chicken, grouse, mallard flank.

Hooks

To the dresser of flies, a hook is far more than simply a connection between man and fish; it is the canvas on which his masterpieces are composed. As such, it is critical, both in the tying of the fly and subsequent use astream.

A fair variety of hooks is available today, many of which are designed expressly for fly-tying and fly-fishing. Some are quite specialized, such as the Keelfly, the Flybody, the elongated streamer hook, and the hump-shanked bass bug hook. We will surely see more innovations as the angling explosion creates a profitable market.

Evaluating Hooks

If I were to seek my fortune in the fly-hook-making business, my first effort would be to try to find out how the superb British hooks of years past were made, and if at all feasible, set up a manufacturing facility to produce a faithful replica. In my opinion, the hooks turned out by the craftsmen of Redditch in the first half of this century have no equal, either before or since. I say this with all due respect to O. Mustad and Sons, the Norwegian firm which has managed to produce a wide range of fine-quality hooks without raising prices any more than necessitated by inflation.

The classic hooks with which I am most familiar are those which were sold under the Ray Bergman label up until approximately 1962. Just prior to the closing of Mr. Bergman's Nyack, New York, shop I was introduced to the Gold Label dry-fly hook by newfound friend Dud Soper, a connoisseur of such items. I called Mr. Bergman, who explained that the hooks were no longer available from his source in England. He had a small stock from which he very generously sold me 8 boxes of 100 in a variety of sizes.

Beautiful as the Gold Labels were, my all-time favorite dry-fly hook is the Sinfalta brand, also marketed by Mr. Bergman. These hooks came in a red package, and were available in both turned-up-eye and turned-down-eye styles. They featured a forged shank and bend, a true model-perfect shape, a small delicate barb with no longer a point than necessary, and a beautifully tapered eye. Though of slightly finer wire, the strength was about the same as a Mustad 94840. They might have been sharper, but that can be said of most hooks, and sharpening is a simple procedure.

And so the Sinfalta remains my personal standard as regards dry-fly hook design, which is like harboring a fondness for the passenger pigeon. Why these hooks aren't in production today I can't fathom, as I am certain they would be very big sellers.

All types of hooks have design characteristics which make them more or less desirable. In my opinion, selection of dry-fly hooks is the most critical, for several reasons:

1. They come in an extremely wide range of sizes, from number 4 down to number 28 (the eyeless size 32 hooks are outside the limits of practicality).

2. They must be sufficiently light to float well, often with very scant dressing; yet they must be strong enough to withstand sometimes heavy strain.

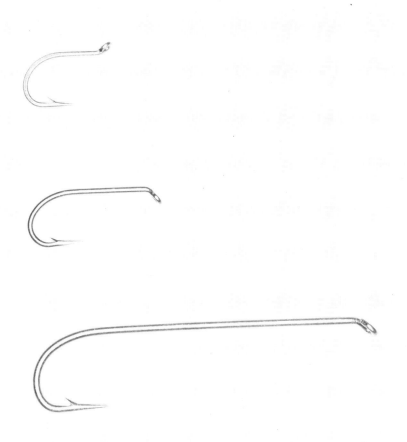

3-1 Hooks: top to bottom: 5X short, regular shank, 6X long.

3. The point and barb must be designed for effective penetration, often with negligible setting pressure.

4. The eye must be sufficiently well made to minimize problems with thread when tying and not to chafe or abrade a leader tippet in the course of a prolonged battle.

5. The barb must not be sliced so deep as to cause a critical weakness in that area.

T. E. Pryce-Tannatt, in his classic *How to Dress Salmon Flies,* brings out some very interesting considerations on hooking and penetration properties, which I suspect were a problem with the large, black-japanned models he employed. They concern the "angle of impact," the angle at which the hook point encounters the fish's jaw, the latter being thought of as a flat plane. Even allowing for the fact that a fish's mouth is *not* a flat plane, there is great validity in the doctor's premise that "problems of engagement" are minimized when the angle of impact falls between twenty degrees and forty-five degrees. This would place the regular-shank hook in the heart of the ambient range, with the extremely short and long hooks falling into questionable areas. (photos 3-1, 3-2) I have always experienced a degree of difficulty in effectively hooking fish on streamers and spiders, and am certain much of it is due to the angle of impact problem. This causes me to wonder what sort of hook Edward R. Hewitt used on his spider-type flies, he having been a technician of high caliber.

In light of this information, one becomes much more critical of hooks, for even in this enlightened "be-nice-to-the-fish" era, the object is to consummate the drama by establishing an indisputably positive connection. If one opts to go barbless and throw slack line so as to aid the fish's escape, great. However, I like to be reasonably certain I could have brought the quarry to net, had I chosen to do so. Incidentally, I never cease to be amazed at how hard it is to lose a well-hooked trout on a barbless hook, even on purpose.

Pryce-Tannatt advances his argument a step further by

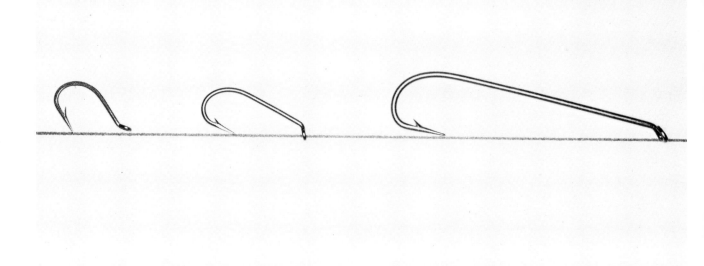

3-2 Note difference in "angle of impact."

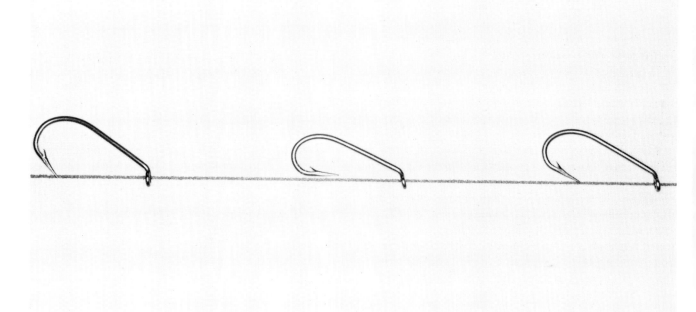

3-3 Setting up for the "angle of impact" test.

commenting on the shape or "bevel" of the point itself. He states that an effectively designed hook will have a point which is neither curved too much inward nor spread outward. This is particularly true of hooks used in fly-tying, as opposed to hooks used with natural baits. The inward-turned point will skid along the plane and probably not engage at all, whereas the outward-turned point will scrape along the plane and not penetrate.

Skeptics can try this simple experiment. Take three size 12 regular shank hooks—Mustad 94840's, let us say—and bend them as shown. Tie each hook onto a foot-long piece of typical leader tippet material, using any knot you prefer. Get a block of balsa wood and give the hooks a head start by sticking them into the wood up to the barb, with the grain. Now pull straight away on the tippet. Use a smooth tug, as you do when striking. (photo 3-3)

First of all, you will likely find it difficult to insert the inward-bent hook at all, even though it hasn't been altered much. Help it out further by pressing it into the balsa from the top. Now, pull on the tippet. The results should tell you something. The outward-bent hook will also give trouble, though of a somewhat different nature. The unaltered hook will engage with convincing efficiency.

Nobody's going to fish with hooks bent inward or outward, as in the exercise. But there are a number of hook designs whose characteristics cause similar results. The extrashort, the superlong, the Flybody (which is an extrashort with a rigid tailbone)—these designs have less-than-optimum hooking properties. The extremes in shank length are responsible.

Yet countless numbers of fish are brought to net on these designs each year. A fish's mouth is not a flat plane. The nooks and crannies offer many hook-holds; no block of balsa wood, this. And there are ways to improve on hook design, especially with short-shanked hooks, where contrary to longer-shanked models, bending the point slightly inward improves the angle of impact. An option on streamers is to use 4X-shanked hooks, going a size larger for length if necessary. This also improves the gap.

Few tiers use the beak-pointed type of hook; don't. Most of us in our bait-fishing beginnings were impressed by the lethal, clawlike appearance of these hooks, and for that purpose they were fine. For fly-fishing, forget it; the beak point simulates the inward-bent hook of the experiment. Incidentally, a similar effect is created by sharpening a hook incorrectly, which will be addressed later in the chapter.

I got somewhat carried away in my hook research, resorting to micrometers, microscopes and the services of a friend who works in a ballistics lab and has access to a computerized scale which is sensitive to one ten-thousandth of a gram. Here is the resulting set of criteria by which I feel dry-fly hooks can be fairly evaluated:

1. Eye: Good workmanship, no rough edges or unclosed eye loops. A tapered eye is ideal, as it allows for maximum aperture with minimum bulk. Turned-down eye is preferred, except for size 20 and smaller, where it begins to interfere with effective hooking. For tiny hooks I prefer the straight-eyed model, but turned-up eye is okay, too.

2. Bend: The model-perfect or semicircular bend allows the full length of the hook shank to be used. Sproat and limerick-type bends, where the hook begins to slope at the rear, tend to force the fly's tail to point downward. I also think the model-perfect is more aesthetically pleasing.

3. Shank Length: A regular shank is preferred for standard dry-fly work. This means the usable length of the shank from eye to bend is approximately twice the gap. This will vary slightly among styles and manufacturers.

4. Point: A straight spear point is recommended. It should not be overly long; this causes penetration problems.

5. Barb: A small, delicate barb is preferred. This minimizes penetration difficulties, cuts down on damage to the fish's mouth, and eases unhooking. Also, a small barb requires less of a slice in the metal of the hook, thereby minimizing loss of strength.

6. Wire: Standard dry-fly fine wire is quite suitable for nearly all applications. Diameter varies with hook size; number 14 wire is around seventeen- or eighteen-thousandths of an inch at midshank. Wire should be of sufficient temper to retain shape under strain but not so hard that it is brittle. It is far better that a hook bend a little than break.

The hook gap, while very important in smaller hooks, is not really a factor in evaluation, for it is the constant which determines hook size and the other parts of the hook are proportionate to it. The gaps on different brands of fly-tying hooks are surprisingly uniform. A size 12 is 3/32 of an inch, or just under 5 millimeters.

Sharpness is certainly a factor, insofar as actual fishing is concerned. No hooks are really outstanding in that department as they come from the factory, though all can be touched up quickly and easily. Even without touching up, the run-of-the-mill dry-fly hook will penetrate well enough, at least when new.

If I were to rate hooks on a scale of one to ten in my six categories I would award my beloved Sinfalta Red Label a ten across the board, for a total of sixty. (photo 3-4) Since it is no longer available, however, I am willing to risk a comparison with the Mustad 94840, which is the most widely used dry-fly hook in America by an overwhelming margin.

1. Eye: Not as finely made or delicately

tapered as the Red Label, but pretty
good.   8.5
2. Bend: Not quite a model-perfect, but
close.   9.0
3. Shank Length: A bit compromised by
the slight slope at the bend, but still very
good.   9.0
4. Point: Could be a bit shorter, but not
bad.   8.5
5. Barb: Slightly larger than need be, but
only that.   9.0
6. Wire about as strong as the Red Label,
but one-thousandth inch thicker. Tends
to vary in temper from batch to batch.   __8.0__
                                                                     52.0

Considering it is mass-produced and comparatively inexpensive, I think the Mustad stands up very well by comparison. Some others do not fare as well, though highly touted and priced accordingly.

There was a period when I used a lot of superfine wire hooks because I thought the difference in flotation was significant. That was before making any weight comparisons. A Mustad 94840 in size 14 weighs .0240 gram, while a 94833, the 3X fine model, weighs .0175. That's about 42 hooks to the gram in the heavier wire and 57 in the lighter. At 31.1 grams to the ounce, that works out to 1296 of the heavier hooks to the ounce and 1777 of the lighter.

With those statistics in mind, it is difficult to believe that a critical difference in flotation exists. I still use the superfine wire hooks for sparsely dressed spent patterns and some versions of the no-hackle, but that's about all. It should be kept in mind that minor variations in quality of wire and strength at the barb are magnified in the superfine models. I have noticed considerable fluctuation between batches.

I hope this exercise encourages and assists the reader in making assessments. In recent years we have seen the entry —and in some cases, rapid exodus—of new hooks in the market place. I suspect we will see more—it's big business now. I would love nothing better than to have the Red Label become available again, but only if it is of the former quality. I intend to scrutinize all new brands of hooks *very* carefully.

Quality of wire is probably the most critical factor in dry-fly hooks. Usually one finds out about the wire in a batch of hooks during the tying process. If the wire is abnormally soft, the tier will notice too much flexibility in the shank, especially in the 3X fine models. Brittleness is not quite as obvious. If the hook point is buried between the jaws of the vise, breakage will frequently occur. This ill-advised practice may also cause hooks of acceptable quality to be damaged to the breaking point by pressure at

the barb from the vise jaws. A better brittleness test is to clamp the hook into the vise as usual, with the barb and point exposed, and push upwards on the eye. If the hook breaks readily without much flexing, you may well have a brittle batch.

A consideration which is particularly critical in very small hooks concerns the angular gap—that is, the space between the point and the front extremity of the eye. The shorter the shank, the worse the problem; that is why extrashort-shank hooks have turned-up eyes. I am critical of overly long points because they reduce the angular gap. On average-sized hooks, the combination of a long spear point and a turned-down eye is generally tolerable, but with 18's, 20's, and smaller, it increasingly causes problems.

Today, small hooks are available with either turned-up or straight eyes, which greatly ameliorates the angular gap problem. (photo 3-5) The straight eye better accommodates the figure-eight turle knot, which I use for tying on dry flies. This knot is most secure when the loop portion is slipped over the ''neck'' of the fly, which is difficult with the turned-up eye.

Another problem with small hooks has to do with the vertical gap—that is, the distance between the point and the shank. There is little enough clearance to begin with, and it is reduced by whatever bulk the body material introduces. Optimally, a very small hook would be designed with a 1X or 2X-short shank, which would accommodate the proper body length for tiny flies while allowing sufficient gap for effective hooking. Since no such hooks are available, I suggest the tier go a hook size larger and underdress the little *Tricorythodes* and *Pseudocloeons*.

While usually not as critical, a similar problem can occur with elongated-shank hooks used for dressing streamers and many nymph patterns. Here again, the body material tends to reduce the vertical gap, accentuating the engagement problems that are inherent in 6X and 8X-long streamer hooks.

The solution is to use less extreme shank lengths and go a size larger to obtain desired proportions. For example, a large stonefly nymph may be dressed on a size 4 hook with a 4X-long shank or a size 6 hook with a 6X-long shank, the same body length resulting. The gap is improved significantly by utilizing the 4X-long. (photo 3-6)

Excepting the gap factor, don't get overly concerned with hook design on wet-fly, nymph, and streamer hooks. Don't agonize over sproat, improved-sproat, or limerick bends; there is no functional difference. I will confess to a weakness for the limerick on streamers, but again, that's subjective. On a more practical note, the loop-eye type of hook is good for certain streamer and salmon patterns, where the broader base offered by the double wire assists in mounting bulky wings. Also, the loop eye eliminates

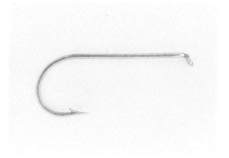

3-4 The Sinfalta Red Label.

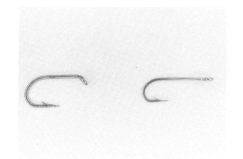

3-5 Note much-improved "angular gap" properties of the straight-eyed hook on the right.

3-6 Hook on left is a 6XL, hook on right is a 4XL in the next larger size. Note gap improvement.

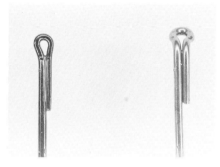

3-7 Left: looped eye on black Japanned salmon hook.
Right: looped eye on bronzed streamer hook.

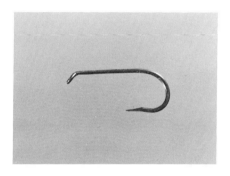

3-8 A typical dry fly hook debarbed by filing.

any problems of the leader being frayed by sharp edges, an important consideration with Atlantic salmon flies. (photo 3-7)

Sharpening and Debarbing Hooks

It would behoove all of us to sharpen our hooks in the vise prior to the fly-tying process. This is time-consuming and somewhat bothersome, and I admit to not always heeding my own advice. Even so, I advocate supplemental sharpening of all hooks, especially the larger ones.

Top-quality fly hooks usually come from the factory reasonably sharp. However, there are variations in sharpness from batch to batch, and even the best could benefit from a bit of touching up. Any hook with a modicum of sharpness will penetrate soft tissue, but as we know, there are places in a fish's mouth which definitely are not soft. All

of us have recollections of hook points grating on gaping jaws.

There are a number of instruments which may be used in the hook-sharpening task, including: fine-grit stones; small, fine-cut files; ceramic wafers, and specially made hones and steels. All of these are effective and have application in various situations. The choice depends primarily on two factors: the size of the hook and how much sharpening is required. For fine honing on small hooks an Arkansas stone is hard to beat, although ceramics are coming fast. However, neither of these would be a good choice for use on a size 2/0 saltwater hook, many of which come from the factory very dull and require extensive sharpening.

The technique for honing a typical fly hook:

1. Mount the hook upside-down in the vise, with maximum exposure of barb and point.

2. Using moderate pressure—about as much as when

shaving—hone the sides of the point, holding to the taper as it exists.

3. Work around the point as much as space will allow. Try to hone from the inside out, so as to avoid rounding the point, thereby creating a beak-style point.

4. Don't overdo, and avoid creating too stubby a point. Finger-test for optimum sharpness, or examine under a 20X loupe.

While honing, it is a simple matter to debarb a hook, which I recommend for several reasons. Besides the quick, easy release of fish, it saves wear and tear on flies. Penetration may be enhanced by removal of the impediment of an overly large barb. In many cases, tissue damage occurs during the playing of a fish as a direct result of the barb being twisted about. Debarbing greatly reduces this, often effecting a better hold than with the barb intact.

I am convinced of the benefits of debarbing on run-of-the-mill trout flies. On oversized or very heavy flies, such as those used in saltwater, the barb is needed. A fish can throw a heavy fly much more readily, particularly the acrobatic species such as tarpon and striped bass.

A hook may be partially debarbed by the simple expedient of squeezing the barb with pliers. This is no problem on larger, heavier-wire hooks. With the delicate dry-fly variety, however, I would advise considerable caution. The barb area is most fragile, and an indiscrete pinch can weaken or break the hook. Hooks will break in the vise if the tier buries the barb. One must wonder how many hooks were impaired in this manner, resulting later in lost fish.

If the tier elects to pinch the barb, he should use minimal pressure, no more than is required to accomplish the task. Squeeze gently, gradually building up pressure until the barb breaks off or is flattened. If there is still more of a bump than is wanted, don't try to squeeze it flat; use a file to finish the job.

Debarbing may easily be done entirely with the file, a method that exerts much less stress on smaller, finer hooks. (photo 3-8) Use the finest-cut file available, as the barb will catch in the grooves of rougher-cut files, again jeopardizing this fragile area. While filing down the barb, be careful to avoid carving a nick into any part of the bend, creating a weakened spot.

Mustad makes a straight-pointed barbless hook, model 94845, which is analogous in all other respects to the model 94840. However, the current list price of the barbless model is $4.05 per hundred, compared to $2.85 for the barbed counterpart. Obviously, there is more expense involved in making barbed hooks, and it makes no sense for those fly-dressers who opt for barblessness to be penalized. When the 94845 is priced at or below the level of the 94840, I will buy it. Until then, I'll keep on filing.

Three Vital Thread-Handling Techniques

4

Virtually every procedure in fly-dressing involves the tying thread, if only to tie on and tie off a piece of material. For this reason, dexterity with thread is perhaps the most valuable skill a tier can have. Incredibly, I still encounter tiers who have been struggling for years to improve their flies without realizing ineffectual thread-handling was preordaining their products to mediocrity.

When a fly-tier affixes material to a hook with thread, one of two things is intended to happen: either the material is to be distributed around the hook or it is to be fastened precisely where the fingers place it. Both executions are essential and should be mastered.

In essence, there are only three fundamental thread-handling techniques: the pinch, the distribution wrap, and the slack loop. They are not difficult to learn, but fly-dressing itself *is* difficult if they are not mastered.

Essential Pinch

The essential pinch is the most important single manipulation in fly-tying for two reasons. It is used more frequently than any other technique, and its faulty execution is the direct cause of a multitude of other serious problems.

In its basic form, the pinch is a two-handed, slack-thread technique—''two-handed'' because both hands manipulate the thread, and ''slack-thread'' because tension is maintained by means other than the weight of the bobbin or the application of tension by the bobbin hand.

By way of illustration, let us analyze a procedure which

is a classic example of the pinch technique, the tying on of quill-section wet-fly wings. Whether or not you fish with these traditional flies (I still find certain patterns very effective) isn't the point: development of this particular skill is what is important. For this purpose, one would be hard put to find a better exercise than winging the wet fly.

Here is a step-by-step description of the pinch (it is assumed the preliminary operations have been completed):

1. With the left hand, position the material on the hook shank exactly as you wish it to be after the tying-on. (photo 4-1)

2. Bring the tying thread to a vertical position directly above the hook shank. (photo 4-2)

3. Slide the thread between the left thumb and index finger so that it is gripped firmly with the material. The lower portion of the thumb and index finger also grip the hook shank. (photo 4-3)

4. *Without exerting lateral pressure on the material,* bring the tying thread directly downward, at the same time slipping it between the left thumb and index finger on the far side of the material. (photo 4-4)

5. You have formed a loop over the material. The entire assembly is held firmly in place by the pinch. There is *no* tension on the thread at this point.

6. Satisfy yourself that the material is in the desired position and that the loop of tying thread will strike the material precisely where desired.

7. With a smooth motion, apply tension directly downward with the bobbin hand. It works best if the pressure is increased gradually, using subtle yet insistent tugs. Keep pinching throughout.

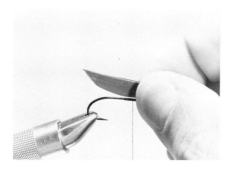

4-1 The pinch sequence: position the wings.

4-2 Bring thread straight upward.

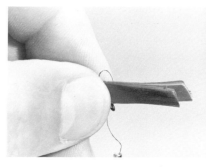

4-3 Slack loop is formed over wings.

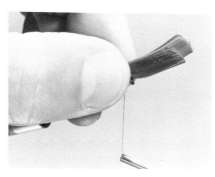

4-4 Apply tension with straight downward motion.

4-5 Wings secured in position.

8. Repeat steps 2 through 7 one or more times to secure the material.

9. Release the pinch and inspect the results. Minor adjustments and repositioning may be made with the fingers. (photo 4-5)

10. Secure the tied-in component further with turns of thread on top of or in front of, but not *behind* the pinched spot.

You may now trim away the excess material and proceed with the remaining operations.

The pinch is used so frequently in fly-tying that after a while it becomes a conditioned reflex. It is the recommended technique for any operation where the objective is to affix a component or piece of material in a precise position and attitude. We will look at many applications of the pinch in the hands-on section of the book.

Distribution Wrap

This technique might be called the antithesis of the pinch, in that the objective is to use the thread in such a manner as to deploy material around the shank of the hook. It is a very simple move which merely allows a natural phenomenon to occur in a controlled manner, the phenomenon being the tendency of most materials to try to escape the pressure of thread under tension.

Probably the best example of the distribution wrap is the tying-on of fibers for nymph and wet-fly hackle. In 1941, James E. Leisenring, America's answer to G. E. M. Skues, published a brief but penetrating treatise on the fishing and tying of subaqueous flies, *The Art of Tying the Wet Fly*. In 1971 Crown publishers, under the watchful guidance of editor Nick Lyons, republished the classic, coupling it with a new section, "Fishing the Flymph," by

Vernon S. Hidy. This pocket-sized volume leaves little to be said about sunken-fly fishing in theory and practice, and if I master its contents in my lifetime, I'll die a happy man.

The "flymph" was one of the three types of wet flies utilized by "Big Jim." This wingless, webby-limbed creation is similar to those advocated by Sylvester Nemes in a present-day book entitled *The Soft-hackled Fly*. They are very simple to construct, consisting merely of a body, which is sometimes ribbed, and a collar of hackle. The latter component makes use of hen hackle, grouse feathers, and a number of other soft, flexible materials which undulate in a life-suggesting manner in the currents of the stream.

Some of the feathers these flies call for can be wound on exactly like dry-fly hackle. Others can be folded and wound in the British tradition. However, some do not readily lend themselves to being wound at all, for various reasons. Consider grouse hackle, for example. The average feather has barbules long enough for a size 8 or 10 fly. Very few are small enough to accommodate a 12. Yet many soft-hackled patterns are most effective in small sizes. What to do?

The distribution wrap enables hackle fibers to be removed from the stem and tied on in a manner so similar to wound hackle that a trained eye would be hard-pressed to tell which method had been used. As an example, we will look at the tying-on of grouse hackle.

1. Strip some barbules from a grouse ruff or body feather.

2. Determine the appropriate length of hackle, and position the barbules accordingly at the neck of the fly, just ahead of the body and on the far side of the hook. (photo 4-6)

3. Instead of pinching, allow the barbules to be forced ahead of the thread as it is wound around the hook shank. Add more barbules as required to fill vacant spots and provide the desired amount of hackle. (photos 4-7, 4-8)

That's it. A few rehearsals and you'll be making excellent hackles with feathers you might have thrown away.

A hint: when hackling flies in this manner, don't leave quite as much shank as you usually would between the front of the body and the eye of the hook. This method requires less space than wound hackle. Too long a neck area will result in an unsightly, elongated head.

The distribution wrap opens up many possibilities for the fly-tier. Feathers that were previously considered of no value or at best suitable for bearded hackle may be used on many killing patterns. Coupled with this enhancement is the monetary benefit of greater utilization, no insignificant consideration in fly-tying these days.

Slack Loop

The third of the essential techniques is indisputably the least known, yet the applications are extremely important for most fly-dressers. The slack loop is actually a continuation of the distribution wrap, with the material distributed entirely around the hook. But it is also similar to the pinch, in that when the final pressure is applied, it is perpendicular to the hook shank rather than around it. This pressure, applied from 360 degrees, tends to fix the distributed material uniformly as it is deployed by the distribution wrap.

A comment is in order on the relatively new prewaxed nylon thread, a product of the late 1960s. This thread behaves quite differently from traditional thread. It has a remarkable "memory," a distinct tendency to remain in place as wrapped. This, coupled with the greater number of wraps employed by most of today's tiers, facilitates the use of the slack-loop procedure. Traditional thread, even well waxed, has a tendency to loosen or unwrap when not under tension.

This is no recommendation for indiscrete or unnecessary relaxation of thread tension during the tying process. The slack loop is a controlled process which is set up by the se-

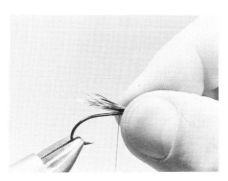

4-6 The distribution wrap sequence: position the material.

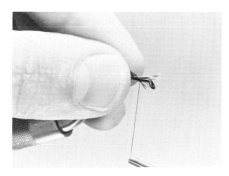

4-7 Thread forces material around hook.

4-8 The result.

4-9 The slack loop sequence: deer hair in position.

4-10 Start the loop.

4-11 Slack loop with material distributed.

4-12 Tension applied.

4-13 The result.

curing of the previous step. That's a proposition quite different from careless technique, which allows thread to go slack at random.

As mentioned, the slack loop has attributes of the distribution wrap and the pinch, depending on just what procedure is being executed. Tying on deer hair for a clipped body of the head of a Muddler Minnow is a good example.

1. Cut off a bunch of deer hair sufficient to generously cover the circumference of the hook shank. (photo 4-9)

2. Start the hair on the top or far side of the hook, using the distribution wrap to deploy the material, helping it along with the left thumb and forefinger, if necessary. (photo 4-10)

3. When the material is evenly deployed, encircle it with a full turn of thread under little or no tension. (photo 4-11)

4. Pull the loop tight with a series of subtle tugs. The hair will crimp and flare uniformly. Secure with additional wraps under normal tension. (photos 4-12, 4-13)

Usually, two wraps are sufficient: first, the distribution wrap, then the slack loop. Where larger quantities of hair are involved, you may wish to use a third, that is to say, a second slack loop. This works out quite satisfactorily, but the application of a third loop does inhibit the tightening of the initial wrap.

As you continue to develop your fly-dressing skills, you will find these three techniques to be of great value. Advanced tiers often use slight variations in solving specific problems. For instance, I may tie on a peacock quill at the bend of a size 18 hook by relaxing thread tension slightly, sneaking the thread over the quill, then resuming normal tension. A classic pinch is not easily executed under those particular circumstances; this "wrap-pinch" combination allows visual contact with the material as it is tied to the hook.

The Quill Gordon Dry Fly

TECHNIQUES TO BE LEARNED

1. Size relationships
2. Positional relationships
3. Quantities of materials
4. Transitional techniques
5. Making things stay put
6. Tying the wood duck wing
7. Tying the typical dry-fly tail
8. Setting up and tying the stripped peacock quill body
9. Setting up and tying the conventional dry-fly hackle

I can hear everyone saying, ''For Pete's sake, if there's one fly I know how to tie properly, it's the Quill Gordon.'' But, my friends, we are not merely going to tie this standard pattern; we are going to study the anatomy of the Quill Gordon. We will examine each step in exhaustive detail, not only to become intimately familiar with handling each particular component but also—and this is of greater importance—to see how it fits into the overall scheme of the fly and how it sets up the tying of the other components. It is essential to realize that the tying of a fly is not simply a matter of affixing individual materials to a hook in an arrangement suggestive of the anatomy of a particular insect. Rather, it is a cohesive, sequential procedure from the first turn of thread to the last. No matter how familiar you are with the basic dry fly, I guarantee the Quill Gordon will seem like a new pattern when we are finished.

I have chosen the Quill Gordon because it is an extremely well-integrated fly; the materials that make up the various components fit together in classic structural harmony, something which cannot be said of all flies. Some patterns call for the use of materials which conflict with each other and, in some cases, fight against the fly-dressing process. Anyone who has tried to tie a size 14 Irresistible can appreciate that statement. Yet one cannot generally say that such flies are poorly designed, for in many cases the effectiveness of the finished product more than justifies the difficulties encountered in the dressing. After all, fly-tying is a problem-solving endeavor, and would be far less intriguing if it were otherwise.

Many of the procedures employed in dressing the Quill Gordon are basic, and will be applied throughout the remainder of this book. As we step through the fly the emphasis on preciseness and deftness of execution is clear.

Wood Duck Drake

This shouldn't create apprehension; on the contrary, fly-tying is more easily executed with precise techniques than slipshod ones. And it is really easy to develop manual skill —awareness is sixty percent of the battle, practice the other forty percent. Start thinking precision, and your tying is guaranteed to improve. This will serve you well, particularly on very small flies where slight miscalculations can create major problems.

COMPONENTS

Hook: Size 14 Mustard 94849 or equivalent
Thread: Olive prewaxed 6/0
Wing: Barred wood duck flank or dyed mallard substitute
Tail: Stiff dun hackle fibers
Body: Stripped quill from peacock eye
Hackle: Feather from top-quality dun cape

TYING STEPS

1. Place the hook in the vise as shown in photograph 5-1. I do not advocate burying the point in the jaws of the vise, because it is easier to learn to work around the point than around the bulky jaws and because pressure on the barb area frequently causes weakness or breakage.

2. Tie on the thread just ahead of the thorax area, about 1/16 inch (2 mm) back from the eye. (photo 5-2)

3. Take five or six turns towards the rear, trim off the loose end, take two or three turns forward to the center of the thorax area, 1/8 inch (3 mm) back from the eye. (photo 5-3)

4. Select a barred wood duck feather with nice even tips. (photo 5-4) There are several methods for gathering fibers for this type of wing, a knowledge of which enables the tier to use up all of his precious wood duck without waste. These will be covered in subsequent notes. For now, we will use the center-section method.

5. Separate a center section with a sufficient amount of fibers in it to make a substantial but not an overly bulky wing. For a size 14, this will take around ¾ to 1 inch (22-26 mm) of fibers, depending on density. (photo 5-5)

6. Fold back the unwanted fibers on either side, being careful not to impair them, as they can be used later for another wing. Be sure the portion remaining is equal on either side of the center stem. (photo 5-6)

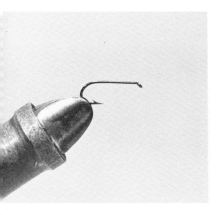

5-1 Quill Gordan Dry Fly: my preference: barb exposed.

5-2 Tie on here.

5-3 Create base of thread.

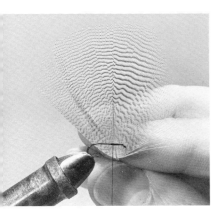

5-4 A prime wood duck feather.

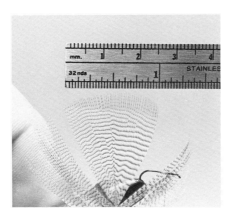

5-5 About an inch of tip will suffice for a size 14 wing.

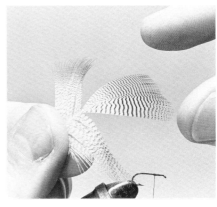

5-6 Folding the wood duck feather, step 1.

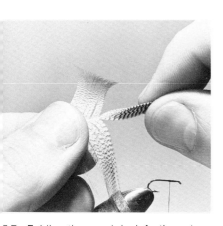

5-7 Folding the wood duck feather, step 2.

5-8 Folding the wood duck feather, step 3.

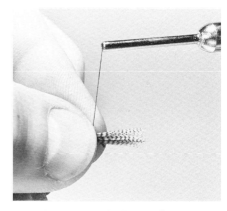

5-9 Tie in with a pinch, step 1.

7. Fold the fibers of the center section into a neat bunch by stroking downward with the right thumb and forefinger, then outward toward the tips to even them up. Secure the bunch by gripping with the left thumb and forefinger. (photo 5-7)

8. Expose about ½ inch (12 mm) of feather ahead of the left thumb and forefinger and position it on top of the hook so that the next turn of thread will pass over the material at the ½-inch mark. (photo 5-8)

9. You are about to execute the pinch. Bring the thread directly up and work it in between the tips of the left thumb and index finger. (photo 5-9)

10. Bring the thread down between the pinch on the far side of the hook, creating a slack loop above the material. (photo 5-10)

11. Snug the loop of thread down over the bunched fibers, pulling straight downward with the thread, pinching all the while to hold them in position. (photo 5-11)

12. If the material has slipped around the hook a bit, reposition it directly on top and repeat the pinch. If necessary, repeat the reposition and pinch procedure once more. *It is essential that the wing material be on top of the hook and perfectly centered.*

13. Take three turns back toward the butt, then three turns forward, returning to the tie-in point, thereby securing the wing material. Now trim off the excess butt on an elongated bias. This helps form the taper of the body. (photos 5-12, 5-13)

14. Begin to stand the wing up by preening it with the fingers. (photo 5-14)

15. Take three or four turns of thread tight to the base of the wing, forcing it back against the tie-in point. Help out the process with the left thumb and forefinger. This should cause the wing to stand up straight. Don't take too many turns; you will create a bump which will cause problems later. (photos 5-15, 5-16) If the wing doesn't stand up perfectly straight after a maximum of, let us say, five turns, don't worry—the following steps will correct that condition.

16. Separate the wing fibers into two equal bunches with the tip of your scissors. (photos 5-17, 5-18)

17. Continue to separate the two bunches by stroking with the fingers. (photo 5-19)

18. You will now execute the crisscross. Make a pass front-to-back with the thread through the V between the two wing sections, holding the near side in position while doing so.

19. Bring the thread under the hook, then make a pass back-to-front through the V, holding the far side in position while doing so. Repeat steps 18 and 19 once if further separation appears necessary. (photos 5-20–5-25)

20. You will now execute the figure eight. First, make a front-to-back pass through the V exactly like the beginning of the crisscross.

21. Hold the far wing firmly by the tip, then make a pass around the very base. (photo 5-26) I find it helpful to invert the bobbin while doing this.

22. *Don't let go of the wing.* Bring the thread back through the V and down to perpendicular position behind the near wing. (photo 5-27) Now release the far wing, keeping only the lightest tension on the thread, *and always in a downward direction.* (photo 5-28)

23. Hold the near wing firmly by the tip and make a pass around the very base. (photo 5-29)

24. Go back through the V, ending up behind the far wing with the thread perpendicular and under light tension. (photo 5-30) Now release the wing, being sure that tension on the thread is *always in a downward direction.*

25. The wings may be perfectly formed and stabilized after one figure eight. If not, repeat the procedure, snugging up the loops and applying slightly more tension than before, so as to discipline the material. (photo 5-31) Avoid figure eighting more than twice, or perhaps three times on a larger fly, as the accumulated bulk will interfere with the hackling procedure later on.

26. Wind the thread evenly back to the bend, binding down the trimmed wing butt in a smooth taper.

27. At the very bend of the hook or even a hair beyond, create a small bump with four or five turns of thread. This will aid in the spreading of the tails. (photo 5-32)

28. Select a small bunch of stiff hackle fibers for the tail. Spade hackle is usually best; saddle hackle and large cape hackle may also be quite satisfactory. Tail material need not come off the same cape as the hackle, but the color should match closely. Eight to ten fibers is about right. Too much material in the tail spoils the silhouette. (photo 5-33)

29. Position the bunch of fibers exactly on top of the hook. Transfer the grip to the right thumb and forefinger and adjust the length. I prefer a tail around ⅜ to ⁷⁄₁₆ inch long (10 mm). (photo 5-34)

30. Regrip the feathers with the left hand, making certain the fibers stay directly on top of the hook. Tie in the tail, using the pinch. (photo 5-35)

31. Wind back a few turns, forcing the fibers against the bump. This should cause them to flair. (photo 5-36)

32. Select a stripped peacock quill with plenty of light-dark contrast. (photo 5-37)

33. Tie in the quill, dark edge trailing, on the side of the hook, using the pinch or the tension variance technique. The tie-in point should be right where the tail begins. The quill should be positioned at an attitude of approximately forty-five degrees to the hook shank, so as to facilitate the beginning wrap. About 1¼ inches (32 mm)

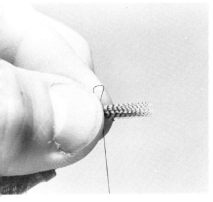

5-10 Tie in with a pinch, step 2.

5-11 Tie in with a pinch, step 3.

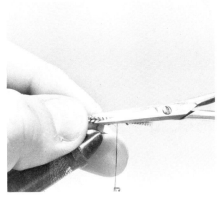

5-12 Trim on bias.

5-13 Material should now appear thus.

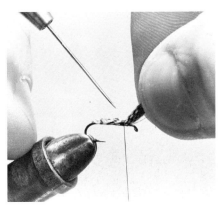

5-14 Adjust to get all fibers on top.

5-15 Pull fibers into upright position.

5-16 Wraps of thread secure feather in upright position.

5-17 Upright undivided clump.

5-18 Divide clump with scissor tips.

5-19 Enforce separation with fingers.

5-20 The crisscross, step 1: bring thread straight up.

5-21 The crisscross, step 2: across and down.

5-22 The crisscross, step 3: pass under hook and behind wings.

5-23 The crisscross, step 4: thread straight up behind near wing.

5-24 The crisscross, step 5: across and down in front of far wing.

5-25 Wings should now appear thus.

5-26 The figure eight, step 1: thread is wrapped around base of far wing.

5-27 The figure eight, step 2: continue thread around base of far wing and back through "V".

5-28 The figure eight, step 3: thread straight down behind wing.

5-29 The figure eight, step 4: seize near wing, start thread around base.

5-30 The figure eight, step 5: continue thread around near wing and back through the "V".

5-31 Completed wings.

5-32 Bump of thread at bend.

5-33 Spade hackle for tail.

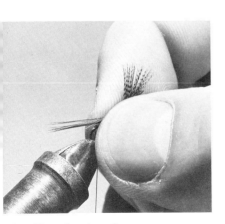

5-34 Mounting the tail.

5-35 Tie in with pinch.

5-36 Bump spreads fibers.

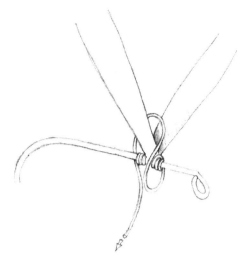

The Crisscross: steps 1, 2, 3

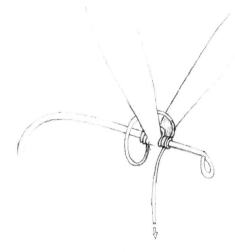

The Crisscross: steps 4, 5

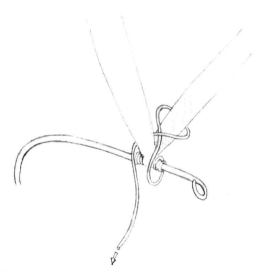

The Figure Eight: steps 1, 2, 3

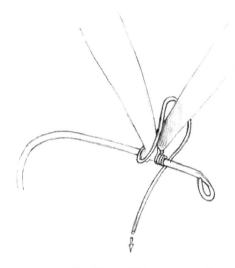

The Figure Eight: steps 4, 5

of quill is required, including an allowance for gripping. (photo 5-38)

34. Wind the thread forward a few turns, further securing the tail and quill. Now trim off the excess tail and body material, cutting on a slight bias just short of the wings. This further contributes to the making of a smooth, well-formed body with slight taper. (photo 5-39)

35. Wind the thread forward almost but not quite to the base of the wings, winding down the excess tail and body material. Use neat wraps which lie precisely against each other.

36. Wind back nearly to the base of the tail, then forward again to a position just behind the wing. You are now forming the underbody. It should be very even and slightly tapered. (photo 5-40) Use the thread discretely to fill in or smooth over any minute fissures.

37. Grasp the end of the peacock quill with a pair of hackle pliers, using a straightforward grip. Be careful not to apply much tension, as the quill will break easily at the tie-in point. (photo 5-41)

38. Wrap the quill, maintaining moderate tension. The dark edge of the quill should lie precisely against the light

5-37 Note contrast in quill.

5-38 Tie in with dark edge trailing.

5-39 Trim excess material.

5-40 Create smooth underbody.

5-41 Begin wrapping quill.

5-42 Dark edge against light.

5-43 Tie off quill.

5-44 Secure as shown.

5-45 Thread positioned for hackle tie-in.

edge of the previous wrap, creating the desired segmentation. As an option, you may leave the slightest space between turns, allowing the olive underbody to peak through. (photo 5-42)

39. Stop the body just short of the wings, tying down the quill on the underside of the hook. (photo 5-43)

40. Secure the quill with two turns of thread just in front of the wings. This effectively locks in the body and smooths out the tie-off. (photo 5-44)

41. Take one more turn of thread, passing it beneath the thorax so as to be in position for the tying-in of the hackle. (photo 5-45)

42. Select one top-quality hackle feather, if you have a cape which will allow this. If not, use two. For this exercise, we will assume the use of one feather. Flex the hackle to determine proper spread. A true size 14 hackle will have a radius of ⅜ of an inch or slightly less (9 mm). (photo 5-46) Strip off the unwanted portion towards the butt. A truly excellent feather will have 1 ¼ to 1 ½ inches (32-38 mm) of virtually web-free hackle which will be almost perfectly true to size throughout. This should allow five to seven turns.

43. Using the tension variance technique, tie in the hackle feather underneath the hook just slightly behind the wings. Hold the feather at approximately forty-five degrees to the hook and take two or three turns of the thread tight to the rear edge of the base of the wing. (photo 5-47)

44. Pass forward under the thorax and continue to secure the stem with close, tight winds ahead of the wing. Traverse the hook smoothly, leaving no bumps. Stop slightly back from the eye, leaving about ⅟₃₂ inch (1 mm).

45. Trim off the butt and observe the area over which you are about to wind the hackle. It should now be obvious why we were so careful earlier with the trimming, amounts of materials, and turns of thread. If all was done properly, we have a small, neat space behind the wing, enough for two or perhaps three turns of hackle. The diameter of the materials in this area should be minimized by a precise execution of the thread and the absence of excess body materials. The diameter of the materials is important here, because excess bulk spreads the hackle, causing it to become oversized, in effect.

The area in front of the wing will taper slightly towards the eye, which can't be helped and if minimal is of no consequence. There should be no bumps, lumps, dips, or crevices which might interfere with the hackling process. If any exist, they may be corrected with a discrete turn or two of thread. If you perceive that a little too much bulk was created back during the standing-up of the wing, you may level off the area with a few turns to the rear, then back forward. It is better to slightly increase the diameter than to have a sharp drop-off.

46. Now for the climax. Seize the tip of the feather with the hackle pliers. As previously stated, I recommend a straight-on grip. Be sure the center quill is grasped firmly, which normally will require taking about ³⁄₁₆ inch (5 mm) of feather into the jaws of the pliers. More than this wastes prime hackle.

47. Square the feather to the hook shank by moving it perhaps fifteen degrees beyond the right angle, then returning to perpendicular. (photo 5-48)

48. Begin the first turn almost but not quite tight to the wings, remembering you will take another turn or two before crossing over to the front of the wings. Tension should be moderate and steady. Keep the hackle pliers extended straight out. Avoid flexing the hackle stem; it will break readily under such stress. (photo 5-49)

49. Take the second turn in the tiny crevice between the first turn and the wing. (photo 5-50)

50. Cross over directly beneath the thorax and take the next turn absolutely snug to the front of the wings. (photo 5-51)

51. Take the succeeding turns—probably three—to where the thread was left hanging, each absolutely tight to the one preceeding. *Do not invade the space reserved for the tie-off and head.* (photos 5-52, 5-53)

52. To tie off the hackle, let the hackle pliers hang loose, then take four or five firm wraps of thread around the feather tip, one atop the other, or nearly so.

53. Using the fingers of the left hand, move the thread out of the way and trim off the remaining feather stem and errant fibers. Try to pull the fibers off to one side before trimming, so as to keep the eye clear. (photo 5-54)

54. Secure and smooth the tie-off point with a few more turns of thread. Whip finish the head, using whatever technique works for you, and the fly is completed. (photo 5-55)

I recommend two thorough coats of Ambroid on the body. (If someone has told you this will make the fly heavy, forget it—a typical drop of Ambroid weighs 12 to 15 ten-thousandths of a gram.) Apply the cement with a bodkin, holding the fly at a forty-five degree angle so the liquid seeps into the thorax area. (photo 5-56) Allow to dry thoroughly and repeat.

One coat is sufficient for the head, but feel free to use two, if you wish. Be very careful to keep the eye clear of cement. Should a drop inadvertently run in, wipe it out by passing a discarded hackle feather through the eye.

WOOD DUCK WING

The technique employed in the preceding exercise is probably the simplest, quickest way to get a neat wing. With wood duck as scarce—and nearly as costly—as spun gold, we must use each precious feather to its maximum.

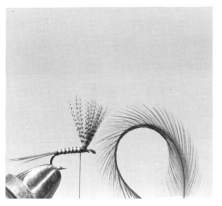

5-46 Flex feather to gauge size.

5-47 Tie in, trim excess.

5-48 Bring feather upright.

5-49 First turn of hackle. Note slight space behind wings.

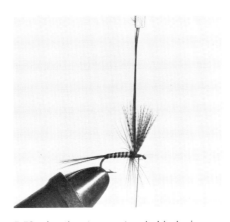

5-50 Another turn or two behind wings.

5-51 Cross over beneath thorax.

5-52 Wrap tight to front of wings.

5-53 Don't obscure the eye.

5-54 Hold thread aside while trimming.

5-55 The completed fly.

5-56 Cement the body.

This requires a knowledge of two additional techniques for handling wood duck.

THE EVENED-UP SECTION METHOD

Assume you have already used the center portion of a feather, and wish to get an additional wing out of each side, which is possible with a large feather of good quality.

1. Preen a section on one side so that the fibers assume a ninety degree angle relative to the center stem. Notice how the tips even up. (photo 5-57) If there are any scraggly fibers of poor consistency near the base, dispose of them.
2. Cut or pull off the fibers, keeping the tips even. They may now be folded or rolled into a neat bunch and made into a wing. (photo 5-58)

THE MATCHED OR SUPPLEMENTED SECTION METHOD

This technique complements the evened-up method and is very similar in execution. It is used where the remaining fibers in a side section are insufficient to make a wing or where the fibers are curved and hard to bunch. Let us assume the latter situation exists.

1. Preen the fibers on one side out to ninety degrees and cut them off neatly. Lay the section aside. (photo 5-59)
2. Do the same with the fibers from the other side, or for that matter, from another feather of similar configuration. (photo 5-60)

3. Carefully pick up the two sections and match them back-to-back, or convex-to-convex. This is a delicate procedure and may require a bit of rehearsal. (photo 5-61)
4. Flatten the bunches with a squeeze of the right thumb and forefinger. They are now ready to be tied on and made up into a wing. (photo 5-62)

Notice that the curvature of the two matched bunches forms a natural division for the wings. Be careful not to disturb this relationship during the tying process.

STRIPPED PEACOCK AND CONDOR QUILL

The object in making a stripped peacock quill body is to create a light-dark contrast which produces a segmented effect. The eyed portion of a peacock tail is made up of quills which, when stripped of their herl, have a light edge and a dark edge. The quills from the stem of the feather are much easier to strip, but lack the contrasting shades.

When buying peacock feathers for quill bodies, one should try to determine the amount of contrast in the eyed portion of the feather. A very good indicator is the amount of lightness which shows on the back of the eye when the quills are pinched between the thumb and forefinger. Simply turn the eye so the dull side is facing you and squeeze, so that the quills are forced to lie flat. If they show a light shade, that eye will produce well-segmented bodies.

The largest-eyed feathers usually make the best quill bodies. They generally have better contrast than smaller, more immature feathers, and their quills are of sufficient length and breadth to make bodies on size 14 and 12 flies. These larger quills are also less apt to break, a frequent catastrophe in the winding of quill bodies.

A number of methods have been suggested for stripping the herl from a peacock eye. Trying to scrape off the herl with a knife, razor blade, or needle point is generally not feasible, as the amount of pressure necessary to remove the herl often damages the delicate quill. Stripping with Clorox, even under the most carefully controlled conditions, makes the quills lose most or all of their contrast, and come out brittle and weakened. The two methods that work best are to rub off the herl with an eraser or to coat the eye with paraffin and strip the quills with a fingernail or dull knife. The procedure for the paraffin method is:

1. In a small saucepan, bring a pint of water to a boil.
2. Drop in a chunk of paraffin the size of an ice cube and boil until the wax is entirely melted.

3. Remove the pan from the fire and let stand for perhaps ten minutes. Being lighter than water, the melted paraffin will spread across the surface.

4. Dip the peacock eye into the pan and withdraw it, repeating two or three times. The paraffin will form a thin coating.

5. Let the waxed eye cool for a few minutes. The quills may now be easily stripped without damage or loss of coloration.

An added benefit of the paraffin method is convenience of storage and transportation. These waxed eyes fit in nicely with a portable tying outfit, and will keep practically forever without moth-proofing.

The eraser method is my personal favorite. The best eraser I have found for this purpose is the ''ink'' end of a combination ink-pencil eraser. The old-fashioned round typewriter eraser is also very effective.

5-57 Evened-up section method: when using side portion, even up ends first.

5-58 Combine fibers in uniform bunch.

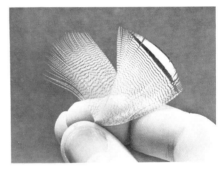

5-59 Matched or supplemented section method: Sometimes one side of a tipped flank feather can be used.

5-60 If feathers are curved, use two opposing sections.

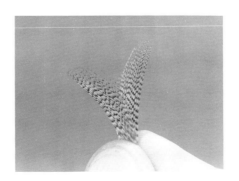

5-61 Match sections back to back.

5-62 Compress before tying in.

The technique is very simple. Merely separate a quill from the eye, hold it against a tabletop or piece of cardboard, and rub off the herl. Several quills may be stripped simultaneously with practice. I like to strip two or three eyes on a lazy winter afternoon, providing enough quills for a typical season.

Condor quill, which is preferred over peacock by some tiers, is quite another matter, as the paraffin and eraser methods are totally ineffective. The only successful method for stripping condor seems to be the Clorox process. I approach this delicate procedure with quaking heart, for a slight miscalculation will ruin an irreplaceable feather in a flash, a most depressing occurrence.

Quite possibly, you will never have occasion to strip a condor quill, for it is doubtful these feathers will become commercially available again. However, there is still a lot of condor in private collections, and if you should aquire some, it is very important to do an optimal stripping job.

1. In a soup dish or similar container, mix 4 ounces of Clorox and 2 ounces of water.

2. In another vessel, mix 2 heaping tablespoons of baking soda with approximately 1 cup of water.

3. Using tweezers or the equivalent, immerse a fairly small section—2 inches, let us say—of condor quill in the Clorox solution, herl side up.

4. Swish the feather around, carefully observing the changes in color of both the quill and the solution. The feather will soon begin to lighten and the Clorox will begin to look like weak beef broth.

5. After about 30 seconds, remove the quill, squeeze out the excess fluid and swizzle the feather in the baking soda solution for 10 or 20 seconds. This will stop the action of the Clorox.

6. Examine the feather to see if the fuzz is gone. If it is, you are done. If not, put it back in the Clorox for 10 or 15 seconds and swish it around some more.

7. When the fuzz has been removed and the bleaching action arrested by the baking soda solution, rinse the feather in plain water, squeeze, and allow to dry.

The all-important factor is timing. The Clorox is cut with water to make the timing factor a little less critical, for straight Clorox is extremely quick. Keep in mind that to remove the feather from the Clorox prematurely does no harm, whereas to leave it in too long causes irreversible damage. You can always repeat the stripping process but you can never undo it.

A properly stripped condor feather will have a distinct dark edge, the lightly shaded portion being approximately twice as wide as the dark. These feathers may be used as-is on patterns calling for natural quill, such as the Quill Gordon, or they can be dyed to whatever color is desired. Here again, caution is advised, for a poor dye job can also ruin a valuable piece of material. The fabric dyes sold in most dry-goods stores and supermarkets work very well on condor.

6

The Adams

TECHNIQUES TO BE LEARNED

1. Hackle-tip wing
2. Dubbed body, single-thread method
3. Winding two hackle feathers

If an angler were forced to choose one pattern to use for life, the Adams would be very hard to beat. The multi-shaded, diffused effect which the mottled materials create apparently has terrific trout appeal. In a wide spectrum of sizes, the Adams will match hatches nearly enough, and is a dynamite attractor pattern as well. The Adams is an exquisitely beautiful creation, when dressed to perfection.

It is not a difficult pattern to tie; however, there are enough complexities to justify inclusion here. We will focus only on that which is different, carrying over the skills acquired so far.

COMPONENTS

Hook: Size 14 Mustad 94840 or equivalent
Thread: Black prewaxed 6/0
Wing: Barred Rock hackle tips
Tail: Stiff barred Rock hackle fibers
Body: Gray dubbing, either soft fur or poly
Hackle: One medium or dark ginger and one barred Rock (grizzly)

TYING STEPS

1. Select two matching grizzly hackle feathers with close, pretty barrings. These need not be the valuable feathers in the "money" portion of the cape. Larger feathers from further back, which have little other value, will do nicely, provided the tips aren't excessively round or the markings too wide. (photo 6-1)

2. The following method for preparing the wings is unique, to my knowledge. First, lay the feathers together with the tips perfectly matched. Either side may face outward, depending on what looks best, but the exposed side must be the same for both feathers. (photo 6-2)

3. Estimate (or measure) the appropriate length, which is ½ inch (12 mm) for a size 14. (photo 6-3)

4. Grasping the feathers by their tips, gently stroke back the fibers until the precise spot is reached where the thread must intersect the stems to form a ½-inch wing.

5. Be sure the tips are still perfectly even. Then fold back the fibers and catch them with the left thumb and forefinger, exposing the wings-to-be. (photo 6-4) The fingers must be in a position to apply the pinch to the exact

Bat at Dusk

point on the feather stems where the thread will catch them.

6. Lay the feathers on the hook with the tie-in point exactly the desired distance from the eye. Suit yourself on this; I recommend ³/₃₂ inch (2+ mm).

7. Tie the wings in with a pinch, followed by a repeat-pinch. (photo 6-5)

8. Under only two turns of thread, the feathers are easily adjusted. With the right thumb and forefinger, gently stand them erect and make whatever subtle adjustments may be necessary to arrange them precisely atop the hook. While doing this, don't release the butts of the feathers, which are being held with the thumb and forefinger. (photo 6-6)

9. Pick up the bobbin again and secure the feathers with a few close turns towards the rear, then a like number back to the tie-in point. If you notice the stems slipping during this process, release the bobbin and adjust as described in step 8. Trim off the butts.

10. Preen the wings into the upright position. If one or two fibers at the base refuse to cooperate, cut them off. (photo 6-7)

11. Barred Rock hackle-tip wings stand up very readily. Two turns snug in front should do it. (photo 6-8)

12. Structurally speaking, the wings are now completed. If more or less spread is desired, simply set the wings in the desired attitude with the fingers, being *very gentle.*

13. Drop of Ambroid, preferably highly viscose.

14. Create the tail, using the technique learned in the Quill Gordon sequence. Smooth out the underbody with wraps of thread, stopping approximately three turns short of the tail.

15. Prepare the thread by applying a thin coating of wax, even if using prewaxed thread. (photo 6-9)

16. Pull off a sparse tuft of material and lay it on the thread, using the thumb and forefinger to get it close to the hook shank.

6-1 Adams: start with these.

6-2 Match convex to convex.

6-3 Establish desired length.

6-4 Expose stems at tie-in point.

6-5 Lay tips atop hook, tie in with pinch.

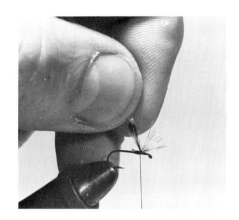

6-6 Preen wings into upright position.

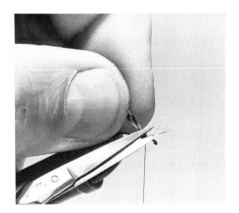

6-7 Eliminate stray fibers.

6-8 Lock wings in position with thread.

17. Twirl the material around the thread, forming a tightly packed, gently tapered worm. (photo 6-10)

18. Pull off a second sparse tuft of material and twirl it onto the thread, overlapping the first bunch somewhat so as to form a worm which is 2 inches (50 mm) in length and tapered at both ends. Caution: do not use too much dubbing, especially when using poly. Polypropylene fibers are extremely strong, and it is practically impossible to remove excess after the body is wound without making a mess of it. (photo 6-11)

19. Observe that the dubbing doesn't quite cover the thread right up to the hook shank—fingers simply can't work that close. This is why we stopped the thread three turns short of the base of the tail, where the body will begin. The dubbing at this point should taper away to nothing. If it doesn't, execute a few twirls to pack it tighter.

20. When satisfied with the worm, wind the thread back to the base of the tail, which should bring the dubbing into contact with the hook.

21. Wind forward, laying each turn snugly against the one preceding. You will probably wish to apply a few supplementary twirls periodically to keep the dubbing tightly packed. (photo 6-12)

22. The body should end 1/32 inch or a scant millimeter in back of the wings. As you near completion, you will see how it's going to come out. If it appears as though you will run over a bit, repack the dubbing and lay your last few turns very closely together. If it looks as though you will be short by a turn or two, try to make the turns slightly less snug. If you must supplement the dubbing, use the most minute quantity. (photo 6-13)

23. Select a ginger feather of the desired shade and a grizzly feather with well-defined markings. Be sure their sizes match, as the barbule spread on a grizzly cape tends to exceed that of a ginger. (photo 6-14) Option: extend the use of your costly barred Rock capes by discrete trimming. A feather with slightly larger barbule spread than the fly calls for may be trimmed to match the ginger with little if any adverse effect on aesthetic appeal or fishability.

24. Tie in the two hackles just as you did the one on the Quill Gordon. (photo 6-15) Don't forget to leave space for the head; this is doubly important when two hackles are used. You will notice that one of the hackle stems lies forward of the other. Take this feather with the pliers and make one turn behind the wing, snug to the base. Cross under the thorax, keep winding to the tie-off point (two or three turns), secure with the thread and trim.

25. Take the second feather and make a turn immediately behind the first hackle. Now pause for a moment and scrutinize your work. If it appears there is sufficient hackle behind the wing, cross over beneath the thorax, take the remaining turns in front and tie off. If it looks as though

the area behind the wing could use another turn, by all means take it. Wind right through the first hackle and take the second turn tight to the wing. If you find you've miscalculated, simply back off, cross under, and complete the hackling process. (photo 6-16)

26. Trim, whip finish, apply Ambroid. (photo 6-17)

THE HACKLE-TIP WING

The traditional method for preparing this type of wing calls for stripping off the excess fibers as though pruning a feather for use as hackle. The method described above is quicker and easier, offers less risk of breaking delicate stems, and gives something to hold onto, which helps to keep the feathers from rolling during the tie-in. Also, errors in judgment are correctible.

WINDING TWO HACKLES

There are no real secrets in winding two feathers. However, a few considerations are worth keeping in mind:

1. When stripping the feathers, don't leave any extra fibers of questionable quality in hopes of getting an extra turn. This would be okay if it enabled one-feather operation, but in this case, you don't need it, and the additional stem will just cause trouble.

2. When winding the first feather, don't strive to pack the turns as tightly as with one-feather operation. Comfortably snug will do.

3. When winding the second feather, be observant. If it appears a particular turn isn't setting properly, back off, wiggle the feather back and forth a bit, try slightly less tension and otherwise feel out the situation. Sometimes the most minute, imperceptible adjustment will cause the turns to meld perfectly.

4. Don't struggle to get that extra turn out of either feather. If the stem is getting short or space is cramped at the head, settle for what you've got and tie off.

OPTIONAL EGG SAC

Many insects are particularly attractive to the trout when ovipositing, that is, depositing fertilized eggs in the stream. The mass of eggs located at the female's posterior becomes highly visible at this time, being quite prominent and in bright shades of yellow, orange, and green. Often the presence of egg-laden insects brings selectivity; the fish want only those flies which are carrying egg sacs.

It pays to carry a few egg-sac flies for such occasions, and the Adams is one of the best. Over the years, the Adams has been outfitted with egg sacs made of yellow chenille, yarn, or dubbing material and they worked okay. How-

6-9 After adding tail, wax thread.

6-10 Apply dubbing.

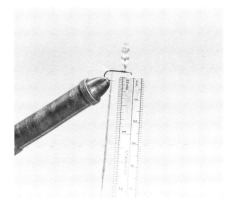

6-11 Note amount of dubbing and thread position.

6-12 Wrap the dubbing.

6-13 Wrapping completed. Note slight space behind wings.

6-14 Select proper size hackle feathers.

6-15 Tie in hackle.

6-16 Winding hackles. Sequence is dresser's preference.

6-17 The completed fly.

6-18 Optional egg sac: tie in egg sac material.

6-19 Make a loop.

6-20 Tighten the loop.

6-21 Completed egg sac with body dubbed over.

ever, Matty Vinceguerra has a far superior method, using polypropylene yarn. It is simple to construct, natural in appearance, and conducive to flotation because the poly yarn doesn't absorb water as readily as the other materials.

Here are the steps for making the Adams egg sac. Keep in mind that this technique can be carried over to other patterns simply by using the appropriate color and amount of material for the particular insect you wish to imitate.

1. Select a narrow strand of yellow poly yarn and tie it in at the bend. The yarn will be too thick for this application as it comes from the card, so it will be necessary to separate whatever amount is appropriate for the hook size involved. (photo 6-18)

2. Form a loop and tie down at the bend. (photo 6-19)

3. Tighten the loop as shown in photograph 6-20.

4. After trimming off the excess and smoothing with wraps of thread, construct the body. The fly will appear as in photograph 6-21.

7

The Gray Fox Variant

TECHNIQUES TO BE LEARNED

1. Stripped hackle stem body
2. Variant-style long hackle
3. Winding of three hackle feathers

The variant type of dry fly represents a departure from conventional proportions and component relationships. The wings are omitted, the hackle is oversized, and the tail is more substantial in order to balance out the longer hackle.

In some of the older fly-tying books, variants are described as having short, stubby wings of various types. Over the years, fly-tyers got away from these abbreviated wings because it became obvious they made no significant contribution to the fish-taking qualities of the fly. The rationale behind the oversized upright hackle of the variant is that it should represent the wing of the natural. Art Flick, one of the foremost exponents of the modern variant style, illustrates this quite clearly in his writings. In *Streamside Guide,* the Dun Variant is used to imitate *Isonychia bicolor,* and the Cream Variant, the *Potomanthus distinctus.* The hackle colors closely match the wings of the natural insects.

In his section of the *Master Fly-Tying Guide,* Art describes the dressing of the Gray Fox Variant I have come to know and love. The current dressing evolved from Preston Jennings's original pattern, which featured a gold body. Art substituted a stripped hackle quill body and embellished coloration by adding a third hackle of light ginger which complements the dark ginger and grizzly of

the Jennings version. A third innovation is the manner in which the hackle is wound. Jennings tied the grizzly in front of the ginger. Flick winds all three hackles into the same area, creating a beautiful mottled effect suggestive of the wings of the *Stenonema* mayflies and others.

The Gray Fox Variant is a pure joy to tie and fish. While I generally limit its use to moving currents, it will sometimes produce on flat pools, especially under windy conditions or in failing light. Usually it is a convincing fly which fish take solidly, but even when it doesn't, it seems they can't resist splashing at the tempting concoction, and many good fish can be located in this manner.

While it is an easy pattern to dress, there are several places where one can get into trouble by imprecise methods or by not setting up the forthcoming steps by proper execution of the previous ones. The stripped hackle stem body and three-feather hackle introduce bulky stems which must be compensated for. We will study ways to do this in the exercise.

The materials and proportions called for in this pattern will cause problems in selection and preparation, not to mention procurement. For this reason, the notes following the tying steps are much more extensive than for previously covered patterns. The reader may wish to go over them before tying the actual fly.

Mayfly Dun

COMPONENTS

Hook: Size 14 Mustad 94840 or equivalent
Thread: Tan or maize prewaxed 6/0
Tail: Preferably multivariant (see notes)
Body: Stripped medium ginger stem from large hackle feather, cape, or saddle, presoaked
Hackle: Three oversized feathers of a size that would normally be used on a size 10 hook, one medium to dark ginger, one light ginger, and one grizzly

TYING STEPS

1. Tie on at mid-hook, wind to the rear, create the bump.

2. Tie in the tail. Use more fibers than you did in the previous patterns, about half again as much. Make the tail longer than normal, ½ to 9/16 inch (12-14 mm) is about right. (photo 7-1) Spread well. Trim on the bias so that the forward taper extends to the original thread tie-in point, being careful not to encroach on the area reserved for hackle. (photo 7-2)

3. Tie in the quill so that the first turn will pass over the base of the tail just ahead of the bump. (photo 7-3) Trim the excess stem on the bias up where the tail excess ends.

4. Wind the thread forward, backward, and forward again, creating a smooth underbody. You will notice there is a slight bump at the rear where the tail and stem were tied in. Compensate for this by supplementing the area ahead of the bump until the underbody is smooth and continuous. (photos 7-4, 7-5)

5. Wind the quill to where the forward taper of the underbody slopes off. (photo 7-6) Tie it down firmly, but do not cut off the excess there. Instead, trim on the bias approximately halfway between the tie-down point and the eye. Use a sturdy pair of scissors or nail clippers, as the stem can impair delicate scissor tips. (photo 7-7)

6. Secure the quill and prepare the area for the hackling process by winding forward to the eye, then back to the forward extreme of the body. Use the thread to smooth out any significant unevenness, but be sparing. Be extra-certain to leave adequate head space. (photo 7-8)

7. Tie in the three hackle feathers in whatever arrangement you find works best for you. There is an advantage to tying the grizzly last. Barred Rock stems are usually quite fine and easier to tie over two previously wound hackles. (photos 7-9, 7-10)

8. When winding the first hackle, don't struggle for closeness as with a one-feather procedure. On the other hand, don't arbitrarily space out the turns. Let them fall naturally, and the succeeding hackles will be accomodated. (photo 7-11)

Art Flick

9. Start the second hackle one turn behind the first, then wind right through it. If slight fighting occurs, ignore it. If excessive disorder is noticed, back off a turn and meld in from a slightly different vector. (photo 7-12)

10. Start the third hackle tight to the forward edge of the body. (photo 7-13) As you begin to wind forward, pay attention to the length which remains and plan the spacing of your turns so as not to run short of feather. This is not to imply one can get away with excessive spiraling or crosswinding, for this will mash down the previously applied hackle. Moderate adjustments in spacing will work out fine.

11. Trim, whip finish, Ambroid. (photo 7-14)

12. Treat the body with two permeating coats of Ambroid. (photo 7-15) If a presoaked quill was used, which is strongly recommended, set aside the flies to dry for several hours before applying the Ambroid.

TAIL MATERIAL

With the Gray Fox Variant, one becomes aware of the difficulty encountered in procuring long, stiff tailing materials, and begins to understand why some fly-dressers drool over capes that have a wealth of spade hackle. (photo 7-16)

Multivariant materials result in the preferred diffused coloration. Multivariant capes and saddles are fairly common in Chinese imports. Usually the feathers are very large, and it is possible to find a supply which fairly well matches the feathers used for Gray Fox Variant hackles.

Naturally, one can mix ginger and barred Rock to get the same effect. The problem here is finding grizzly feathers of adequate length and quality. These feathers tend to be soft, and the spade hackles are usually very disappointing. As if this isn't enough, the saddles seldom amount to much either, at least as far as tailing material is concerned.

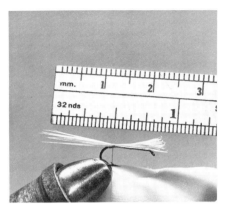

7-1 Gray Fox Variant: tail should be longer than usual to complement hackle.

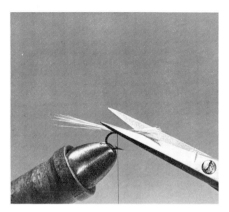

7-2 Trim excess on bias.

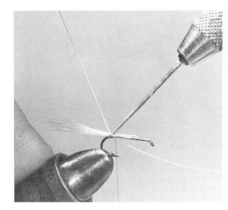

7-3 Tie in quill thus.

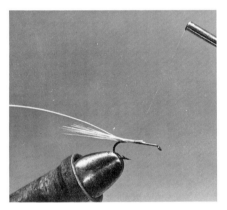

7-4 Create a smooth base.

7-5 Leave plenty of room ahead of body.

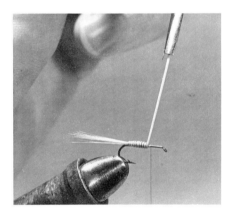

7-6 Wind quill body.

7-7 Trim excess.

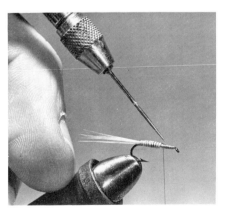

7-8 Create smooth base for hackle.

7-9 Three hackles tied in.

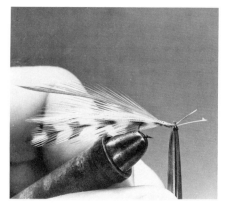

7-10 Trim stems neatly; do not obscure eye.

7-11 Wind first hackle.

7-12 Intersperse second hackle with first.

7-13 Third hackle will find niches.

7-14 The completed fly.

7-15 Cement the body.

If appropriate material for either of these two techniques cannot be located, it is advisable to use straight ginger. Top-quality barbules in this shade aren't so rare, and a solid-color tail of great stiffness is better than a mottled one that is soft. The variant style depends heavily on the tail, and it is not a good idea to compromise stiffness.

When searching for tail material, don't overlook the large hackles further back on a cape. While seldom if ever in a class with spades, they sometimes are surprisingly stiff, especially outside of the webbed center area. When using the barbules from these feathers, be sure to position the tie-in point so that the web is on the waste end that will be cut off or wound down to form the underbody.

You will encounter some difficulty in keeping the barbule tips evened up when removing variant tail material from the feather, much more so than with material for smaller flies. It is helpful to fold the feather first, stroking

the fibers so that the shiny sides are laid back against one another. In this manner, a bunch can be gathered in a small area. (photo 7-17)

BODY MATERIAL

Several excellent flies call for this type of body, notably the Red Quill Hendrickson and the Gray Fox Variant. It sounds simple to prepare, and it is. The tricky part lies in the selection and acquisition of feathers which readily lend themselves to this process.

The first thing to look for, of course, is color. If you have in mind a particular shade, it is a simple matter to match it up with the stem coloration of the feathers you are examining. Large cape hackles and saddle hackles have stems suitable for making quill bodies. Try to select those which have pure color, rather than a dark streak up the center, for even though the stem appears to be of proper coloration, it may turn out to be dark when wrapped around the hook. Also, try to select stems whose color extends almost to the end of the butt. Some stems, especially those from light ginger capes, become almost white in the butt portion, which produces an undesirable effect.

After having stripped the fibers, examine the stem closely to see if the stripping process has left white edges on either side. The best test is to wrap the stem around a hook and observe the effect. If a lot of whiteness appears, you can assume the other feathers on that saddle or cape will have like characteristics. You may either search for another bunch of feathers or supplement the coloration of the ones in hand.

Stems can be colored with either dye or felt markers. The felt marker is far more convenient than mixing up a batch of dye for a bunch of quills, even a large bunch. Select a color that is a shade or two lighter than the quill itself, as this will tint the white areas you have exposed in the stripping process a bit lighter than the quill proper, producing a segmented effect.

The technique is simple enough: merely press the quill against a piece of cardboard with the tip of the marker and draw it through a few times. Be sure to use a high-quality waterproof marker, such as the Pantone brand, which may be obtained from artist supply stores and some fly-tying material houses.

It is very important to soak the stems before use. It takes awhile to thoroughly soak the stems, at least an hour. A large number of quills can be stripped and stored in olive jars full of water. How long they will keep I cannot say, but the ones I'm using presently have been in water for several months and are in excellent condition.

When using the presoaked quills, remove them one at a time as needed, using a pair of tweezers. Wipe the excess fluid from the stem by drawing it against a blotter or some other absorbent surface. After tying, set the flies aside for awhile to allow the bodies to dry thoroughly. Then apply a protective coat of Ambroid or some other high-quality cement. Treat all quill bodies in this manner, so as to obtain some protection against damage by the trout's teeth.

Anyone who has been tying hackle-stem quill bodies for

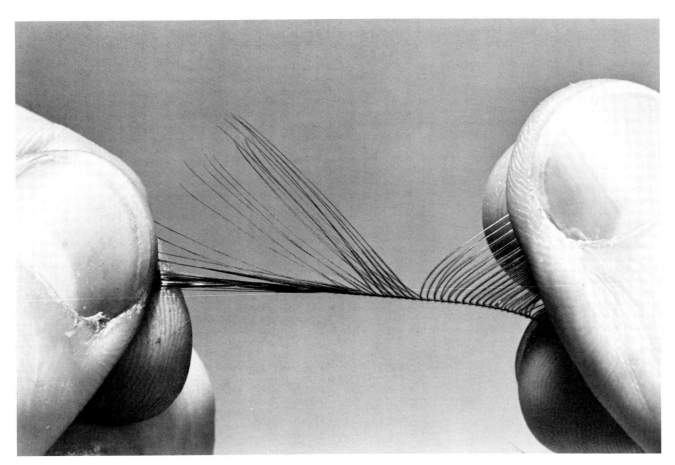

7-16 Tail material: best is near tip of spade hackle.

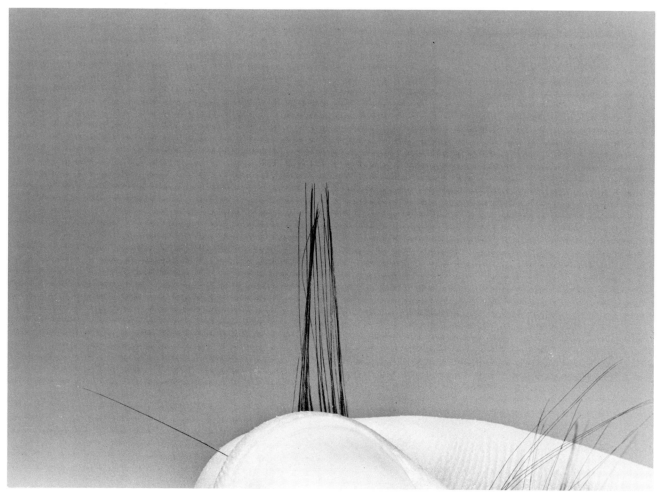

7-17 Tail material: even up tips before tying in.

awhile becomes aware that some stems are flexible enough to be wound without breakage. They should be soaked anyway. While an unsoaked quill may be wound satisfactorily, its natural tendency to straighten may cause subsequent breakage from stress such as casting or removal from a hooked fish. A soaked quill takes the shape of the hook and has far less tendency to break later on. Also, a thoroughly soaked quill is soft, and will compress nicely when tied off. A dry quill can leave a bulky lump when tied off, a potential source of trouble when the hackle is wound.

The three quill-body materials we have discussed thus far have unique properties which should be taken into account when tying. For instance, peacock quills are quite narrow, lie flat, and tie off with the least bulk of the three. This makes them most suitable for delicate work on smaller flies. Condor quills have the most pronounced contrast and are usually somewhat wider than peacock. They also have a more abrupt taper, which the tier can take advantage of to produce progressively wider segments. Condor quills tend to have a thicker edge on the dark side, which

can cause difficulty on smaller flies. Hackle-stem quills come in a number of natural colors, are very inexpensive (they are a by-product), and are the easiest to prepare. They offer a wide range of thicknesses, depending on the size of the stem itself and at what point it is tied in. This can be an asset or detriment, depending on the tier's proficiency with hard-to-handle materials.

It is important to tie in the stem at a point which will allow completion of the body without getting into the fat, pithy butt portion of the stem, but which is not so far towards the tip of the stem that the prime portion of the quill is lost. As a rule of thumb, a stem which is around 4 inches (100 mm) in length after the tip is discarded should be tied in at around the ¾-inch (20 mm) mark. This will allow the 10 to 12 wraps required for a size 14 body without running into the bulky portion of the feather.

HACKLE FEATHERS

As with tail material, the acquisition of feathers suitable for the hackle of the variant style requires some searching, particularly where grizzly is called for. The gingers aren't such a problem, especially if our relationship with mainland China continues to improve. Some recent imports of capes have been eminently suited for variant work; in fact, they were good for little else. Occasionally, a cape comes through in true multivariant coloration, which allows the Gray Fox Variant to be tied without grizzly. Such rare capes should be treasured. I hope our emerging upper echelon of domestic breeders will develop some crossed strains of superior quality.

Grizzly need not be of the best quality, provided the gingers are truly excellent. Spade hackles would yield the best grizzly, but they are not plentiful and probably never will be. So, the tier can resort to saddles and large cape hackles.

In either case, it is extremely important to strip off all of the webby hackle; actually, not much more than the tips are used. As the tip area of a large hackle feather is still 1 ¼ to 1 ½ inches (32–38 mm) long, it will be quite adequate, considering that three feathers are used. Besides the obvious deterioration in quality, another important reason for using just the tips is to avoid the thicker stem further down, which presents difficulties in winding, tying off, and trimming.

8

The Dorothea Dun Cut-Wing Parachute

TECHNIQUES TO BE LEARNED

1. Upright cut or shaped wings
2. Parachute-style hackle

Ephemerella dorothea, which is also known by pale evening dun, sulphur dun and other aliases, is one of my favorite hatches. In fact, I can think of several streams where it is *the* favorite, without qualification. The Willowemoc, lovely sister stream of the more famous Beaverkill, has a tremendous emergence of dorotheas and the trout adore them. As evening shadows lengthen, the spinners return, falling amongst the emerging subimagos, often stimulating feeding long after one can no longer see the quiet rise forms.

As mayflies go, Dorothea is on the small side of medium, generally running to the equivalent of a size 16. The period of emergence runs from mid-May to mid-June, when most eastern and midwestern streams are clear and somewhat subdued. These conditions of good visibility, coupled with six or eight weeks of almost constant encounters with ersatz snacks, cause heightened erudition on the part of Friend Trout. A skillful presentation is necessitated, and a convincing imitation.

I generally use a parachute-style fly for this hatch. The horizontally wound hackle lends itself particularly well to small, sparsely dressed patterns that are fished on the gentle water where Dorothea abounds. Consequently, this is an ideal pattern with which to demonstrate the parachute technique.

COMPONENTS

Hook: Size 16 Mustad 94840, 94833, or equivalent
Thread: Yellow prewaxed 6/0
Tail: Pale watery dun hackle fibers
Body: Sulphur-yellow poly
Wings: Pale watery dun feather tips. These may be hen hackle, rooster hackle, body feathers, or duck breast. (see notes)
Hackle: One pale watery dun feather

TYING STEPS

1. Tie on near bend, make the bump and tail, traverse the hook shank to the eye, then back twenty-five to thirty percent.

2. Tie in the wing feathers, after selecting and preparing them as described in the notes following. The technique is virtually the same as for the hackle-tip wings on the Adams described earlier. Length should be approximately ⅜ inch (10 mm) See photographs 8-1 to 8-4.

3. Before standing the wings up, trim off the butts, leaving only enough excess to ensure an effective tie-down. Secure with a few snug wraps.

4. Stand up the wings, as with the Adams. Be sure they

are on straight. Minute adjustments may be made at this point by wiggling the feathers ever so slightly. (photo 8-5)

5. Tie in the hackle feather shiny side down with the stem just ahead of the wings and the tip pointing off towards the back, as shown in photograph 8-6. This positions the feather to be wound counterclockwise.

6. Tie down the stem securely and trim.

7. Return to within a few turns of the bend—you *are* remembering to leave a bit of space to engage the body, aren't you? Spin on a thin layer of poly dubbing 1¾ inches (44 mm) long. (photo 8-7)

8. Create the body and take one or perhaps two turns ahead of the wing and tight against it, forming a mini-thorax. Keep it small, because the hackle has to be tied off in front of it. Refer to photograph 8-8.

9. We will now wind the hackle. The choice of whether or not to use a gallows tool is up to the reader (see hackle note). I prefer it for all save the stiffest wings and shall employ it in this exercise. Grasp the two wing feathers gently by the tips with the gallows tool pliers. (photo 8-9)

10. Begin to wind the hackle counterclockwise. Use very light tension and drop the hackle pliers slightly below horizontal when at ninety degrees to the hook shank, front and back. Remember that each turn should go just below and slightly on top of the one before. (photos 8-10, 8-11)

11. Sometimes it isn't possible to use up the entire feather. This is fine; parachutes shouldn't have a lot of hackle. When the feather is expended or the hackle begins to creep upward, tie off by holding the hackle up out of the way with the left thumb and forefinger and taking five or six snug winds of thread. Trim. (photo 8-12)

12. Smooth the hackle back into the position and cut a V out of the front. (photo 8-13)

13. Whip finish, Ambroid on the head, also a small drop at the base of the wing where the hackle is wound. (photos 8-14, 8-15)

CUT OR SHAPED WINGS

As previously indicated, cut wings may be made from a number of feathers. Assuming proper color, the following considerations should be taken into account. A cut wing should be all web, with no scraggly barbules around the edges. First-quality hen capes have optimum webbiness, some rooster capes do, also. Body feathers of chickens and other birds—ducks, geese and pheasants, to name a few— are nearly all web. Cut wing construction is greatly complicated by thick, stiff, center quills. Take the wings from the portion of the feather out away from the thicker quill near the butts. Hen hackle feathers have the finest, softest stems of all, which makes them the easiest to use. Body feathers, particularly those from a duck or goose, tend to have heavier stems which may roll when being tied down.

They do make beautiful wings, however. Be sure the wings sit straight when in the upright position, or casting difficulties will ensue.

Cut wings may be treated with an adhesive or put on as they are. Restraint is the byword, for cut wings which are virtually converted to plastic will almost certainly twist the leader tippet during casting. I prefer to use a bit of Krylon, applied as follows:

1. After selecting the feathers, hold them with tweezers and spray on a very light mist from 10 to 12 inches away, covering the sides.

2. Set the feathers aside and allow them to dry *thoroughly*. It is best to anticipate your needs and do a bunch an hour prior to tying.

3. Cut the feathers to shape in matched pairs, either all at a time or as required.

The feathers may be cut to shape first and sprayed afterwards; however, they trim more nicely when pretreated. Of course, a second misting may be applied after the trimming. This is a bother, as another drying interval is required.

There are several ways to trim. Either scissors or toenail clippers may be used. I prefer scissors—try both and find out which suits you.

The most expeditious method is to lay two well-matched feathers together spoon-style, as they would lie on the bird. Be sure the center quills are perfectly in line, then trim the feathers to shape simultaneously, making symmetrical the amount of material on either side of the stem. This method saves time, and matches the wings perfectly.

Some of the more advanced fly-dressers like to closely match the natural silhouette of a mayfly wing, which means the quill will not be centered. Since the feathers are placed back-to-back for tying-in, this asymmetrical cutting requires that the two wings be shaped separately. This is more work, and the trout couldn't care less. However, the effect is quite lovely, and on larger flies, there is less tendency towards twisting the leader during casting.

A new tool just on the market is the nuts for making shaped wings—the Orvis wing cutter, or more accurately, wing burner. Actually, this is a set of tools with three sizes to accommodate a full range of hook sizes. The technique is very similar to fletching arrows; heat is used to burn away the unwanted portion of the feather. The brass tongs, which are shaped at the tip like a wing, protect the feather while the exposed portion is burned away. A clean flame is required, such as that of a butane lighter or alcohol lamp. (photos 8-16–8-19)

Notice that the tips of the tools are slightly asymmetrical to facilitate the making of a realistic wing. This is a good feature, but it makes it more difficult to prepare two wings

8-1 Dorothea Dun: select wing feathers.

8-2 Shape the wings.

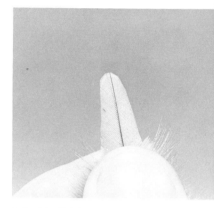

8-3 The finished product.

8-4 Tie in like the Adams. About 3/8 inch is the correct height.

8-5 Reinforce wings with wraps around base.

8-6 Tie in hackle thus.

8-7 Use about 1 3/4 inches of dubbing.

8-8 After completing body/thorax.

8-9 Pliers suspended from gallows tool.

8-10 First turn of hackle around stems.

8-11 Drop pliers below horizontal at this point.

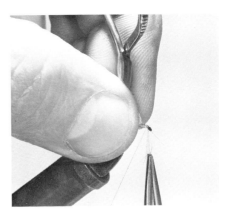

8-12 Tying off hackle.

8-13 Cut "V" from front.

8-14 Drop of cement at base of wing.

8-15 The completed fly.

at a time. Where there's a will, there's a way, however—two, in fact: insert the feathers cup-to-cup or back-to-back, as they will be positioned on the fly; or insert the feathers spoon-fashion with the stems perfectly matched, but off-set so the wings come out symmetrical. The tools cool immediately, allowing the burnt edges to be smoothed off with a rub of the finger. The result is a perfect set of wings every time, with no fuss, and in short order.

With the Adams wings an option was left open on whether to fold back the excess when tying in or to strip the quill bare. If tying cut wings untreated, one retains this option. Once treated, stripping works best.

PARACHUTE-STYLE HACKLE

The parachute technique is simple and easy if a few basic rules are carefully observed.

1. Be sure to select fine-stemmed hackle. Remember,

there is no rigid hook shank around which to bend a recalcitrant quill.

2. Use one feather; two complicates matters. It can be done—I dress parachute March Browns with a mixture of brown and grizzly hackle. These flies are much larger, of course, which facilitates the winding of two feathers.

3. Tie in the feather in such a manner that it is naturally started in the direction you want to go. In the exercise, we set up the feather for counterclockwise operation, which happens to be my preference. To wind clockwise, simply tie in the feather ahead of the wing with the tip pointing towards instead of away from you. I want to be clear on the reason for this detail, which on the surface may seem inconsequential. What we are doing is setting things up so that the quill is not doubled back over itself. I've broken many that way, to my great vexation.

4. Wind with minimal tension.

5. Drop the pliers well below horizontal on each pass around the far and near side; this keeps the feather pro-

8-16 Wing cutter: prepared feather and burning tool.

8-17 Feather inserted in tool.

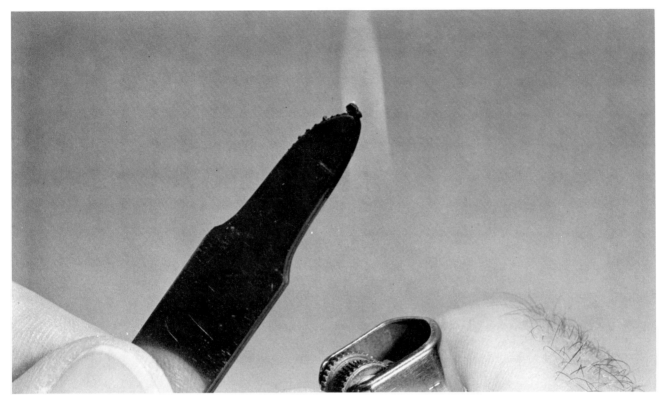

8-18 Squeeze tight, burn off all edges.

8-19 The beautiful finished product.

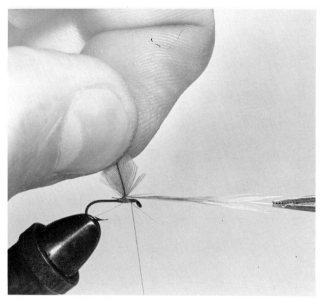

8-20 Hand-winding hackle: first half-turn of hackle. Left hand grips wings.

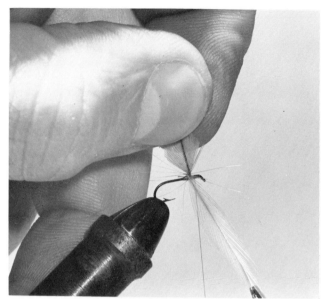

8-21 At this point, switch hands.

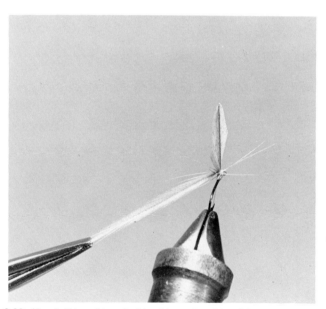

8-22 Use left hand to wind hackle to far side of fly.

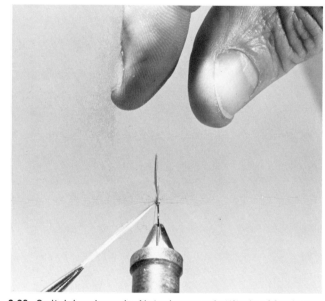

8-23 Switch hands again. Note downward attitude of feather.

gressing in a downward direction. When passing over the hook shank fore and aft, don't raise the pliers more than is absolutely necessary. Remember, with parachute hackle each successive turn goes beneath and *perhaps* slightly overlaps the previous one. You must feel your way. If the hackle flares upward, back off a turn and try again, paying strict attention to proper execution. If the flaring occurs a second time, back off and tie off—you're through.

6. Don't try to get too many turns of hackle. The snow-shoe effect of the barbules lying flat on the water obviates

the need for a lot of hackle, which tends to clutter the silhouette anyway.

7. Be particularly attentive to thorough trimming of the center stem and excess fibers around the eye. Parachute hackle tends to clutter more than conventional.

There is no need to use premium-grade hackle on parachutes. Average dry-fly grade is completely satisfactory. It is also permissible to use hackle that is slightly oversized. For instance, if you are dressing a size 16 and happen across a feather which is a scant 14, use it and don't worry.

The tying steps mentioned the gallows tool, a device which certainly makes life easier when smaller flies with supple wing stems are being worked on. Be careful to treat the delicate wing tips gently when engaging the pliers, and don't use too heavy a counterbalance.

The gallows tool is not an absolute necessity, however. It is quite feasible to hand-wind hackle around cut wings size 16 and even smaller, once proper technique is learned and a delicate touch acquired. Here is the procedure.

1. Using your master hand, take a half-turn around the wing base while holding the tips with the thumb and forefinger of the other hand. (photo 8-20)

2. With very light tension, hold the pliers in a downward attitude approximately thirty degrees below horizontal and at ninety degrees to the hook shank.

3. Change hands by releasing the wing, transferring hands on the pliers, and grasping the wing tips with the hand you have freed. The light tension and downward attitude of the bobbin must remain constant throughout this delicate maneuver, and one shouldn't be dismayed if a bit of practice is necessary. See photographs 8-21 and 8-22.

4. Repeat the change-of-hands process with each half-turn until sufficient hackle has been applied. (photo 8-23)

As an option, several turns of thread may be taken around the base of the wings immediately after standing them up, thereby adding to the stiffness of the stems. This is a good practice on larger flies. With a size 16, to avoid creating any additional bulk only apply this technique if the wings seem to be overly wobbly. If the gallows tool is used, the added rigidity is of little consequence. When executing the hand-hold technique, it can be helpful.

The Hendrickson Thorax **V** Hackle

TECHNIQUE TO BE LEARNED

Thorax "V" Hackle

An interesting characteristic of certain hatches—or more precisely, the trout's reaction to certain hatches—is that after a few days, feeding becomes picky. The fish stop gorging themselves with gluttonous abandon and become cautious and selective. Often, the same emergence which brought fish-a-minute action when it first appeared produces spotty feeding, numerous refusals, and great frustration among the angling contingent.

The Hendrickson hatch is archtypical in this respect, or at least I have found it so on the rivers I fish. Just this past spring, a young fisherman of my acquaintance, after a banner *Ephemerella* day on the Battenkill, commented that the Hendrickson was a wonderful hatch for the beginner because the fish would take anything. I suggested he try the same water again in a few days and give me a report, which he did. It was quite a different story. The same trout which had eagerly gulped any fly he cared to present were now drifting eyeball-to-hackle with his best imitations, then turning up their noses in an endless series of rejections. It was a sobering experience.

When trout manifest such behavior, it helps to have a truly convincing fly on the end of one's leader. The thorax-style **V** with a well-defined wing silhouette has proved to be that kind of fly. Russell George, who has a cottage on the big Beaverkill, raves over the effectiveness of these flies on the heavily fished no-kill waters, where the trout see more fishhooks in a day than does a factory-worker at Mustad. And Gardner Grant, who has access to some private

water on the upper Beaverkill, gloats over the times he has one-upped a visiting superstar using the **V** hackles I tied for him.

I believe the success of this style of fly is attributable primarily to two characteristics: a relatively clean silhouette in the all-important thorax area and stability during floatation, which maintains the wings in an upright attitude. The divided hackle is the key. It allows exposure of the thorax in a more natural manner while functioning as a set of outriggers to keep the fly on an even keel.

We will now employ several of the techniques examined in preceding chapters to dress the thorax-style **V** hackle. However, don't get the idea that because the Hendrickson was chosen for this exercise, the fly type is confined to that pattern. The **V** hackle style may be used to create convincing imitations for any mayfly the angler wishes to represent. Simply vary the size and coloration.

COMPONENTS

Hook: Size 14 Mustad 94840 or equivalent
Thread: Rusty brown prewaxed 6/0
Wing: Slate hen hackle feathers or comparable substitute
Tail: Stiff dun hackle fibers
Body: Rusty dubbing, either fur or synthetic, similar to body shade for Art Flick's Red Quill
Hackle: Dun

98

9-1 Hendrickson Dry Fly: position wings 1/3 shank length back from the eye.

9-2 Wings, tail, and body completed. Note thread position.

9-3 Cut a "V" out of the hackle.

9-4 Apply dubbing for thorax.

9-5 Take a turn or two of dubbing in front of hackle.

9-6 Pass through "V" front-to-rear.

9-7 Pass over top behind hackle, come back through "V".

9-8 The completed fly, side view.

9-9 The completed fly, front view.

Red Fox

TYING STEPS

1. Dress the wings, tail, and body as done in preceding exercises, leaving a bit more space ahead of the wing than with conventional dressings. (photos 9-1, 9-2)

2. Cut a **V** from the hackle at the thorax (photo 9-3)

3. Apply dubbing to thread, about fifty to sixty percent of the amount used for the body (photo 9-4)

4. Take a turn in front of the hackle. (photo 9-5)

5. Cross the dubbing under the thorax and through the **V**, coming out behind the hackle at the near side. (photo 9-6)

6. Wrap the dubbing over top of the hook shank just behind and tight to the hackle, integrating the material with the body. Then cross under the thorax and through the **V** again. (photo 9-7)

7. If necessary, repeat steps 5, 6, and 7 to obtain the desired effect.

8. Take a final turn or two of dubbing ahead of the hackle, then tie off with a whip finish and cement the head. Your fly should resemble photographs 9-8 and 9-9.

THORAX **V** HACKLE

Several techniques are essential to the successful construction of this style of fly:

1. Correct positioning of the wings at the outset.

2. Correct proportions in the body. Don't dress the front portion too heavily, as it will be supplemented by the thorax material.

3. Proper amount of material for the thorax. Keep it relatively thin and firmly packed. More can always be spun onto the thread as required.

This fly type creates opportunities for the innovator, as the thorax may be varied to produce desired effects. It definitely need not match the body—many natural insects have contrasting shading in the thoracic and abdominal areas. In fact, the body could be of another type of material, such as quill, and the thorax could be of synthetic yarn, such as polypropylene. This technique is used on the deer-hair extended body flies which we will explore in a later chapter.

10

The Leadwing Coachman Wet Fly and Nymph

TECHNIQUES TO BE LEARNED

1. Peacock herl
2. Tying the wet-fly quill section downwing
3. Adaptations to the nymph style

The first trout I ever caught on a fly took a wet Leadwing Coachman which was dangling ineffectually in the current below me while I tried to psych myself up for another go. The incident occurred on the Esopus Creek back in the mid-1950s, and if it hadn't been for that compulsive little rainbow I'd have been back to bait and spinning tackle that afternoon.

Since then, the Leadwing Coachman in nymph and wet-fly styles has taken countless fish for me. I enjoy experimenting and coming up with new flies which work, but why throw away old flies which also work, especially those which are easily tied out of inexpensive, readily available materials?

I have tied the Leadwing Coachman in many sizes, ranging from a number 10, 3X long nymph to a number 18 winged wet fly. All have worked when conditions were favorable. My favorites are 3XL size 12 for the nymph and size 10 standard for the winged wet. A lot depends on the particular stream and water type, of course. In turbulent streams, such as the Esopus and the West Branch of the New York Ausable, larger sizes are generally more productive. Conversely, the smaller sizes have worked better on more placid waters. This holds true for most patterns.

In this case, the Leadwing Coachman's success might be attributable to the faith I hold for the pattern—Theodore Gordon said, "Cast your fly with confidence." Speaking objectively, though, it's the peacock herl body that does the magic. This lovely, iridescent material suggests a number of dark nymphs and emerging forms, and is so textured that the current can cause the herl to undulate like a gill. It's simply great stuff, and the bird doesn't have to be killed in order for the feathers to be obtained.

We will discuss peacock herl in depth in the notes following the instructions for tying. Incidentally, the dressing described is not the original for this pattern. The dressing generally accepted as "authentic" calls for no tail and a gold tinsel tag. I call my dressing the Catskill Mountains version.

Wet Fly

COMPONENTS

Hook: Any standard-length, turned-down-eye hook having medium to fairly heavy wire, size 10
Thread: Black or dark brown, 6/0 prewaxed
Tail: Dark brown hen or soft rooster barbules
Body: Peacock herl (see notes)
Wing: Slate-colored duck or goose quill sections (see notes)
Hackle/Legs: Dark brown hen or soft rooster barbules

TYING STEPS

1. Tie on at the rear, creating a small thread-covered area for the seating of the tail, but no bump.

2. Tie in a tail approximately ¼ inch (6 mm) in length. It should be webby but not overly bulky. Trim the excess on a long bias to avoid an unwanted bump.

3. Wind down the excess and prepare for the body by running the thread to the eye and back.

4. Tie in a piece of the tying thread at the base of the tail, 5–6 inches long (130–150 mm). This may be done by making an elongated spinning loop and cutting off one side. See photograph 10-1.

5. Select four or five well-herled peacock fronds from a mature tail; the longer the fronds, the better. Tie these in by the tips. Wind the tying thread forward to about ¹⁄₁₆ inch (2 mm) short of the eye, or perhaps a hair more. (photo 10-2)

6. Dab a tiny bit of wax onto the right thumb and index finger. Then begin to twist the herl and the piece of thread together, taking only a few twists. You are, in essence, forming a peacock-herl chenille. (photo 10-3)

7. Take a turn of the herl around the body, imparting a few more twists in the process. (photo 10-4) Don't do more twisting than is called for, as this will cause the herl to break. *Be sure to keep the thread tight at all times,* as it provides the strong core this operation requires.

8. After completing the first turn, impart a few more twists. Then take the second turn, twisting once or twice more in the process. (photo 10-5)

9. Continue to twist-turn-twist until the body is completed. Tie off and trim the excess. Be sure to avoid creating any bumps on top of the hook where the wing will be placed. It may be necessary to smooth out this area with a few discretely applied wraps of thread, but don't build up unnecessary bulk. Maintain the ¹⁄₁₆-inch (2 mm) working space. It is very important that the wing have enough clearance; otherwise the forward extremity of the body will force it upward at an unsightly angle. See photographs 10-6 and 10-7.

10. Select two well-matched duck or goose quills from opposing wings.

11. Cut a section from each, slightly in excess of ³⁄₁₆ inch (5 mm) in width. (photos 10-8, 10-9)

12. Lay the sections concave to concave and match up the tips so they appear as one. If difficulty is encountered, try this little trick. (photos 10-10–10-13)

   a. Take hold of the sections with a three-fingered grip, as illustrated. The section which will form the near side of the wing is held between the tips of the right thumb and index finger. The other section is held between the tips of the index and middle fingers.

   b. Squiggle the fingertips back and forth until the tips match, using a chopsticks-like technique.

   c. When the match-up is perfect, seize the wings with the thumb and index finger of the left hand, then transfer them back to the right hand.

13. Match up and fine-tune the width of the sections by pulling a fiber or two off the bottom edges, using a bodkin or sharp scissors point to separate. (photo 10-14) As stated, ³⁄₁₆ inch (5 mm) is about right for a size 10.

14. Set the matched quill sections precisely atop the hook shank with the tips pointing upwards. They should extend to a point directly above the rear extremity of the bend of the hook, or *very* slightly beyond. Refer to photograph 10-15.

15. When the wings are positioned exactly where they should be, tie them on with a pinch followed by a re-pinch. This is perhaps the most critical application of the pinch technique, and execution must be extra-precise. (photos 10-16, 10-17)

16. Observe the wings and see that they sit precisely atop the shank. Adjust if necessary. Secure with five or six firm wraps at and very slightly ahead of the tie-in point. Do not make any wraps behind the tie-in point; this will mess up the beautiful down-wings you have created. Wings should now appear as in photograph 10-18.

17. Take a generous pinch of barbules from a very soft, webby, dark brown feather. You will probably wish to employ the folding technique. Be sure to keep the tips even. (photo 10-19)

18. Hold the barbules against the throat of the fly and gauge proper length. The hackle should extend just about to the inside of the hook at mid-bend, making it *very* slightly longer than the body. (photo 10-20)

19. Tie in the hackle bunch with an upside-down pinch just barely ahead of the wing tie-on point. The turns of thread used to secure the wings form the base for the hackle, and should cause it to protrude downwards from the throat at an angle of thirty to forty degrees relative to the hook shank. Secure with several firm wraps, trim without cluttering the eye. Refer to photographs 10-21 and 10-22.

20. Form a neat head, whip finish, Ambroid. (photo 10-23)

Nymph

MATERIALS AND COMPONENTS

Hook: Nymph hook, size 12, 2X or 3X long, regular to medium-heavy wire

Thread: Black or dark brown prewaxed 6/0

Tail: Very webby fibers from hen hackle, grouse hackle, body feathers or similar source, medium to dark brown

Back Stripe (optional): Heavy white cotton thread

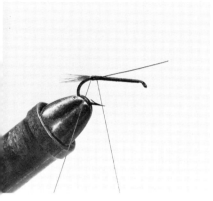

10-1 Leadwing Coachman Dry Fly: tail and supplemental thread in place.

10-2 Tie in peacock herl.

10-3 Take a few twists.

10-4 First turn of herl.

10-5 Twist some more.

10-6 Keep twisting and turning.

10-7 Tie off beneath hook shank.

10-8 Matched wing feathers, several sections removed.

10-9 Matched sections.

10-10 Conforming the wings: first grip sections thus.

10-11 Bring tips together like chopsticks.

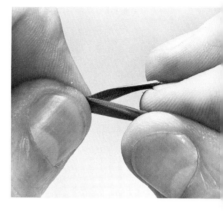

10-12 Seize with left thumb and forefinger.

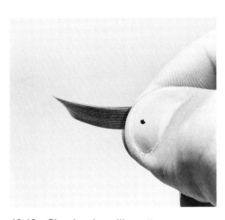

10-13 Classic wing silhouette.

10-14 Reducing width of sections uniformly.

10-15 Positioning wings atop hook.

10-16 Tie in wings with two or more pinches.

10-17 Wings tied precisely.

10-18 Trim excess, prepare area for hackle.

10-19 Typical bunch of hackle fibers.

10-20 Position fibers beneath throat.

10-21 Upside-down pinch.

10-22 Trim excess.

10-23 The completed fly.

Body: Peacock herl, bronzy-purple coloration, extralong
Hackle/Legs: Webby dark brown hen hackle
Wing Case: Very dark gray duck or goose quill section

TYING STEPS

1. Tie in a short, thick tail, approximately ³/₁₆ inch (5 mm) in length.

2. Tie in the white thread for the back stripe dead center on top of the hook over the base of the tail. (photo 10-24) Secure in material clip.

3. Tie in the herl and the thread for twisting, secure in material clip. (photo 10-25)

4. Wind the tying thread to the eye, then back ³/₁₆ inch (5 mm). See photograph 10-26.

5. Tie in the wing case material and the hackle feather. (photo 10-27)

6. Wind the thread forward to a point near the eye, leaving sufficient space to tie off the bulky material and the thread itself.

7. Create the body as described for the wet fly, winding and twisting forward over the abdomen section. (photo 10-28)

8. Work around the wing case and hackle material, form the thorax, and tie off. (photo 10-29)

9. Wind the hackle over the thorax in a spiral (palmer) style. (photo 10-30) Four turns should suffice. Tie off.

10. Fold the wing case over a bodkin or needle. (photo 10-31) The herl thorax doesn't fill out the area very effectively, and this little trick helps create a good-looking thorax silhouette. Tie off, as in photograph 10-32.

11. Bring the back stripe thread all the way forward, center it precisely over the hook shank, tie down. (photo 10-33)

12. Fold the thread over backwards, secure with a few more tight wraps. Whip finish.

10-24 Leadwing Coachman Nymph: tail and white thread for stripe in place.

10-25 Tie in herl and thread for twisting.

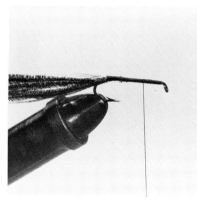

10-26 Advance thread to this position.

10-27 Tie in wing case and hackle material.

10-28 Wrap thread to front, create herl body.

10-29 Complete herl thorax, tie off.

10-30 Wind hackle, trim off top fibers.

10-31 Fold wing case over a needle.

10-32 Tie off wing case.

10-33 Bring back stripe thread forward, tie down.

10-34 Cement on top.

10-35 The completed fly.

13. Apply two coats of rather tacky Ambroid to the entire back of the nymph, peacock area included. (photo 10-34) Be careful not to gunk up the sides and underside of the body. Allow thorough drying between coats. Smooth down the peacock herl back with a finger. The finished fly should resemble photograph 10-35.

The optional back stripe is intended to represent the whitish stripe on the nymph of the mayfly, *Isonychia bicolor*. The fly is quite effective without it, so don't view this component as crucial. None of the other major *Isonychias—sadleri, albomanicata, harperi*—have a stripe distinctive enough to warrant imitation.

PEACOCK HERL

The tail-feathers of a peacock vary greatly in many respects. The characteristics that most concern us in this exercise are length of fronds and thickness of herl on the fronds. A large tail-feather will have fronds of around 6 inches (150 mm) in length. For average to large-sized flies, the longer the better. Remember, we are tying in the fronds by their tips, and there is a very good reason for doing so. The center quill is much finer at the tip, which makes for more effortless twisting when forming the chenille-type body. The herl is just about uniform in thickness over the length of the frond, so the herl-to-quill ratio is much more favorable, producing a soft, dense body. The further out towards the tip, the better the quality of the herl and the greater the ease of execution.

The density of the herl, not the number of turns, should dictate the fullness of the body. Do not use layers or overwraps to build up a herl body; the results are unsightly and unsatisfactory. Fronds with thicker herl are found nearer the eye of the feather, those with thinner herl nearest the butt. Sometimes a single feather will have a range of herl thicknesses which allows tying sizes from 10's down to 18's. If your large feathers don't yield suitable herl for small flies, it is a simple matter to obtain small feathers with thinly herled fronds at minimal cost.

A word about color. Fresh peacock tails are usually very green, whereas the shade preferred by most fly-dressers has a distinct bronze or purplish cast. Green peacock will take this hue if set before a window where the sun can shine on it. Allow several weeks to a month.

The thread-twist method for creating the chenille-herl body was shown to me by Matt Vinciguerra, my star photographer. Bodies thus formed are very evenly herled and practically indestructable. Even more strength may be obtained by substituting a piece of fine monofilament for the thread, but this is not needed, and the thread is nicer to work with. Formerly, I used either a stout thread or fine copper wire reverse ribbing to protect peacock herl bodies. The twist method produces much better results from all standpoints.

WINGS AND WING QUILLS

The name "Leadwing Coachman" is highly suggestive of the shade of quill required for the wings. I have found this pattern to be far more effective when dressed with feathers having a heavy lead or slate coloration.

The perfect quills for this pattern come from the wings of a black duck—the black duck species, not some bird which has been dyed jet black. This canny member of the migratory waterfowl family is quite populous on Atlantic and eastern flyways, and is a great favorite of the serious duck-hunter. It is wise to court the friendship of these

10-36 Wings and wing quills: secondary flight feathers.

10-37 Primary flight feathers, or pointers.

dedicated fanatics, because wild black duck feathers may not be sold commercially, and the birds will not domesticate.

In addition to color, black duck quills have other properties which are of benefit to the fly-dresser. Usually the curvature is fairly moderate, so that one isn't fighting the feathers' tendency to cup. Also the texture of the quills is ideal, even though the black duck is one of the largest. The feathers are soft and workable, yet the fibers hold together very well under stream conditions, and retain the shape in which they were tied.

The nicest feathers for winging wet flies—and this applies to all waterfowl—are the secondary flight quills. (photo 10-36) The primaries, or pointers, may also be suitable; however, these tend to be rougher in texture and have less usable quill area. This is due in part to the very fibrous portion nearest the center stem, which extends much farther out into the feather on pointers. (photo 10-37) This portion is only suitable as a handle with which to manipulate the quill sections. The tie-in point should be outside the rough area.

The tertiary, or inner flight, feathers are also very good,

10-38 Inner or tertiary flight
feathers.

10-39 Removing excess curvature
by ironing.

Canada Goose

especially for smaller flies. (photo 10-38) Two problems may present themselves: the quills may be badly cupped or they may be a lighter shade. The latter is solved by merely selecting one of the many tertiaries with a beautiful lead shade. Neither is the curvature problem difficult to resolve. Considerable success results from ironing out the feathers with a steam iron. (photo 10-39) Steam alone is adequate to reshape the feather; the key is to not use high heat. The method works equally well on pointers, secondaries, and tertiaries. It can also render usable feathers that have been crumpled or messed up by packaging and shipping. The curvature will not always flatten out completely from ironing, but this is as it should be; a moderate amount of opposing curvature causes the wings to match up and hold together in the desired manner.

On the underside of the wings near the shoulder are many smaller feathers which are somewhat palmeate in shape, the smaller, the more so. These feathers are extremely finely textured and make great wings on small wet flies. They also lend themselves admirably to the no-hackle dry-fly style, a technique that has been well-documented in a number of books and periodicals.

Notice that the stems of small feathers around the base

of the pointers and secondaries on the inner side of the wing are more or less centered. This allows matched sections to be taken from either side of the stem. The curvature, such as it is, is generally opposing, so the sections behave in a manner similar to those taken from right and left wing quills. (photos 10-40, 10-41) The only real problem is a tendency for the fibers to separate. Careful handling ameliorates this to a large degree. A light misting of Krylon also helps, particularly for dry-fly work. Be very sparing in application.

Sometimes these small feathers have angular fibers. In other words, the attitude of the fibers from the center quill is sharply upward, rather than predominately outward. This may occur in flight quills, to a lesser degree. The problem is that sections cut from such feathers are too pointed, and produce ill-shaped wings.

It is a simple matter to correct the angle of the fibers by preening until they assume the configuration of the better secondary quills. (photos 10-42, 10-43) Some smaller feathers don't respond well to this treatment, because their tips tend to fray. These will make poor wings and should be discarded.

Incidentally, the preening technique is very effective in

10-40 Inner feathers with centered quill can yield matching wing sections.

10-41 Matching wing sections on another inner feather with centered quill.

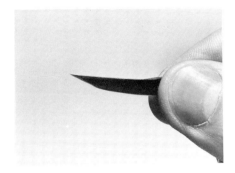

10-42 Shape too pointed.

10-43 Corrected by preening.

10-44 Covert feather, wing case, and cut wing.

10-45 Separation of fibers caused by tying in quill sections with tips pointing downward.

preparing quill sections for use in making nymphal wing cases. The sections behave more uniformly when the fibers lie straight with the shank of the hook. Preening is done while the adhesive is being applied with the fingers. If a spray is used, preen beforehand, get the fibers pointing as desired, then spray.

On larger flies, an excellent substitute for black duck is Canada goose. In fact, these quills are every bit as good as black duck, providing the goose was a fairly small one. The big old honkers have coarser quills than one might wish, also more curvature. They are also not as responsive to ironing as the softer duck quills.

Quills from the wings of other waterfowl, such as mallard, teal, and wood duck, are suitable for wing-making in varying degrees. The colors are considerably lighter, which is fine for patterns which call for such shades but not so good for the Leadwing Coachman. Mallards sometimes are fairly dark and have qualities similar to black duck, in-

cluding size. Teal, wood duck, and other smaller birds generally have very fibrous quills which, coupled with small size, generally limits their use.

On the upper side of the wing in the shoulder area are located a large number of small, palmeate feathers called covert feathers. (photo 10-44) These are often used in an alternative method of making nymphal wing cases. An application of some adhesive—Krylon, vinyl cement, or whatever—is applied, and after this has dried thoroughly, the coverts are trimmed to shape with scissors, nail clippers, or other instrument. This method can produce very realistic wing case silhouettes, particularly from a top perspective. Feathers can be cemented together or laid one atop the other to create special effects, such as simulation of the dual wing cases and large prototophorax of the stonefly nymphs. When used in this manner, the feathers are given a thorough adhesive treatment.

Covert feathers also make excellent cut wings. To avoid

excessive curvature, it is desirable to select those which are of substantial size and set in from the leading edge of the wing. The feathers are well-shaped and take on a most realistic appearance with minimal trimming. The stems are generally not as contrary as those of the more widely used breast feathers, though they might look that way. Usually coverts tie up into a properly aligned upright wing with little or no trouble, provided one avoids using the lower portion, where the stem is usually thick and cantankerous.

A final note on quill section downwings, as these are called: in step 14 I specified the quill sections be tied in with the tips pointing upward. There is a school which advocates just the opposite, on the grounds that the wings lie down flatter and are more suggestive of an emerging insect. However, when the wings are inverted with tips pointing down, the thread intersects the quill sections at such an angle as to cause the fibers to separate and flair. (photo 10-45)

Proper technique will cause the wings to lie in the proper attitude, even with the tips pointing upward. Here are several helpful suggestions:

1. Be sure to create a smooth, flat area on which to seat the wings.

2. Don't carry the body too far forward, as this will produce a bump which will cock the wings. If possible, build in a gentle forward taper.

3. Be conservative about the width of the quill sections.

4. Avoid the fibrous portion of the quill section near the center stem.

5. Option: allow the quill sections to slip down *very slightly* over the shoulders of the fly on either side. Don't overdo this, or the wings will tend to cover the body, a most undesirable situation.

It is obvious by now that a pair of matched wings from a black duck or Canada goose can provide a great deal of valuable fly-tying material. Anyone interested in dressing wet flies and nymphs will do well to acquire at least one pair of wings, preferably from the same bird. If that isn't possible, left and right wings from different birds of similar size and coloration will do. Learn how to handle the various types of feathers and the many applications of them. The result will be a great many attractive, effective, inexpensive flies.

Extended Deer-Hair Body: T-Bone

Extended Deer-Hair Body: Coffin Fly

Extended Deer-Hair Body:
Blue-Winged Olive Parachute

Gray Fox Variant

Hendrickson Cut-Wing, V-Hackle,
Thorax-Style

Blonde Haystack

Ausable Wulff (Tied by Francis
Betters, the originator)

Brown Haystack

Adams, Plain

Buff Gangle-Legs

Quill Gordon

Adams, Egg Sac

Hendrickson, Pheasant-Tail Spent

Dorthea, Cut-Wing, Parachute

Black Gangle-Legs

Rusty Orange Spent

Light Dorato Hare's Ear

Dark Dorato Hare's Ear

Plain Hare's Ear Nymph

Spent Gangle-Legs

Gold-Ribbed Hare's Ear Nymph

Isonychia (Lead-Wing Coachman) Nymph

March Brown Nymph

Dark Cahill   Muddler Minnow   Leadwing Coachman

          Perla Stonefly, Orange   Perla Stonefly, Yellow

Grouse and Green   Alternative   Orange Fish-Hawk

Hornberg

Blacknosed Dace

Gray Ghost

Mickey Finn, Synthetic Hair

Black Ghost Marabou

Beady-Eye

Metz Cape Medium-Dark Dun

Small Indian Cape Cream/Ginger

Bill Tobin Cape (Trout Brook
Hackle Co.) Cream

Large Chinese Cape Ginger Variant

Light Multi-Variant Cape

Dark Multi-Variant Cape

Red Variant Cape

Wet-Fly/Nymph Hackle Feather Grouping:

Woodcock   Hen Pheasant   Guinea   Orange Guinea

Tipped Wood Duck   Brown Mallard   Gray Hen

Grizzly Hen   Gray Mallard   Grouse

Grouping Showing Color Contrast, Fronts and Backs of Adjacent Feathers from Same Capes:

Front, Back Coachman Brown   Front, Back Ginger   Front, Back Dun

Underwater shot: Nymph before "fuzzing" process. Note opaqueness.

Underwater shot: Nymph after "fuzzing" process. Note translucency.

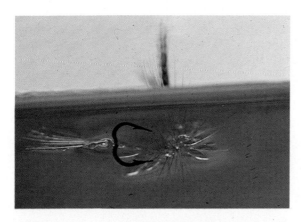

Underwater shot: Standard Quill Gordon Dry Fly. Note indistinct wing silhouette and lack of visible thorax.

Underwater shot: Hendrickson Dry Fly, Cut-wing, V-Hackle, Thorax style. Note cleaner silhouette.

Natural crane fly

Spent Gangle-Legs dry fly. A pretty convincing imitation.

11

The Dark Cahill Wet Fly

TECHNIQUES TO BE LEARNED

1. The spinning-loop dubbing method
2. The imitation wood duck downwing

The Dark Cahill is another traditional pattern which has been tied and fished with telling effect throughout the greater Northeast for several generations. It is a nonspecific pattern, not corolating with one particular insect. Still, it is a handsome, productive concoction.

This pattern is dressed both as a wet and dry fly. Here we are examining the underwater version. We will dress the fly on a size 10 hook, a popular size for wet flies of this type. The Dark Cahill is a great pattern for night fishing, and is often tied on very large hooks—6's, 4's and even 2's, for nocturnal use. The nice thing about the Dark Cahill is that the materials are very plentiful and inexpensive, and lend themselves readily to the dressing of extra-large flies.

COMPONENTS

Hook: Size 10, standard-length shank, average to medium-heavy wire
Thread: Black or dark gray prewaxed 6/0
Tail: Medium brown fibers, same shade as hackle
Body: Soft, dark gray fur, such as muskrat or rabbit
Wings: Mallard flank feathers dyed wood duck color
Hackle: Medium brown, very soft and webby

TYING STEPS

1. Tie on at the tail. Don't worry about covering the hook with thread; you will do that in the normal course of tying the fly.

2. Tie in a bunch of hackle barbules for the tail. These should be fairly short, about ¼ inch (6 mm). Trim on the bias, tapering off around the thoracic area.

3. Now we will execute the spinning-loop dubbed body. Expose 4 to 5 inches (100–125 mm) of thread and apply a bit of supplementary wax, if desired. Note: do not leave space for a few turns of thread towards the tail, as was done in the case of single-thread dubbing.

4. Begin to apply the fur in thin layers, spinning it onto the thread as described earlier. Work up into the area around the hook as closely as possible.

5. If necessary, work the fur in close to the hook by sliding the dubbing up the thread.

6. Use somewhat more dubbing than with the single-thread method, as the twisting of the loop will greatly compact the material. When ready for twisting, the dubbing for a size 10 should resemble an elongated cigar approximately 2½ inches (63 mm) in length, 1/16 inch (2 mm) in diameter at the thickest point, and tapered at both ends. (photo 11-1)

11-1 Dark Cahill Wet Fly: about 2½ inches of dubbing is needed for a wet fly size 10.

11-2 Create the spinning loop.

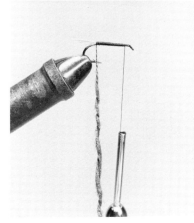

11-3 After winding thread to front, begin twisting the loop.

7. Seize the thread with the hackle pliers ³⁄₁₆ inch (5 mm) beyond the end of the dubbing.

8. Expose a length of thread sufficient to form the loop, approximately 3 inches (75 mm) in this case.

9. *Maintain tension with the hackle pliers.* Pass the thread over the hook at the exact terminal point of the dubbed thread (photo 11-2), then wind forward with neatly aligned wraps to the point where the forward extremity of the body will terminate. Allow ¹⁄₁₆ inch (2 mm) or a hair more for the wings, hackle, and head.

10. Begin to twist the loop under moderate tension. (photo 11-3) You may twist clockwise or counterclockwise.

11. Keep twisting until the spirals in the dubbing disappear and the thread is buried in the fur of the worm. This will require quite a few twists, around sixty to seventy. Once the desired effect is obtained, stop twisting, or you may break the thread where the loop meets the hook.

12. Wind the dubbing to form the body, maintaining moderate tension. Take a few supplementary twists in the process, if required. (photo 11-4)

13. If the process was properly controlled, you should run out of dubbing precisely upon reaching the waiting tying thread. Tie off on the bottom of the hook shank. Trim off the excess thread; form a smooth base on which to mount the wing. Refer to photograph 11-5.

14. Dyed mallard is handled in almost the same manner as the genuine wood duck used for the wings of the Quill Gordon Dry Fly, except that the fibers must point to the rear, which means the hands are reversed. Select a center section, hold it with the thumb and forefinger of the right hand, and fold it with a downward stroke of the thumb and forefinger of the left hand. (photos 11-6, 11-7)

15. To improve the shape of the bunch of fibers, preen

them upwards at an angle, thus working the tips into a more winglike conformation. See photograph 11-8.

16. Position the wings on the hook, adjust so that the tips extend to the rear extremity of the bend. (photo 11-9)

17. Tie in with a pinch, a repinch and a few tight wraps for security (photo 11-10)

18. Tie in the beard-type hackle, like with the Leadwing Coachman. (photo 11-11)

19. Whip finish, Ambroid. The fly should resemble photograph 11-12.

THE SPINNING LOOP

Even a fairly simple procedure like the spinning loop can be made easier by precise execution and attention to detail, and conversely, can be complicated by slipshod methodology.

DO

1. Work the dubbing up tight to the hook where the body starts, thus avoiding the creation of an unsightly mass of twisted thread.

2. Put the material onto the thread in small quantities. The fibers should lie lengthwise on the thread. Natural fur goes on much smoother if it has been fluffed in a blender first.

3. Be sure the material is spread evenly and uniformly, with no lumps, bumps, or hollows.

4. Leave only enough space between the end of the material and the point of seizure to permit tying off the twisted thread, without any bulky dubbing to produce a bump.

1-4 Wrap the body, twisting as you go.

11-5 Leave space for wing at front.

11-6 Grip feather.

1-7 Fold the feather.

11-8 A good silhouette.

11-9 Position wings for the tie-in.

1-10 Tie in with two or three pinches.

11-11 Tie in the hackle.

11-12 The finished fly.

11-13 Alternative method of forming loop: using crochet hook.

5. Tie off on the bottom of the hook.

6. If other components are to be tied in subsequently, as is usually the case, be very attentive to the forward taper of the body and the work area up near the eye. Where the wet-fly type of wing is employed, it is absolutely essential that no excess material build up on top of the hook immediately behind the tie-in point, as this will certainly force the wing to slant upwards at too steep an angle.

DON'T

1. Don't use overly heavy thread, except possibly on very large flies. Twisted thread creates bulk.

2. Don't use a thread color which will alter or contradict the body color. If the tying thread being used is wrong for the body, tie in a separate piece of appropriate color in the form of a spinning loop. Hold the loop open with the fingers of the left hand, apply the dubbing, then twist as usual.

3. Don't use too much material—not even slightly. Remember, it is infinitely more desirable to tie off thread than dubbing.

4. Don't use the spinning loop on small flies, as it creates too much bulk. A size 16 wet or nymph is about as small as is practical, and that with great circumspection.

5. Don't twist too much or under excessive tension. The

thread will knot up and break at the point where the loop meets the hook.

A common crochette hook may be employed as an aid in twisting the loop. It is readily obtainable in any store which has a sewing and knitting section. Use a fairly small-headed model, such as a number 2. The loop is formed by hooking the thread with the crochette hook, rather than seizing it with the hackle pliers. Everything else remains the same.

The crochette hook greatly increases the ease of twisting, and makes it more enjoyable—one can really go like hell! When sufficient twisting has been accomplished, the thread is seized with the hackle pliers, the hook slipped out, and the procedure carried through to completion. While this does introduce an additional step, it is compensated for by the speed and ease of twisting. (photo 11-13)

IMITATION WOOD DUCK WING

We should all be very grateful to the ubiquitous, easily domesticated mallard for growing barred flank feathers which are in most respects similar to those of his exotic relative, the wood duck. How could the fly-dressers of the world manage without a plentiful, low-cost substitute for the wood, or commercially speaking, the oriental Mandarin duck? The American species was accorded game-bird status many years ago, and its plumage is no longer available commercially.

Apparently the great fly-tying explosion, which began in the late 1960s and is still growing, has caused severe depletion of the Mandarin duck. In this case, the shortage seems more real than contrived, for supply has become a greater problem than price. Few catalogs list Mandarin, and even fewer offer complete skins. Those which do asked $20.00 or more per skin in the summer of 1977. Pairs or small packets of barred flank feathers are bringing 10 to 15 cents per feather, on the average. And to think that in the early to mid-1960s, we could get all the prime Mandarin skins we wanted at $2.50 to $3.00 each.

Even when wood duck flank was relatively inexpensive, I saved it for my dry flies and used dyed mallard or teal on the wets. For the downwing style, mallard is perfectly suitable. This material may be purchased predyed or can be bought in the natural shade and dyed. This is very easily done, as today's dyes are excellent and inexpensive. I have used the Veniard brand with outstanding results, and there are others of comparable quality.

The shape and conformation of mallard flank feathers are generally similar to that of wood duck, and the methods for handling sections and bunches of fibers are, for all intents and purposes, the same. As mentioned, down-

wings are tied on with the tips pointing backwards, so the roles of the right and left hands are the opposite of the dry-fly procedure. Still, the rationale is to utilize the center and side portions of the feathers to produce the silhouette.

As one might expect, the actual forming and tying-on is much easier than with dry-fly wings. We don't have to stand the fibers up, divide them equally, and secure them in position. All that's required is to affix a bunch of material to the hook in a winglike arrangement. From a purely utilitarian standpoint, practically any method, however rudimentary, will suffice. Many of the old-time country fly-tiers simply rolled the fibers into a bunch and tied them on. The flies took trout. However, my penchant for aesthetics drives me towards more sophisticated techniques.

In my opinion, the most attractive and effective silhouette for this type of wing is one which suggests a natural mayfly wing laid back over the body as it might be positioned during emergence. To get this shape, the fibers must be stacked vertically, rather than rolled or flattened out over the body of the fly. With a modicum of adroit handling, this is easily accomplished.

The wings of this pattern are so constructed as to form one unified silhouette, as opposed to the divided configuration of the corresponding dry fly. Consequently, when feather sections are folded or matched to form a downwing, they are handled with that result in mind. Sections with curvature are matched concave-to-concave, rather than convex-to-convex, the dynamics being similar to the matching of opposing wing quill sections. The natural alignment of the fibers must be maintained throughout the entire procedure. In other words, the sections, either folded or matched, are so manipulated as to maintain their vertical flatness when stood on edge and tied onto the hook. This is a real test of one's pinch technique. The wings' appearance is enhanced if the fibers form a rough ellipse, like the natural. This is affected by simply stroking the fibers upward with the left thumb and forefinger while holding the butts with the right thumb and forefinger.

That's really about all there is to it—unless one wishes to get fancy. As the tier becomes intimately familiar with mallard flanks, he will notice the presence of certain large, well-formed feathers of a type which do not occur in natural wood duck. These feathers have a well-conformed edge which is somewhat reminiscent of the shape of a wing quill. Only one edge of a feather has this, and which edge it is depends on which side of the bird the feather was taken from. So we have once again a situation of opposing curvatures, as with wing quills. (photo 11-14)

Sections may be taken from these feathers and made into wings, using the same method as with flight quills. Of course, feathers of similar conformity from opposite sides

11-14 Alternative method of forming loop: using opposing sections.

of the bird are required to produce matched sections. These feathers are not as rugged as flight quills, and require very careful handling to prevent the sections from falling apart. A light misting with Krylon helps.

The real problem is obtaining these great flank feathers in matched pairs. Bulk purchases of mallard flanks—two or three ounces—will probably contain a number of these feathers. It is then a matter of sorting out and matching them. A simpler and better method is to obtain a mallard skin with the flank feathers in place.

Wings created by this method are quite pleasing to the eye. From a utilitarian standpoint, however, they are no better than the common variety. So if someone elects to go to the trouble of wading through bags full of feathers, then tying the delicate sections into a wing, he should be aware that the rewards are purely artistic, not piscatorial.

 # The Orange Fish-Hawk Wet Fly

---

TECHNIQUES TO BE LEARNED

1. Floss wet-fly body
2. Tinsel ribbing over floss
3. Folded and wound hackle

Simply dressed wet flies, some having only two components, have been widely used on the chalk streams of Great Britain for centuries, apparently with excellent results. It is doubtful that many British anglers of antiquity had a precise knowledge of what they were imitating, but the dressings that evolved indicate that some certainly did. Dame Juliana Berhers used them, and so did Charles Cotton. Hundreds of years later, G.E.M. Skues was duping the sophisticated browns of Hampshire with such patterns as the Devon and the Yorkshire. Skues brought it all together in his extremely perceptive and literate writings on the nymphal and emerging forms, of which soft-hackle wets are most suggestive.

The American counterpart to Skues was, of course, James E. Leisenring, whom Ernest Schwiebert has dubbed, "the wet-fly wizard of the Brodheads." Big Jim's excellent book, *The Art of Tying the Wet Fly,* is now back in print, with a new introduction by Ernie and a second section, "Fishing the Flymph," by Vernon S. Hidy.

Leisenring was a great exponent of the emerging form style of fishing. A long career on very demanding waters motivated him to develop his technique to a level few anglers have ever achieved. The subtle movements imparted to the fly as it approached the trout were referred to by the master as "making the fly deadly." The fact that his reputation lives on is a tribute to how very great his skills must have been.

The Leisenring book is a must for anyone who hasn't committed himself to dry-fly purism. All of Jim's favorite nymph and wet-fly patterns are in there, along with a wealth of tying and angling information. While I feel some of the processes are slightly out-of-date, I would not be so rash as to challenge a word. Whatever Big Jim did was right, obviously, and the fact that clever innovation in recent years has enabled us to produce the same effect more easily detracts not a whit from the validity of his methods.

A contemporary exponent of soft-hackle patterns is none other than our current empirical genius, Ernie Schwiebert. The caddis section of *Nymphs* is full of such references, as Ernie recommends this type of fly for imitating caddis pupae. In a number of cases he has supplemented and expanded upon the original patterns, in order to create a more realistic image. Those which I have used have been dynamite, and are now permanent additions to my subaqueous inventory. *Nymphs* is another book no serious angler and tier should be without; there's simply no other work which even remotely approximates it.

Trout Feeding on Emerging Flies

The first of the two soft-hackle flies in this book is an old friend from my fledgling days astream. The Orange Fish-Hawk, while somewhat improbable in appearance, is effective enough to be worth carrying, and is perfect for demonstrating the techniques in question. Some people feel it is probably an American pattern carried over from the brook trout era, but several British patterns have orange bodies, so the origin is somewhat uncertain.

Caddis Pupa

COMPONENTS

Hook: Size 12, regular shank, medium wire
Thread: Light orange or yellow
Tail: None
Body: One strand medium or two strands fine orange floss
Ribbing: Narrow gold tinsel, 1/64 inch (1 mm) in width
Hackle: Golden or cream badger, folded

TYING STEPS

1. Tie on 1/8 inch (3 mm) back from the eye, cover the hook with thread to the bend.

2. Cut off a 3-inch (75 mm) piece of tinsel, tie it in with two turns of thread. (photo 12-1)

3. Position the tinsel by tilting it upwards at as steep an angle as is feasible, approximately sixty degrees. Then take a turn or two of thread over the tinsel, working back towards the bend, thereby forcing the tinsel to begin to wrap around the hook.

4. Secure the tinsel by winding over the excess, working forward to within 1/8 inch (3–4 mm) of the eye. The thread should form a perfectly smooth underbody for the floss which is to follow.

5. Tie in a 7-inch (175 mm) piece of floss with two or three wraps of thread, and trim off the excess. *Be sure your fingers are clean.*

6. Secure the floss and smooth out the tie-in area with a few more wraps of thread.

7. Begin wrapping the floss back towards the bend. If the material shows a tendency towards unevenness or excessive spreading, twist it a few times. This problem is more apt to occur in thicker strands. Partially cover each previous wrap for maximum smoothness.

8. At the bend, cover the tie-in of the tinsel with one turn of floss and begin to wrap the material back over itself towards the eye. (photo 12-2) At this stage it is doubly important to partially overlap the winds so that each turn of floss slides off the preceding one and settles smoothly onto the hook. Smoothness can be further enhanced by wiggling the floss laterally, as required.

9. Wind the floss a turn or two past the original tie-in point, creating a smooth forward taper.

10. Secure the floss with several tight wraps and trim off the excess, leaving a slight stub to enable a secure tie-off.

11. Wind forward to the eye and back, tying down the floss firmly. This is important. Floss is a slippery material, and will pull loose if not tightly secured.

12. Saturate the body with well-thinned clear cement. Do not use Ambroid, as it has a tendency to discolor the floss.

13. Begin to wind the tinsel ribbing by taking a tight wrap around the butt end of the body, tilting the floss in a forward direction so it climbs up onto the rear taper.

14. Take five turns of tinsel, maintaining as much tension as the material will permit. Keep the spacing as uniform as possible. (photo 12-3)

15. Tie off with a series of *very* firm wraps of thread—tinsel is even more slippery than floss. Work the thread into a position approximately 1/16 inch (2 mm) back from the eye, or perhaps a hair more.

16. We will now prepare a folded hackle. Select a size 12 feather from a soft cape or saddle. This pattern calls for badger, a type of hackle which is cream or straw-colored with a black center stripe.

17. Affix a pair of hackle pliers to the stem down towards the butt and hold in the right palm. Hold the tip of the feather with the left thumb and forefinger. *The dull side of the feather must be facing downward.* See photograph 12-4.

18. Starting near the tip, begin to stroke the barbules on each side of the center stem upward and back at a forty-five degree angle. In other words, fold the bright side of the feather against itself. Repeat until the barbules form a single row sticking straight upwards from the stem. Refer to photograph 12-5.

19. When a sufficient length of hackle has been folded, release the pliers and strip off the excess, as with a dry-fly hackle. The feather should now appear as in photograph 12-6.

20. Tie in with the barbules pointing back towards the bend. (photo 12-7)

21. Wind the hackle dry-fly style, stroking the barbules back as the turns are taken. (photo 12-8) Four or five wraps should be sufficient; excessive hackle detracts from this fly's appearance and effectiveness.

22. Tie off and whip finish. Before applying head cement, take a black felt pen and blacken the head of the fly on all sides. (photo 12-9)

FLOSS

Floss is an inexpensive material which comes in a wide range of colors, including fluorescent ones. Usually it comes on spools and is available in several weights or thicknesses. One type has four extrafine strands wound together on a spool; the tier can use a single strand or multiples for smaller and larger flies, a convenient feature.

Today the most common materials used in producing floss are nylon, rayon, acetate, and the traditional silk. I prefer nylon and rayon because they are inexpensive, colorfast, and stain-resistant. Acetate has an interesting property—it may be soaked in Acetone solvent and squeezed with pliers to form a flat body. New silk is the most beautiful of materials, but it will soil easily and has limited shelf life.

As all flosses are harmed by light, storage in a dark place is recommended. If you must store your spools on a peg board at your tying desk for convenience, at least devise a dust cover. Common household dust really damages exposed floss.

Today floss bobbins are advertised in the catalogs and periodicals of the trade. After experimentation, I have decided to stick with the manual method. There are both pros and cons. One advantage is that the fingers do not touch the floss (except during tie-on), which eliminates discoloration from dirt or sweat. On large streamer hooks, the use of a bobbin eliminates working with a long piece of floss. Waste is cut down drastically, and great speed and control are possible, given proper technique.

However, it is not feasible to use multistrand floss, unless all four strands are used simultaneously. Every turn of floss with the bobbin method produces a twist in the material, which must be removed every few turns by rotating the bobbin in the reverse direction. Last but hardly least, there is the matter of what to do with the thread bobbin while the floss bobbin is in use. I've tried working around it, and forget it—no way! All you can do is tie off the thread, then tie back on again after the winding of the

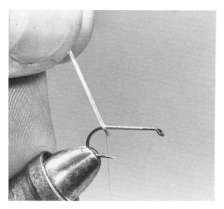

12-1 Orange Fish-Hawk Wet Fly: tie in tinsel at rear.

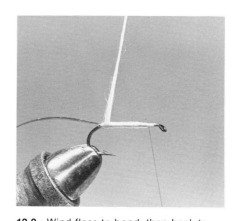

12-2 Wind floss to bend, then back to front.

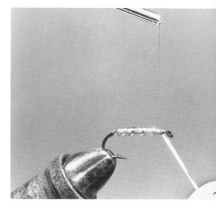

12-3 Wind tinsel ribbing while cement is wet.

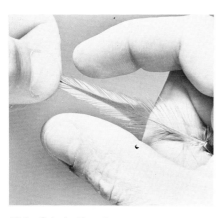

12-4 Grip feather thus preparatory to folding.

12-5 Preen fibers upward.

12-6 A nicely folded feather.

12-7 Tie in hackle as shown.

12-8 While winding, preen hackle fibers towards rear.

12-9 The finished fly. Blacken head with marker.

floss is completed. This is unwieldly, consumes time, and creates bulk.

These disadvantages, the last one in particular, have influenced me to stay with the finger-wrapping technique for floss. However, every fly-dresser should give it a try and draw his own conclusions. If you like the rotating vise (I don't), the floss bobbin is the greatest thing since the repeal of prohibition.

There are three critical points in the creation of a floss body: the tie-on, the reversal, and the tie-off. It is during the execution of these operations that slipping, spreading, and slackness can occur. The last phenomenon can be most detrimental, as it produces unsightly bunches of loose filaments. In extreme cases, slackness can cause the outer layer of floss to slip off the inner layer, ruining the fly.

Slackness is caused by a marked difference in tension on the various filaments during the wrapping process. As mentioned, this problem is most noticeable when thick floss is used, an argument for the stranded variety. A major contributing factor is the manner in which the tie-in is executed. Unevenness here will almost certainly be carried over into the wrapping process.

I have a small trick which I employ at the point of tying-in which sets up the floss and gets the body off to a good start. Simply leave about ½ inch excess and pull it back under the two or three turns of thread used to tie the floss in. This helps even up the tension on the filaments and also eliminates the need to trim, providing the butt is neatly cut to begin with. A few rehearsals may be necessary, so you don't pull the butt end all the way through. This is a minor tragedy; just tie in the floss again. A miniscule stub should protrude, and should be tightly wound down to secure the floss.

The reversal, or turn-around, occurs at the bend, where the floss is started back over itself. Faulty execution can cause slackness at this very vulnerable point, as the floss is most likely to slide backwards in this area. A few hooked and released fish, or even the mere act of casting, will precipitate this unraveling, which utterly destroys a fly perfect in all other respects.

Perhaps the key factor in keeping slackness out of the reversal is to make certain there is none as the bend is approached. By the time the shank has been traversed, any minor imperfections should have been manicured out, and the floss should be virtually flowing onto the hook. The reversal should be executed smartly with one turn. Layers of floss here will almost certainly slip later. Maintain firm tension, and control excessive spreading with a few twists, if necessary.

''Spreading'' refers to the tendency of floss to flatten out along the hook shank. Like many things in life, a little of this is beneficial, a lot is detrimental. A moderate amount of spreading helps smooth out the body. Too much creates uneven filaments, and thus slack. Spreading is controled by simply imparting a few discrete twists to the floss, as required.

The tie-off is the third area of concern, primarily because the last few turns of floss are made in such a manner as to produce a forward taper, which may cause the material to slip, slide, and otherwise misbehave. The critical factor is preparation; one must create a smooth, gentle slope with the thread immediately after tying on the floss, so as to eliminate any sharp drop-offs. Then, after the body has been created, it becomes simply a matter of catching the floss with the thread in such a manner as not to cause unevenness or induce slackness.

A good little technique is to be certain the thread is waiting *exactly* where the body is to terminate. Take the final wrap of floss tight to the thread, actually working right up against it. This tends to minimize spread, slippage, and slackness, and sets up a firm, well-controlled tie-off.

There are still a few purists in the fly-dressing game who object to the application of cement to a floss body, claiming that cement discolors and dulls the material. This is not true, unless an inappropriate substance is used. In fact, a thorough permeation of clear cement will protect the body from becoming waterlogged, which dulls it plenty. As mentioned earlier, don't use Ambroid or any other nontransparent adhesive. And be sure the cement is well-thinned, or an unsightly crust may form and spoil the appearance of the body.

When using light, bright flosses, such as the orange of this pattern, the color of the tying thread becomes a factor. On large streamers and wet flies with thick bodies, one can wrap pale floss over dark thread and get away with it. Not so on thin-bodied flies. And many pattern specifications call for very slender bodies, even on streamers. The Gray Ghost is a prime example.

Match the shade of the thread to the floss, or failing that, go a shade or two lighter. The array of thread colors available today makes this a simple matter. Usually the head of the fly should be dark, in fact, black in many cases. This improves the fly's appearance, and seems to improve its effectiveness. A felt pen effects this transformation in short order. Don't get sloppy; apply the pen to the thread only. And be sure to use the waterproof variety.

TINSEL

Even staunch traditionalists now agree, albeit grudgingly, that mylar has it all over even the best of the old-fashioned tinsels. After acknowledging this, they proceed to use their old tinsel anyway. I'm as bad as any of them, because I haven't yet been able to come to grips with disposing of my large supply of tinsel, which is still in excellent condition. Years ago—around 1963, I would guess—I bought a selection of the Henri Verdura tinsel from Herter's on one-ounce spools. You wouldn't believe the amount of material one of those spools holds! Fortunately, the tinsel is of superior quality, and is still bright and untarnished. This is a mixed blessing. If the stuff would deteriorate, I could restock with mylar, unencumbered by my penchant for insignificant frugalities.

Mylar ties on better, is easier to start, wraps more smoothly, ties off neater, and never discolors. In fact, it climbs up onto the rear taper of a floss body so well the reader may wish to forget my neat trick in step 3 for positioning the tinsel.

For the type of fly in this exercise, I prefer a narrow tinsel and a conservative number of wraps. It is generally agreed that the body is the main attraction and the ribbing an embellishment. Just what the tinsel rib might represent to the fish is anyone's guess. One school of thought claims it simulates the minute gas bubbles which are present during the emergence of certain nymphs and pupae. I have noticed that some days the trout go for ribbed patterns and at other times prefer the same pattern unribbed. The Hare's Ear is a case in point.

To create a tough, durable rib which will hold its position, wrap the tinsel immediately after applying the cement to the floss. Apply firm tension throughout the procedure, especially during tie-off. An instant of carelessness here, and the entire rib is lost. Totally secure the material before trimming off the excess.

FOLDED HACKLE

Folded hackle has been used in the British Isles for centuries. It is employed on streamers and salmon flies as well as traditional wets. Some very beautiful effects can be created with folded hackle, particularly on the salmon patterns. (I do prefer the ''bearding'' method for most winged wet flies and simple nymphs, however: it is much easier, neater, accommodates small flies, and can be done with practically any material.)

Folding a hackle feather is usually quite easy if one remembers to stroke the barbules so that the shiny sides come together while the duller sides form the exterior. Feathers fold very reluctantly when stroked the other way, if indeed they fold at all. When stroking, be careful to keep the barbules on their respective sides of the stem; do not allow any of them to cross over. Some tiers like to spread the barbules before folding. I don't feel this is necessary, but if it helps you, by all means do so.

Using hackle pliers as a handle is a valuable aid with smaller feathers. Longer ones may be held securely without this prop. The pinky and fourth finger of the right hand are the ones which do the gripping, thereby leaving the thumb and forefinger free for stroking. The left hand merely holds the tip under moderate tension. Be careful —it's quite easy to snap off the tip during the folding process.

Fly-dressers who employ the folded-hackle technique extensively will soon learn that some feathers fold with ridiculous ease—one stroke will do it—while others are less compliant. Sometimes only part of a feather folds well. If most of the barbules fold, simply induce the remainder to behave accordingly by effective stroking during the winding of the hackle. Usually the end result is completely satisfactory.

Folded hackles may be tied in by either the tips or the butts, to meet the requirements of the pattern. Many streamers and salmon flies need a collar of hackle which gets progressively longer as it nears the head. This is made by tying in the hackle by the tip, which is first trimmed to expose the stem. Simple patterns like the Orange Fish-Hawk may also benefit from this technique, which is a bit more difficult than the common method. It is not essential, however, unless the feather has an abnormally thick butt.

13

The Grouse and Green Wet Fly

TECHNIQUE TO BE LEARNED

The distribution-wrap hackling method

Over the years, literally millions of trout have been taken on very simple flies, and for that matter, still are today. I well remember banner days on Catskill and Adirondack rivers using such patterns as the Gray Hackle, the Brown Hackle, the Orange Fish-Hawk, and the Bread Crust. I didn't know about the Grouse and Green back then, and wish I had.

In 1975 a gentleman named Sylvester Nemes produced a charming little book named *The Soft-Hackle Fly*. It contains patterns, tying instructions, fishing hints, historical references, and a generous number of anecdotes. Some of the traditional British patterns are depicted; several are dressed with a supplementary fur thorax. This embellishment lends itself readily to the hackling technique the exercise will cover, and if the tier wishes to add this component, he is completely at liberty to do so. Mr. Nemes refers to the fly as the Partridge and Green. Since I use hackles from our native Ruffled Grouse, I defer to that matchless gamebird in naming the pattern.

COMPONENTS

Hook: Size 16, standard shank, medium wire
Thread: Olive prewaxed 6/0
Tail: None
Body: Bright green dubbing
Hackle: Grouse

TYING STEPS

1. Cover the hook shank with thread to the bend, then dub on sufficient material to make a body which will extend almost to the eye.

2. Create the body. When nearing the forward extremity, pack the dubbing in such a manner as to cause a sharp drop-off. A gentle forward taper is not wanted here. Leave only 1/32 inch (1 mm) of space between the front of the body and the eye. Refer to photograph 13-1.

3. Strip off a bunch of barbules from a grouse hackle feather, first being sure to even up the tips. (photo 13-2)

4. Position the bunch of barbules against the far side of the hook (photo 13-3) so that the tips extend slightly beyond the rear of the body.

5. Tie in the hackle material with a distribution wrap, causing the barbules to distribute around the under side, near side, and top of the hook. (photo 13-4) A supplementary pinch or two of grouse barbules may be required, but keep them sparse. (photo 13-5)

6. Take a few turns of thread, causing the hackle to continue to distribute evenly around the hook. If it is reluctant to do so, help it along with the fingers.

7. Trim the excess and secure with a series of tight wraps. (photo 13-6)

8. Hold the bobbin in the left hand, and with the right thumb and forefinger stroke the hackle material forward

13-1 Grouse and Green Wet Fly: the completed body. Note stubbed shape at front.

13-2 Grouse hackle fibers.

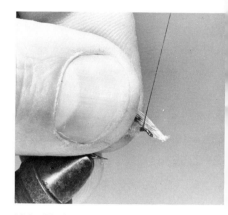

13-3 Tie in on far side.

13-4 Allow thread to distribute fibers around hook.

13-5 Supplement as required.

13-6 Trim neatly and carefully.

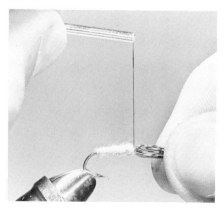

13-7 Preen hackle forward, wrap thread behind to produce flared effect.

13-8 The completed fly.

Ruffled Grouse

over the eye. The thread will thus be positioned behind the collar of hackle.

9. Take a few turns of thread tight to the rear of the collar by passing the bobbin over the top with the left hand, releasing it, then reaching under and catching it again. See photograph 13-7.

10. Release the hackle. With a bit of manicuring it should protrude from the hook shank at something approximating a right angle, or perhaps will slightly drape back over the body.

11. Whip finish, darken the head with a felt pen if required, Ambroid. The completed fly should resemble photograph 13-8.

DISTRIBUTION-WRAP HACKLE TECHNIQUE

Traditionally, grouse or partridge hackle was wound on just like any other hackle. The small feathers were tied in by the tips and two turns, or possibly three on a good-sized fly, were taken. This is perfectly okay, provided the feather matches the size requirements of the fly being dressed. This the crux of the entire matter. Very few grouse hackle feathers have barbules short enough to dress anything smaller than a size 14. And the soft-hackle patterns are very effective in small sizes; Schwiebert recommends them down to size 22. Even if grouse hackles that small were

available, it would be difficult indeed to wind them on such miniature patterns.

With the distribution-wrap method, any size feather can be used for the smaller flies. This allows the use of a vast array of material which would not be suitable otherwise. Not only do all the hackles of a grouse ruff become usable, but also the body feathers. So is the plumage of many other birds, as was mentioned in the chapter on hackle. Hen pheasant body feathers are particularly attractive.

The distribution-wrap technique is so easy that nothing else needs be said. The important points are:

1. Tie in with a sloppy pinch, so the material begins to distribute immediately.

2. Don't use too much hackle; keep it sparse.

3. Use the thread and perhaps the fingers to create an even distribution.

4. Secure the barbules before stroking them forward over the eye.

5. Make those wraps of thread behind the collar very snug to the hackle fibers, so they are supported in a flared position.

This is a classic application of one of the basic thread-handling techniques which were covered in Chapter 4.

The Hare's Ear Nymph

14

TECHNIQUES TO BE LEARNED

1. Fuzzy dubbed body
2. Quill section wing case
3. General formation of nymphal silhouette

Nymphs are strange. It is easy to tie a rough model which is generally suggestive of underwater insect life, and which will take fish under average conditions when presented with a degree of skill. However, when the angling situation or the demands of the fly-dresser's vanity call for more realism, frustrating problems arise. I feel a truly realistic nymph is harder to construct than any other fly. The fish sees an underwater insect pretty much as it is, without distortion from reflection and refraction. Except where fast, diffused currents interfere with vision, the fish gets a good opportunity to pass judgment on the naturalness of nymphal imitations.

The Hare's Ear Nymph is an appropriate entry into nymph tying. It is an adaption of an ancient British wet fly pattern which has been used with deadly effect on the chalk streams for centuries. While not truly imitative of any particular nymph, the Hare's Ear is representative of many underwater forms, which must be why it works so well, particularly in fast currents or failing light.

This is an easy pattern to tie, but there are many poorly tied examples in the boxes of experienced tiers. It is ideal for demonstrating the fuzzy dubbed body, a most important procedure in the dressing of many subsurface patterns.

COMPONENTS

Hook: Size 10 or 12 standard wire
Thread: 6/0 prewaxed tan or brown
Tails: Fibers from grouse feather, wood duck flank, or brown mallard
Body: Rough tan-gray-brown dubbing, such is found on the face of a rabbit
Ribbing (optional): Fine gold tinsel
Thorax: Same as body
Wing Case: Dark gray or grayish-brown section from duck or goose wing quill which has been treated with an adhesive
Hackle/Legs: Grouse ruff or any soft feather of similar mottled coloration

TYING STEPS

1. Coat the hook with thread and create a bump to spread tail fibers.

2. Tie in the tail. It should be sparse, a half-dozen fibers at most, approximately ⅔ or ¾ of the length of the shank.

3. If ribbing is opted for, tie it in now, secure in material clip. (photo 14-1)

128

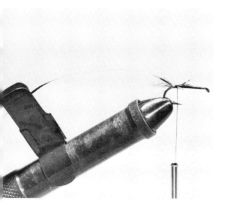

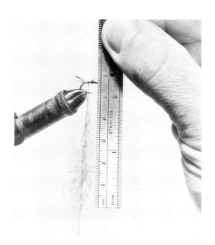

14-1 Hare's Ear Nymph: tail in place,
tinsel tied in.

14-2 Apply dubbing loosely.

14-3 Body should be rough.

4. Dub the body, using the spinning loop method. It should be about ⅔ of the shank length. On a size 10 hook, this will require approximately 2 inches (50 mm) of material, spun loosely onto thread, as shown in photograph 14-2. Don't twist the loop too tightly; this detracts from the fuzziness. (photo 14-3) Tie off the body thread beneath the thorax. If using ribbing, wind it now. (photo 14-4)

5. Tie in the wing case material. (photo 14-5) For a size 10, the section should be 3/16 inch (4 mm) wide. Avoid using the coarse portion nearest the center stem; it splits readily. Be sure the quill section is centered on the shank, and is forced tightly against the forward extremity of the body. In fact, a few wraps of thread up over the body will help spread the wing case in a realistic manner.

6. Dub the thorax, using spinning loop or single thread. This dubbing should be tightly packed. For a size 10, you will require about 1¼ inches (32 mm) of material. (photo 14-6) The thorax should be slightly wider than the abdomen's widest point, in order to fill out the wing case. It should abut the wing case material tightly, and may in fact slightly overlap the wraps of thread which go back over the front of the abdomen. See photograph 14-7.

Caution: leave some space ahead of the thorax for the hackle and the tie-off of the wing case. Remember, the quill section is somewhat bulky and therefore requires a bit more tie-off area than softer materials. Approximately .04 inch (1 mm) should suffice.

7. Tie in the hackle, using the distribution wrap technique so that the material protrudes from the sides and throat. (photo 14-8)

8. Fold the wing case forward over the thorax. If a more spread-out or squared-off effect is wanted, fold the quill section over a pin, as shown in photograph 14-9. Don't use this ploy unless the quill section was thoroughly treated

with Krylon, Pliobond, vinyl cement or other adhesive. Also, don't overdo it; a large loop or slack area in the wing case is not desirable. When tying the wing case down, hold it flat with your thumb, as shown in photograph 14-10.

9. Whip finish, tint the head with dark brown felt pen if desired, apply Ambroid to head and also the wing case if it appears that additional protection is required. The fly should resemble photograph 14-11.

FUZZIER BODIES

The dubbing on this type of body may be deemed fuzzy enough by the tier. If enhancement is wanted, there are several methods.

1. The fine-toothed saw blade method, a la Poul Jorgensen. An Exacto saw, hack saw blade, or saber saw blade will do. Scrape the body lengthwise, using a light stroke to avoid cutting the thread.

2. The wire brush method, a la Dick Talleur. This was dreamed up to facilitate fuzzing up dubbed bodies with tinsel ribbings. Obtain a small wire brush as depicted. (photo 14-12) Brush crossways to the hook shank, so as to avoid disturbing the tinsel. This method also works very well on unribbed bodies.

3. The traditional dubbing needle method. A stiff bodkin or needle is used to scarify the body. When ribbing is used, it is necessary to pick out the fur between the ribs, a delicate and tedious procedure.

4. Dr. Horvath's super dubbing Twister-Teaser, a remarkable little tool which has just come out. The Twister-Teaser is the brainchild of Dr. Fred Horvath, the piscatorially oriented dentist from Connecticut, who has also blessed us with Andra dubbing material and polypropylene felt soles for waders. It is an ingenious device, not a gimmick,

14-4 Don't wind ribbing too closely.

14-5 Treated feather section tied in for wing case.

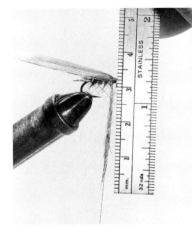

14-6 Preparing to dub thorax.

14-7 Force dubbing against wing case material.

14-8 Thorax completed, hackle in place.

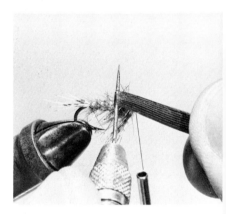

14-9 Fold wing case over needle.

14-10 Flatten wing case with thumb while tying down.

14-11 The completed fly.

14-12 Using a wire
brush to enhance
the fuzziness
of a fur body.

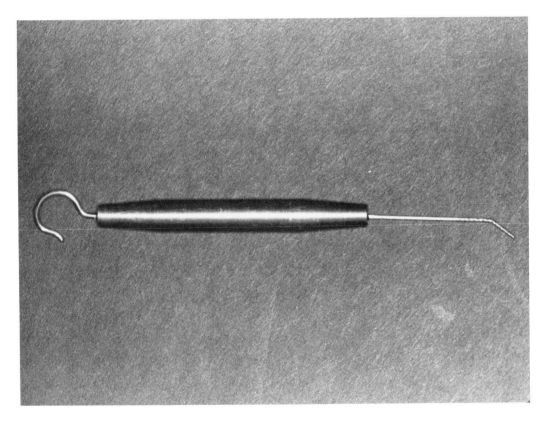

14-13 Dr. Horvath's
Super Twister-
Teaser.

14-14 A close-up of the teaser, showing the barbs.

and a real boon to the fly-dresser. On one end is a hook for twisting the spinning loop. On the other is a wire probe covered with small barbs, which is used to pick out dubbing. (photos 14-13, 14-14)

The tool is very simple, and its operation is self-evident.

One word of caution, however: go easy, so as to avoid fraying or cutting the thread that is buried inside the body material. And be particularly careful when working on a ribbed body, as an errant pass with the teaser can sever tinsel, especially mylar.

The March Brown Nymph, Weighted

15

TECHNIQUES TO BE LEARNED

1. Three individual spread tails
2. Strip method for weighted underbody
3. Oval monofilament rib

The March Brown Nymph is an extremely productive pattern on rivers that have one or more of the several important mayflies in the *Stenonema* group. It is also suggestive enough of certain stonefly nymphs that fish will often take it for one.

As with most nymphs, shading will vary somewhat with locality, stream-bed coloration, instar cycle, and proximity to emergence. Familiarity is the best guide to accuracy in this regard, and some elementary entomology in the form of rock-rolling is of considerable benefit. Color also varies within the *Stenonema* group, with March Brown (*S. vicarium*) the darkest, Gray Fox (*S. fuscum*) slightly lighter and Light Cahill (*S. ithaca and canadense*) lighter still.

Size also varies according to the circumstances stated above. A mature March Brown nymph—one which has completed all of its instar cycles—will generally be about ⅝ inch in length (15–16 mm), not counting the tails. Gray Fox averages ½ inch (13 mm), the other two about the same or slightly smaller. For the Gray Fox (*Stenonema ithaca* and *fuscum*), tie this nymph a shade or two lighter on a size 12, 2XL hook.

COMPONENTS

Hook: Size 10 or 12, 2XL, standard wire
Thread: 6/0 prewaxed tan or light brown
Tails: Cock ring-necked pheasant tail fibers (3)
Underbody: Lead wire, .003–.0035 inch (approx. 1 mm)
Body: Amber dubbing or yarn
Ribbing: Cortland cobra oval monofilament, 15-pound test, dyed dark brown
Thorax: Dark brown fur or synthetic substitute
Wing Case: Section from darkly marked turkey or pheasant feather, treated with Krylon or similar adhesive
Hackle: Mottled brown ruff feathers from grouse or hen pheasant body feathers with similar coloration

TYING STEPS

1. Coat the hook with thread, ending up at bend.
2. Tie in center tail fiber. (photo 15-1)
3. Create bump with thread, five or six wraps. (photo 15-2)

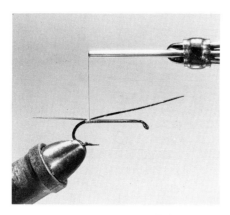

15-1 March Brown Nymph: tie in center tail fiber.

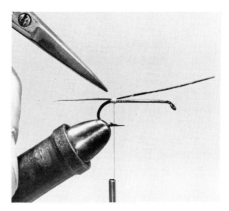

15-2 Create a bump.

15-3 Tie in exterior tail fibers.

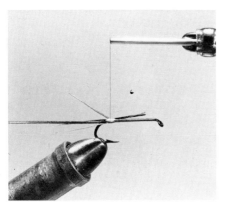

15-4 Tie in monofilament for ribbing.

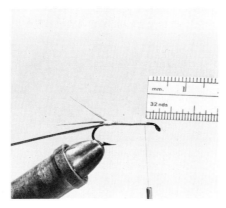

15-5 Position thread ⅛ from eye as shown.

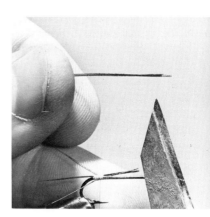

15-6 Slice lead wire to long, tapered point.

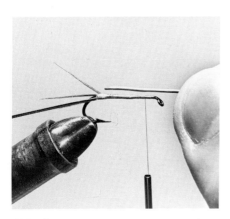

15-7 Position wire.

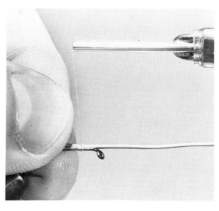

15-8 Tie wire against side of hook.

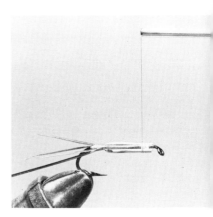

15-9 Repeat on opposite side of hook.

15-10 Create dubbed body.

15-11 Wind ribbing evenly and fairly close.

15-12 Tie in wing case material.

15-13 Thorax in place.

15-14 Hen pheasant body feather fibers.

15-15 Hackle tied in with distribution wrap.

15-16 Wing case should be flattened to its full width.

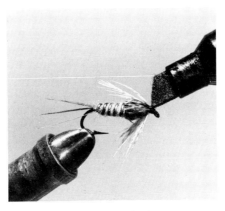

15-17 Tint thread, if desired.

15-18 The completed fly.

4. Tie in each exterior tail fiber separately. Either may be tied in first, according to the tier's preference. See photograph 15-3.

5. Slice the oval mono on a long bias and tie in the tip of the slice, leaving some sliced section exposed as an aid to starting the rib. Secure the mono in the material clip. See photograph 15-4.

6. Wind thread to ⅛ inch (3 mm) from eye. (photo 15-5)

7. Slice a piece of lead wire on a long bias. Lay it alongside the shank on the far side of the hook, with the point of the slice not quite reaching the base of the tail. See photographs 15-6 and 15-7.

8. Tie in the wire with six or eight wraps, being careful to exert only moderate tension, so as not to cause the wire to roll or slip. (photo 15-8)

9. Cut off the wire on a bias, leaving approximately ¹⁄₁₆ inch of space for the head.

10. Tie in a second piece of lead wire on the near side of the hook, making it a mirror image of the first piece. (photo 15-9)

11. Traverse the hook with wraps of thread back to the end of the underbody, forward to the eye, then back to the rear again. Keep tension moderate, hold wire in place with fingers. Leave slight spaces between wraps to facilitate permeation of cement, which is applied upon completion of the underbody.

12. Create the body, using whatever dubbing method and material you prefer, or yarn, for that matter. (photo 15-10) The nymph illustrated has orangish-amber poly dubbing, because the March Brown Nymphs in the northeastern streams I fish are that shade, especially when emergence is imminent. I haven't concerned myself with fuzziness, as the gills on the *Stenonema* nymphs are not that pronounced.

The shaping of the lead wire will help create a tapered effect. If more is desired, simply taper the dubbing on the thread. Be sure to start the body at the very base of the tails. Do not make the abdomen overly long, as it isn't so on the natural. About sixty percent of the shank will suffice.

13. Wind the ribbing, using six or seven turns from bend to front of abdomen. Space the ribs evenly and exert firm tension. Tie off the mono underneath the thorax area, taking care to effectively secure this slippery material. Refer to photograph 15-11.

14. Tie in the section of turkey feather for the wing case. (photo 15-12) It should be approximately ³⁄₁₆ inch (5 mm) wide for a nymph of this size. Wrap the thread slightly back over the front of the abdomen, so the feather is fully spread.

15. Make a thorax out of medium to dark brown dubbing. It should be slightly thicker than the front of the abdomen and should abut the wing case feather tightly where they meet. Maintain this thickness nearly to the head, tapering abruptly where the underbody drops off. (photo 15-13)

16. Tie in a generous wisp of mottled brown hackle material on each side, allowing some of the fibers to distribute into the throat area. The hackle should be fairly long, ⅜ to ½ inch (approx. 10 mm). Refer to photographs 15-14 and 15-15.

17. Fold over the wing case, using the needle or hand technique, whichever you prefer. Flatten the wing case feather to its full width with your thumb as you tie it down. (photo 15-16)

18. Whip finish the head. For a more realistic effect, tint the thread with a dark brown felt marker. Coat the head with Ambroid, and also the wing case if you feel additional protection is warranted. (photos 15-17, 15-18)

16

The Perla Stonefly Nymph

TECHNIQUES TO BE LEARNED

1. Preparation and use of pheasant body feathers
2. Underbody-overbody method of creating two-toned effect
3. Overlaid grouse hackle for legs

Stonefly nymphs are convincingly represented by any number of simple patterns such as the Montana, the Bitch Creek, and the Girdle Bug. These well-proven flies have accounted for a great many trout, particularly in the swift free-stone rivers of the West. It seems, however, that these and other suggestive patterns need a measure of assistance from rapid, broken currents and other circumstances which hinder the fish's perception. Here in the Northeast, where artificial flies may soon outnumber naturals, much greater success is had with more lifelike patterns.

The Perla Stonefly Nymph is an amalgam of components borrowed from various other patterns. It isn't a precise imitator; in fact, it suggests two well-distributed stoneflies, *Perla capitata* and *Perla immarginata,* which are similar in size and color. It is a reasonable compromise between rough representation and model-making, and the fish this pattern has accounted for over several years allow recommendation without equivocation.

Stonefly nymphs are distinguished from mayfly nymphs by several unique characteristics. The two invariable ones are that the stonefly nymphs have two wings cases, mayfly nymphs have one; and that the gills of a stonefly nymph are located in the thorax area, whereas the gills of a mayfly

nymph are in the abdominal area. Other less distinctive stonefly characteristics are two tails (most mayfly nymphs have three, the genus *Epeorus* being a notable exception); a long abdomen with a very gradual taper (which some mayfly nymphs also have); and long, pronounced antennae.

Certainly the general size, shape, and color of stonefly nymphs are of interest to the fly-dresser. I also feel the representation of gills, which is accomplished by the use of a fuzzy thorax, is significant. The legs, which are prominent, would seem to be important. Other parts of the anatomy—antennae, eyes, protothorax, etc.—are, I believe, of secondary value in lending credibility to the fly-dresser's product.

Another characteristic which stoneflies often have is a marked difference in coloration between the back and underside of the abdomen. This is particularly true of the two in question. The underside of the *Perla capitata* runs to a rich yellow, while *Perla immarginata* is more orange. This accounts for the choice of the underbody-overbody technique for this pattern. A thread ribbing is used to imitate the abdominal segments, protect the overbody, and create the desired silhouette. This fly may be tied in sizes 6 to 12 on 4XL hooks. The proportions stated are for size 8, 4XL.

137

Stonefly Nymph

COMPONENTS

Hook: Size 8, 4XL, heavy wire
Thread: Tan or brown prewaxed
Tails: Fibers of grouse or hen pheasant body feather which have been treated with Pliobond
Foundation: Lead wire strips, .035 inch (1 mm)
Underbody: Dull maize or pumpkin-colored poly dubbing
Overbody: Hen pheasant body feather
Ribbing: Cotton sewing thread, same color as underbody
Thorax: Tan or light brown rabbit dubbing or soft fur same color as underbody
Hackle/Legs: Grouse
Wing Case: Hen pheasant (continuation of overbody)
Head: Brown fur or poly dubbing

TYING STEPS

1. Select a fairly long hen pheasant body feather on which the markings are not overly dark or pronounced. Apply a smear of Pliobond and preen with fingers to obtain the needed shape as illustrated in photographs 16-1 and 16-2. Be sure to preen immediately; Pliobond dries in seconds. Stop preening when material becomes tacky, or you will make an awful mess. Set the feather aside.

2. Tie in the strips of lead wire. Be sure to leave a bit of space at the head. Apply cement.

3. At precisely the beginning of the bend, tie in the tip of the treated pheasant feather. (photo 16-3) Be careful to secure it neatly, with no foldovers.

4. Affix the tails, one on each side of the hook. These will protrude from either side of the butt of the abdomen. Refer to photographs 16-4 and 16-5.

5. Tie in the ribbing thread, secure in material clip.

6. Apply the dubbing, using the single thread technique with a bit of wax. Use the poly blending method to obtain the desired shade. About 4 inches (100 mm) of dubbing are required for this size hook.

7. Wind the dubbing about sixty percent of the shank length. (photo 16-6)

8. Fold the pheasant feather over the underbody. (photo 16-7) When tying off, hold the feather down over the sides of the abdomen to prevent the edges from folding back over themselves. At this point, the body shape does not look like a stonefly and you probably think one of us has goofed.

9. Wind the ribbing, using spacings of about 1/16 inch. After tying off, you will notice the body has suddenly become stoneflyish. (photo 16-8)

10. Fold the overbody feather back over itself and take a

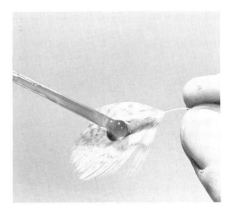

16-1 Perla Stonefly Nymph: apply Pliobond to hen pheasant feather.

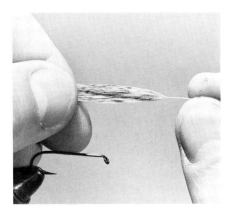

16-2 Preen to shape.

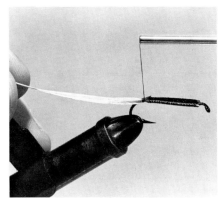

16-3 Tie in treated pheasant feather.

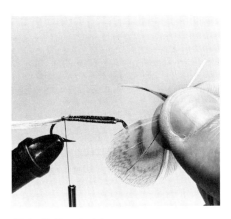

16-4 Tail material.

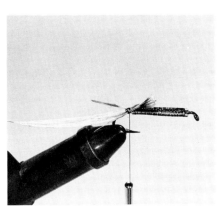

16-5 Tails tied in.

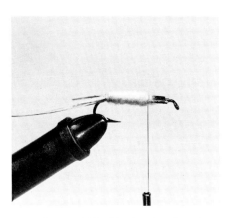

16-6 Create dubbed body, stopping at thorax.

16-7 Fold the pheasant feather over the back.

16-8 Ribbing in place.

16-9 Fold back and secure remaining pheasant feather.

16-10 Prepare feather for legs.

16-11 Test for length, manicure if necessary.

16-12 Tying in the legs feather.

16-13 Create a thorax.

16-14 Fold the legs feather over the thorax.

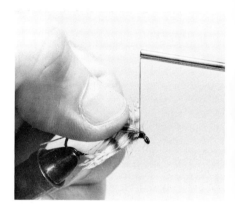

16-15 Fold the wing case over, trim, secure with thread.

16-16 Create a fur head.

16-17 Cement the back and wing case.

16-18 The completed fly.

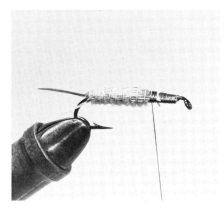

16-19 Fancy version: after completing steps 1–9, trim off excess wing case.

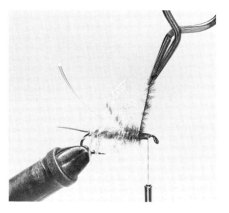

16-20 Wrapping ostrich thorax.

16-21 Shaped feather for rear wing case.

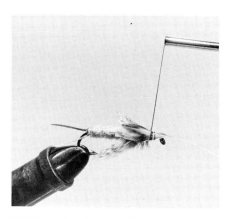

16-22 Tie in wing case thus.

16-23 Tie in forward wing case.

16-24 Antennae in place.

few turns of thread back over the front of the abdomen. (photo 16-9)

11. Select a grouse hackle feather with fiber spread of the desired dimensions, in this case about an inch (26 mm) when the fibers are flared at ninety degrees from the stem. Trim back the tip on either side, as illustrated in photograph 16-10.

12. The grouse feather is to be laid over the back of the thorax to form the legs. The barbuled section should extend from the absolute rear of the wing case to the neck, just behind the eye of the hook. Measure by laying the feather over the thorax area, then trimming or pulling off fibers until the desired amount remains. (photo 16-11) Be sure the two sides are uniformly stripped. Tie in at the extreme rear of the wing case area with the feather extending backward. The tying thread should touch the edges of the first barbules. (photo 16-12)

13. Dub a fuzzy thorax, using the spinning loop method. (photo 16-13) Leave yourself some space at the head.

14. Fold the grouse feather forward over the thorax and tie off, making sure the stem is centered. (photo 16-14)

15. Fold the remaining hen pheasant feather over to form the wing case and tie off. (photo 16-15)

16. Create a head out of light brown fur or poly, dubbing the material tightly and without fuzz. (photo 16-16) If you don't have enough room for the head, forget it, just tie off with a whip finish.

17. Treat the entire back of the fly with two coats of Ambroid or equivalent, allowing thorough drying between coats. (photo 16-17) The completed fly should resemble photograph 16-18.

Fancy Version

The Perla Stonefly as described will take fish like crazy,

16-25 The completed fly.

given reasonably skillful presentation. If the tier wishes to dress up the fly to impress friends, here's how:

1. Complete steps 1–9.
2. Instead of folding back the overbody feather, cut it off and tie down the end. At this stage, the fly should appear as in photograph 16-19.
3. Prepare the wing case feathers by coating two hen pheasant or grouse feathers with Pliobond. Do not preen these feathers into an elongated shape; the fibers should lie in their natural position. Set the feathers aside to dry.
4. Prepare the legs/hackle feather as previously described and tie in at front of abdomen.
5. Tie in a thick ostrich herl at the front of the abdomen. This can be light brown or the same color as the underbody, whichever you like. Wind evenly to the head area, forming the thorax. (photo 16-20)
6. Fold over the legs/hackle feather and tie off.
7. Trim one of the treated feathers into the shape and size of a wing case. (photo 16-21) It helps to have a model in front of you. I use the color plates in Schwiebert's *Nymphs.*

8. Strip off the front fibers until the feather is the size of the entire wing case area, front to rear. Tie in over the thorax, being careful to center the stem. (photo 16-22)
9. Trim the other treated feather to shape. Strip off fibers until only enough is left to form the second or forward wing case. Tie in over the first feather, being careful to center the quill. (photo 16-23)
10. Tie in the two antennae on either side of the hook just behind the eye. These are pheasant or grouse fibers treated with Pliobond, like the tails. Refer to photograph 16-24.
11. Create the head as described, whip finish, Ambroid. The completed fly should resemble photograph 16-25.

NOTES ON THE PERLA STONEFLY

The feathers for the tail and antennae are prepared in advance simply by coating the pheasant or grouse feathers with Pliobond. Don't preen into a streamlined shape; merely distribute the adhesive with the fingers. After drying, the fibers can be separated with a bodkin and strips pulled off of desired thickness. Two or three fibers are about right for the average size Perla.

When preparing the overbody feather it is important to get the proper width. The idea is that the feather should cover the sides of the underbody, leaving only the abdomen showing. Naturally, this will vary with hook size. For a size 8, the feather should be ⅛ inch (3 mm) wide at the point where it is tied in and about ¼ inch (5–6 mm) in the wing case area.

The folded-over hackle technique is tricky. The secret is to leave as much fibered area as the size of the fly will allow, and to tie the feather in so that the fibered portion extends as far back as possible. This is why the tying thread should actually touch the edges of the fibers, so that when the feather is folded forward the fibers are locked in place.

17

The
Black Ghost Streamer

TECHNIQUES TO BE LEARNED

1. Wrapped lead wire weighted body
2. Application of floss over wire
3. Tinsel ribbing over floss
4. Marabou wing, with bucktail underwing

Streamers, technically speaking, are not flies—they are fly-rod lures. With the possible exception of a small Muddler fished as a wet fly, there's no way a streamer resembles an insect. In fact, many streamers don't resemble anything in the known universe. They are strictly attractors, products of the fly-dresser's imagination, designed to create an effect and draw the impulsive strike.

There is a faction in fly-rod angling circles which disapproves of streamer fishing on the grounds that it is non-purist, unsporting, and rather gauche. Then there are the streamer maniacs, touting streamers as the best type of fly for day-in, day-out productivity. I like streamer fishing. It has turned many a dull day astream into a wild extravaganza. But alas, like other patterns, they are no panacea; all in the right place and time.

I also love to dress streamers. It is such a pleasure, after days and weeks of acting like a neurosurgeon over tiny hooks and minute scraps of feathers and fur, to clamp a number 6 long-shank hook into the vise and whip up something which resembles a New England hillside in autumn. As I tie in the delicate cheeks and shoulders of a Gray Ghost, my mind conjures up visions of Carrie Stevens

in her Maine cabin. It is winter, and the snow has crept halfway up the window panes. Outside, all is quiet, even the massive brook trout which passively fin away the winter in the Upper Dam pool, waiting for spring and rejuvenation.

Inside, there is peace and amity. The fireplace radiates comfort, providing necessary warmth to speed the supple fingers in their intricate ballet, danced upon the miniature stage of a hook shank. The gaily colored streamers accumulate in the boxes—Gray Ghost, Colonel Bates, Allie's Favorite, Shang's Special—each a carbon copy of its brother, perfect in every detail. Carrie exchanges smiles with her husband, the guide. They know spring will come, and with it, the fishermen, restless from a long bout with the mundane affairs of the city. The flies will be ogled at and raved over. Then they will be taken away to lakes and pools at which the ice has been out only a few days, where they will form bright links between hungry trout and worshipful men.

The Black Ghost Marabou streamer with optional weighted body is fairly simple to construct, yet instructive in a number of techniques. It is also a damned effective lure, for reasons which are not totally clear, as it is hardly an imitative pattern. I was introduced to it by Bill Dorato, a resourceful angler who has a knack for coming up with weird flies which work. Bill must have been a fish in one of his previous lives.

As the fly-dresser gets into the tying of streamers, he soon discovers it is time-consuming. This is to be expected —there is a lot of hook to cover. Of course, the amount of time varies considerably with the complexity of the pattern and the size of the hook. Don't rush it. Get into the spirit of the thing, don't make unwarranted compromises, and the result will be flies of great beauty in which one may take justifiable pride.

COMPONENTS

Hook: Size 6 streamer, 6X long
Thread: Black prewaxed 6/0
Tail: Yellow hackle fibers
Ribbing: Flat silver tinsel, $1/32$ inch (1 mm) in width
Underbody: Lead wire, .020 inch in diameter
Body: Black floss, medium thickness
Underwing: Stiff white bucktail
Wing: White marabou
Throat Hackle: Yellow hackle fibers, very soft

TYING STEPS

1. Tie on at the throat, cover the hook with thread to the bend, and create a wet-fly type tail approximately 3.8 inches (96 mm) in length. (photo 17-1) Trim excess on bias to avoid creating a bump.

2. Tie in a piece of tinsel 6 inches (150 mm) in length, using only one or two turns of thread. Then tilt the tinsel into a position from which it can later be wrapped around the rear of the body to start the ribbing. Start the tinsel in the proper direction by taking a turn or two of thread behind the tie-in point while holding the tinsel in the desired attitude.

3. Secure the tinsel with a series of tight wraps, working up the shank approximately $1/8$ inch or a bit more (3–4 mm). If the old-fashioned tinsel is used instead of mylar, the excess may want to reverse-wrap itself around the shank as it is wound down. If so, help it along with the fingers. Put the tinsel in the material clip, taking care not to disturb its relationship to the hook at the bend.

4. Cover the hook with thread to the eye, winding down any excess tail material in the process, then wind back down the shank to a point $1/4$ inch (6 mm) from the eye. (photo 17-2)

5. Tie in a piece of .020 inch diameter lead wire, 8 inches (200 mm) in length. (photo 17-3) The end should be cut

on an angle so as to minimize bulk. The tying thread should end up $3/16$ inch (4 mm) back from the eye.

6. Wrap the lead wire around the hook shank, working backward toward the tail. The wraps should abut each other, with no gaps in between, however minute. (photo 17-4)

7. Stop at a point $1/4$ inch from the bend and cut off the excess wire at an angle, so as to minimize bulk. (photo 17-5)

8. Cut off a piece of medium-weight black floss 36 inches (90 cm) in length and double it. Cut the loop to create two equal lengths. Tie them in together where the tying thread was left. (photo 17-6)

9. Wind the two strands of floss together, working backward up onto the lead wire. Do not permit the strands to separate; they should go on almost as one wide strand. If little ridges appear, flatten them out by wiggling the floss back and forth.

10. Wind to the tie-in point of the tinsel, then back over the body again wiggling and smoothing in the process. It is rather difficult to create a perfectly smooth body when winding over lead wire; however, the two-strand technique plus some adroit wiggling should reduce unevenness to negligible proportions. (photos 17-7, 17-8)

11. Wrap the floss to a point just beyond where it was originally tied in, leaving $1/8$ inch (3 mm) as a work area. (photo 17-9) Tie off on the bottom of the hook.

12. Using a small artist's brush, coat the body thoroughly—but not excessively—with clear cement, well-thinned. (photo 17-10) The substance should permeate the body, leaving no blobs. Don't use Ambroid, which will dull and discolor the floss.

13. Immediately, while the cement is still wet, wind the tinsel ribbing. For a fly of this size, a spacing of $1/16$ inch (2 mm) is about right. The wraps should be quite tight and the spacings uniform. See photograph 17-11.

14. Tie off beneath the shank, whip-finish or use a few half-hitches, and cut off the tying thread. Lay the finished body aside, suspending it from something or impaling the hook point in a block of cork, foam plastic, or balsa wood, so the body does not contact any surface. Tie some more bodies or go do something else for a while. Allow enough time for thorough drying, apply a second coat of cement, let it dry completely.

15. When the body is one hundred percent dry, remount the hook in the vise and tie on the thread $1/8$ inch (3 mm) behind the eye. Create a smooth base for the wing.

16. Tie on for the underwing a sparse bunch of stiff white bucktail. The tips should extend to the rear extremity of the bend. (photo 17-12) The purpose of the underwing is to inhibit the marabou from wrapping around the hook during casting. Stiffness may be enhanced by tying in the bucktail $1/2$ inch (12 mm) long, then cutting it off

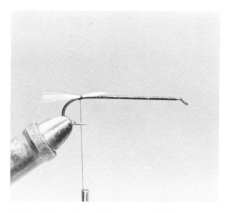

17-1 Black Ghost Streamer: tail in place.

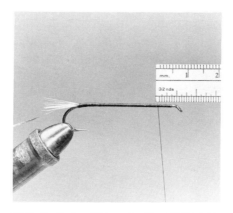

17-2 To tie in ribbing, position thread as shown.

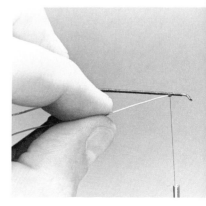

17-3 Tie in lead wire.

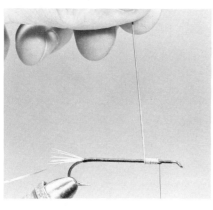

17-4 Wrap wire evenly.

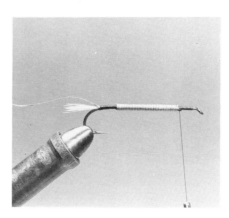

17-5 Terminate wire well short of bend.

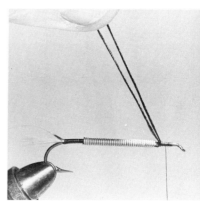

17-6 Tie in floss in this position.

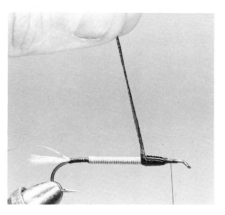

17-7 Wraps of floss should be smooth and contiguous.

17-8 When wrapping back over, smooth out bump caused by wire.

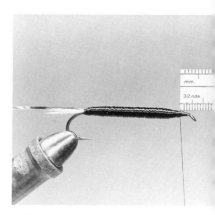

17-9 Leave adequate space ahead of body.

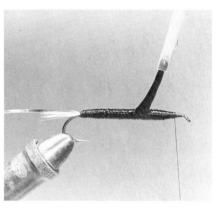

17-10 Saturate with clear laquer or cement.

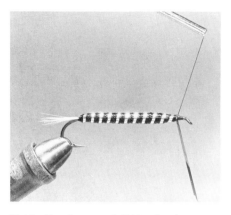

17-11 Evenly spaced ribbing in place. Tie off at throat.

17-12 Bucktail underwing in place.

17-13 Marabou should be about 25 percent longer than underwing.

17-14 Be sure marabou is precisely on top of hook.

17-15 The completed Black Ghost.

square to the required length. The effect will be hidden by the marabou.

17. Select a bunch of marabou fibers of sufficient length for the wing, which for this hook size is approximately 2 inches (50 mm). See photograph 17-13. Do not use a larger bunch than can be easily handled, as supplemental amounts may easily be added.

18. Tie on the marabou with a couple of pinches (photo 17-14) followed by several tight security wraps, and trim off the excess. Be very careful not to cut the thread while trimming, as the soft marabou tends to obscure it.

19. A marabou wing should be quite full, as it will slim down greatly when wet. If additional material is desired, simply repeat the process just described. The fibers will meld as though tied in as a single bunch.

20. Tie in a beard-style throat hackle of soft yellow barbules, just as with a wet fly.

21. Whip finish; apply two coats of black head cement

or laquer, allowing thorough drying between coats. The completed fly should resemble photograph 17-15.

MARABOU

Originally, marabou plumage came from a stork of that name. Today feathers from the rump area of the white turkey are used. This fact should not distress the fly-dresser at all; it is one of the few cases where nothing is lost in substitution.

There are a few tricks to working with marabou. The most important one is selection of plumage. Marabou feathers vary considerably in size, configuration, texture, and density. Nearly all are suitable for one application or another. The important thing is to select the material in accordance with planned use.

The two main types of marabou feathers are shorts and full plumes. (photo 17-16) The shorts are usually tied in

17-16 Long and short marabou plumes.

whole. With the plumes, bunches of fibers are gathered, cut from the stem, and tied onto the hook.

Of the two, I prefer working with the shorts, simply because they are more or less the right shape and require less preparation. (photo 17-17) The fibers are very soft and dense, and behave in a most enticing fashion underwater. The only difficulty is the thickness of the center stem near the butt of the feather. Select a feather of sufficient length that the butt is cut off as excess.

The plumes also make up into excellent streamer wings, with a bit more effort. The main technique to remember is to work with fairly modest-sized bunches. (photo 17-18) As a rule of thumb, limit bunches to one inch (25 mm) of fibers, measured along the center stem. It is far, far easier to handle two or three successive one-inch bunches of fibers than a single two- or three-inch bunch, and the material ties in more securely. As a matter of fact, tying in thick bunches of any material—hair, feathers or whatever —is poor practice. As the tying thread only grips the outer

layer, the inner fibers are held on by those which are bunched around them. A few casts, and look, Ma, no wing!

The fibers on the ends of plumes are usually skimpy. They do have their applications, however. (photo 17-19) Keith Fulsher recommends them for tying the Marabou Shiner pattern in his Thunder Creek series. They are also useful as wings on miniature streamer patterns.

When purchasing marabou feathers, one should be aware of the size of the streamers on which the material will be used. As stated, the plumage varies considerably in size. A small plume will tie wings up to 1½ inches (36 mm) in length; an exceptionally large one, twice that. Very large flies may be created by tying in a long marabou tail and a wing of the same color. The two components behave as one when wet, giving the effect of an elongated wing. This method is commonly employed in dressing saltwater patterns.

17-17 Shorts tied in whole produce a beautiful effect.

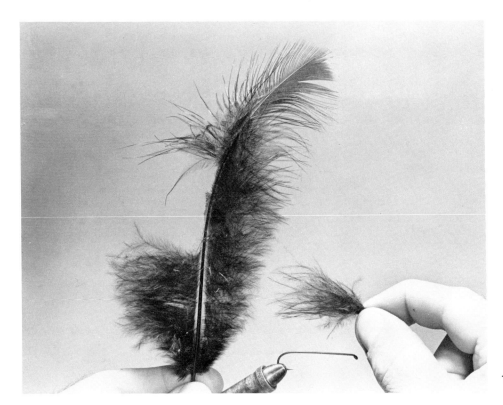

17-18 Bunches are taken from full plumes.

17-19 Tips are suitable for certain delicate operations.

18

The Blacknosed Dace Bucktail

TECHNIQUES TO BE LEARNED

1. Multiple-layer hair wing
2. Silver tinsel body with oval tinsel ribbing
3. Yarn butt
4. Natural and artificial hair

The first flies I ever attempted to tie were bucktails, because someone told me they were easy. What hogwash! Handling all that hair and tinsel is in no way easy, and I still have to think carefully at every step in order to avoid creating big trouble.

Originally, the term "bucktail" applied to those streamer flies on which deer tail hairs were used as wings. Now, it refers to a wide range of hair-winged, fly-rod lures. Several types of hair have been used in place of bucktail over the years, and we will briefly examine a few of them in the notes following the tying instructions.

The Blacknosed Dace was originated by one of the Catskills' great masters, Art Flick. Few men know their rivers as Art knows his beloved Schoharie, and he perceived early on the significance of the pretty, black-striped minnow as a forage fish for larger trout. The continuing effectiveness of the resulting Blacknosed Dace streamer on today's over-fished rivers bears eloquent testimony to his success.

Art's development of the Blacknosed Dace was a significant advancement in the evolution of the bucktail from pure attractor to convincing imitator. Not that there's anything wrong with attractors; they are still extremely pro-

ductive in the right environment, and are a sheer joy to tie. The point is that much of the time, in "civilized" angling environments, the fish insist on something which looks real. This requirement spawned a new generation of streamer fly-dressers, including men like Keith Fulsher and Dave Whitlock, who put as much effort into creating realism in their area of expertise as the nymph and dry-fly gurus do in theirs.

The Blacknosed Dace covers the essential techniques and procedures of bucktail fly-dressing. It has the additional advantages for this exercise of being composed of relatively inexpensive, easily obtained materials and being a great fishtaker.

Incidentally, I have read a number of articles over the years touting streamers as being the "best" type of fly for day-in, day-out productivity over a season. I distinctly remember one article in which the writer avowed that if he were permitted only one fly with which to fish for the rest of his life, it would be a streamer. And, I have heard quite a few credulous anglers repeat these sensational statements in the blissful belief that whatever gets printed in a major outdoor publication must be gospel.

151

Brown Trout, Blacknosed Dace

In my opinion, arbitrary statements of this type are misleading by their very nature. No statement about flies or fly-fishing can be that general or unqualified. I would love to talk to the fellow who made the "streamers forever" comment after a season on the Henry's Fork or the LeTort, provided he wasn't in a locked ward under heavy sedation. Streamers are certainly wonderful lures, but in the right place, at the right time! They do not work miracles, and on certain types of water, such as the two limestone streams previously mentioned, are seldom, if ever, effective.

COMPONENTS

Hook: Size 6, 6X long, medium or heavy wire
Thread: Black 6/0, prewaxed
Butt: Red yarn, either wool or synthetic, fairly thick
Body: Flat silver tinsel of medium width, $\frac{1}{16}$ inch (2 mm)
Ribbing: Oval silver tinsel
Wing: Layers of white, black, and light brown bucktail or substitutes (see notes)

TYING STEPS

1. Before tying on, be sure your vise is properly adjusted to receive the large hook and hold it securely.

2. Tie on near the bend, then cover the hook with thread up to the eye and back towards the rear approximately $\frac{1}{4}$ inch (6 mm). The turns should abut each other perfectly, so as to form a smooth foundation. (photo 18-1)

3. Tie in a piece of red yarn a few inches (70–80 mm) long. Trim off the excess in front of the tie-in point, cutting on a bias. (photo 18-2)

4. Secure the yarn to the hook shank with close, evenly spaced wraps all the way to the bend. Use the left hand to keep tension on the yarn, and to keep it centered atop the hook. The wraps need not abut—that's very tedious—but a smooth foundation must be created. (photo 18-3)

5. After wrapping to the bend, cut off the yarn so as to leave a short butt of approximately $\frac{3}{16}$ inch (4 mm), as in photograph 18-4.

6. Tie in a 4-inch (100 mm) piece of oval tinsel. (photo

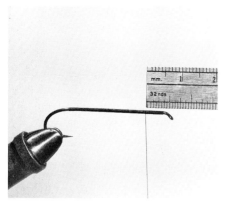

18-1 Blacknosed Dace Bucktail: position of thread at start of tying sequence.

18-2 Tying in and trimming wool yarn.

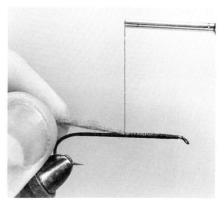

18-3 Formation of underbody.

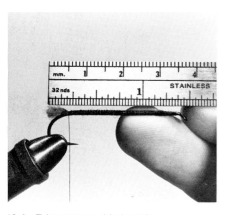

18-4 Trim yarn to this length.

18-5 Ribbing tinsel in place.

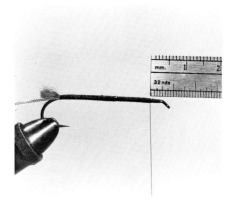

18-6 Come forward with thread to this position.

18-7 Tie in flat tinsel for body.

18-8 Wrap smoothly to bend.

18-5) Wrap the excess flat and tight against the underbody, so as to maintain a smooth foundation.

7. Using close wraps, wind the thread forward to a point ⅛ inch (3 mm) from the eye, or perhaps a hair more. (photo 18-6)

8. Tie in a piece of the flat tinsel approximately 10 inches (250 mm) long. (photo 18-7) Position it for wrapping as previously described for the Orange Fish-Hawk. A hint: when tinsel of this width or greater is required, mylar is overwhelmingly easier to work with than traditional tinsel material.

9. Wind the tinsel back to the bend, under firm tension. (photo 18-8) The turns should touch each other. A helpful trick is to slightly overlap the previous turn, then coax the material to slide off onto the hook shank.

10. At the bend, reverse the tinsel and wrap forward to the tie-in point. Be very precise, with each turn abutting the previous one. Tie off on the bottom. (photo 18-9)

11. Wind the oval tinsel ribbing under firm tension, keeping the spacings even at about 1/16-inch (2 mm) intervals. Tie off on the bottom. (photo 18-10)

12. Prepare for the wing by smoothing out the tie-in area with wraps of thread, creating a gentle forward taper. (photo 18-11) If there is a bump where the final turn of tinsel passed over the top of the hook, flatten it with the back edge of a pair of scissors, or whatever is handy.

13. We are now ready to build the wing. Keep in mind that on this pattern, the idea is to create a three-layered effect, with each layer retaining its purity; that is, the bunches should remain separate, rather than mix with the adjoining layers.

14. Cut off a small bunch of fine white bucktail. Strip out the shorter hairs near the base by holding the outermost portion with the left thumb and forefinger and preening with the right thumb and forefinger. (photo 18-12)

15. Even up the tips with a hair-tamping tool of some sort. Any small cylinder will do, such as an empty pill bottle. Simply insert the hair tip ends down and tap the container against a tabletop a dozen or so times. If the tips aren't perfectly even, all the better. A moderate amount of unevenness creates an attractive tapered effect.

16. Give the bunch of hair its final preening, eliminating any extraneous or unruly hairs. The bunch should be substantial enough to retain its identity after the other two layers are tied on, and no more. Refer to the illustrations.

17. Set the bunch precisely atop the hook shank, using the right hand so adjustments in positioning can readily be made. On this size fly, the tips should not protrude more than ½ inch (13 mm) beyond the rear of the bend. A wing which is too long tends to twist around the hook during casting. (photo 18-13)

18. As you prepare to tie on the bunch of hair, keep in mind that the bottom layer of hair extends slightly further forward than the two succeeding ones, and forms the tapered "nose" of the fly. Therefore, the thread should be positioned towards the rear of the tie-in area.

19. To tie in the hair, hold it slightly above the hook and pass a loop of thread around just the hair itself. Then snug it down onto the hook and secure with eight or ten tight wraps. The loop-around method keeps the hair from slipping around the shoulders of the fly and aids in maintaining definition between the layers of wing material. (photos 18-14, 18-15)

20. Cut off the excess at approximately a forty-five degree angle. The bottom fibers should just about reach the rear of the eye. (photo 18-16)

21. Tie down and smooth out with a series of tight wraps. Don't be afraid to use plenty of winds; this will help keep the white layer separated from the one to follow. Create a base for the next layer by *slightly* building up some thread at and just to the rear of the tie-in point. Do *not* wind back too far; an elongated head is unsightly. The entire head should be ⅛ to 5/32 inch (3 mm) long.

22. Cut off a bunch of fine black bucktail approximately ⅔ the bulk of the white bunch. Repeat the preening and evening process.

23. Position the thread at the point where the white layer was tied on.

24. Position the black bunch so that it is slightly shorter than the white bunch, as shown in photograph 18-17.

25. Tie in the black bunch, using the loop-around method previously described, and secure with a series of tight wraps. (photo 18-18) Do not wind back beyond where the thread securing the white bunch stops, as this will force the black hairs downward, causing them to mix with the white hairs. Also, don't wrap forward too far, you will hinder the next step.

26. Cut off the excess on the bias, at about forty-five degrees. (photo 18-19) As far as possible, the trimmed ends should form a continuation of the taper begun with the previous layer.

27. Smooth out with a series of tight wraps (photo 18-20), setting the stage for the tie-on of the top layer. Again, don't wind any further to the rear than was previously done.

28. Prepare a bunch of tan or pale brown bucktail in the prescribed manner. It should be of approximately the same bulk as the white.

29. Be sure the thread is situated in the same position as for the tying-in of the first two layers.

30. Position the brown bunch so that it is the same length as the white. (photo 18-21)

31. Tie the bunch on with a loop-around and secure with tight wraps, following the same rules as before. (photos 18-22, 18-23)

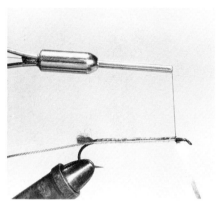

18-9 Tie off tinsel at throat.

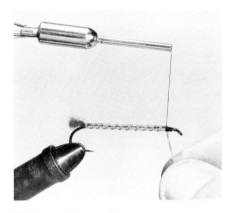

18-10 Ribbing in place.

18-11 Thread base for wing.

18-12 Manicure the hair.

18-13 Position hair atop hook.

18-14 Pass thread completely around hair.

18-15 Snug hair down and secure.

18-16 Trim on forward slant.

32. Form a neatly tapered head with a couple of layers of tight wraps from the eye back to the rear extremity of the head. It is usually necessary to build up the area just behind the eye, in order to get the thread to climb the taper.

34. Whip finish, two coats black lacquer. The finished fly should resemble photograph 18-24.

BUCKTAIL SILHOUETTES

In this exercise, particular emphasis was placed on keeping the layers separate and distinct, so as to maximize the brown-over-black-over-white effect. The loop-around technique is of great assistance here. The separation is important with any pattern which is similar in construction, such as those in Keith Fulsher's Thunder Creek series and Sam Slaymaker's Little Brook, Little Brown, and Little Rainbow Trout. The garish but sometimes lethal Mickey Finn is another pattern which relies very heavily on it to obtain the desired effect.

The other important style point has to do with the amount of flare one builds into the wing. Bucktails with nicely flared wings are certainly more attractive visually, and will be granted a stamp of approval in streamer-dressing circles. They also have better action in the water than overly slender, tightly bunched models, as the flared hair tends to pulsate with the currents of the river and the movements imparted by the angler. After comparisons over a number of seasons, I can definitely report a marked preference on the fishes' part for bucktails dressed in the manner prescribed.

This is the reason for emphasizing the preparation of a thread base for the wing which inclines slightly upward towards the rear. When the hair is mounted on such a plane, it will naturally spread or flare a little, whereas hair mounted onto a flat plane has a tendency to bunch more closely and cling tightly to the hook shank. This is true of single-bunch wings as well as the multilayered variety.

One further note on technique. In the Marabou Black Ghost exercise, the streamer wing was built up with multiple bunches, rather than one thick bunch of material. In the case of hair, this is doubly important. The Blacknosed Dace is composed of three colors, so the multiple bunch technique is mandatory. However, many bucktails have a solid-color wing, and there is a great temptation to expedite the process by tying it on in a single bunch. On a small fly, this might be okay, but where greater bulk is required, two or three layers are advised. This permits the thread to contact a high percentage of the fibers, locking them securely in place.

With the Blacknosed Dace, we used the tying thread to set up each succeeding layer in such a way that it remained separate from the adjoining layers. When building up a single-color wing with two or three bunches, don't create so much definition. Tie in each bunch securely, and prepare for the succeeding bunch by creating a slight forward taper, so the completed effect is that of one bunch, nicely flaired. This can be accomplished by using the loop-around technique on the first bunch and the pinch technique on succeeding bunches. This keeps the lower portion of the wing from sliding down around the shoulders and body while allowing the succeeding layers to blend in.

HAIR

Hair is important to the fly-dresser from both a functional and aesthetic standpoint. We all want our flies to be beautiful, both in our eyes and those of our peer group. We also wish concurrence on the part of the quarry. And we want to facilitate and simplify the fly-dressing process as much as possible. Careful choosing and preparation of hair are essential to the attainment of all these goals.

The most popular hair for the bucktail type of streamer is still the original deer tail, and for good reason. Deer tails (either sex will do) are plentiful and of reasonably low cost —they are a byproduct of the annual Bambi chase. The hair comes in white and various shades of brown, some of which closely match the coloration of certain forage fish. The hair is easy to dye in all shades except black, and that can be done also with proper dyes and methods.

Deer tail is a relatively easy material to handle. There is considerable variance in length and texture of hair from tail to tail, which allows the tier to select that which best suits the size and style of fly he intends to dress. Long, coarse hair from large animals accommodates very large lures, particularly saltwater patterns. There is general agreement among devotees of the brine that no other material can match deer tail for appearance and durability. These people crave top-quality tails the way dry-fly aficionados drool over prime capes.

The finer, softer hair from smaller tails is perfect for average-size freshwater bucktails such as the Blacknosed Dace. The hair is fine enough not to create unwieldly bulk, yet it flares nicely and retains its shape when in use. Small bunches are all that are needed, and one fair-sized tail goes a long way. After the natural colors on a tail are used up, the remainder may be dyed.

Unfortunately, many deer tails are thrown away each year. Most hunters are not aware of the value of the tail and the deer skin itself, or just don't want the problem of getting it into the proper hands. If the tier has friends who hunt, or better yet, knows a butcher who cuts up deer in the fall, he should by all means arrange to obtain some tails plus whatever body and facial hair he might require. A complete body skin, scraped and salted, will supply several average noncommercial fly-dressers for years. The

18-17 Black layer is slightly shorter than white. Note thread base.

18-18 Black layer in place.

18-19 Trim black layer on forward slant.

18-20 Secure and create base of thread.

18-21 Brown layer is as long as the white.

18-22 Tie on with loop-around technique.

18-23 Trim on slant.

18-24 The completed fly.

mask, while somewhat difficult to skin out, provides incomparable material for hair wings and special effects, such as the Comparadun series designed by Al Caucci and Bob Nastasi.

It is very simple to dress out a deer tail and preserve it for long storage. Simply lay the tail on a counter or cutting board and expose the cartilage by making an incision from the base to the tip. The elongated carrot-shaped cartilage is removed and discarded. Then tack the tail to a board in such a manner as to spread and fully expose the tissue. Cover the exposed area with a generous layer of coarse kosher salt and store in a cool, dry place. After a week or so, check to see if the tail is thoroughly cured. If it is very dry and crusty, remove the excess salt with a stiff-bristled brush and store with a few paradichlorobenzene moth nuggets in a container which will tolerate this chemical—glass and wood are best. If the tail is still slightly moist, replace the salt and give it a few more days.

Washing will improve the appearance of deer tail hair and make it more pleasant to have around. A thorough washing is absolutely necessary if the deer tail is to be dyed. Do not wash the tail until it is completely cured. Then place one or several tails in a mesh onion bag and wash them in a clothes washer, just as you would your socks. When the entire cycle is completed, the hair will be damp and the skin moist. Lay the tails on a wire mesh, so the air can get at the hairs, or hang in a dry spot, away from pets and mice.

In lieu of the automated procedure, deer tails may be washed by hand. Soak them for a half-hour in a strong solution of dish detergent and hot water. Throw out the solution, prepare another batch, and wash the tails thoroughly. Use very hot water and wear rubber gloves to protect the hands.

Quite a variety of hairs are employed in streamer dressing, either as a substitute for deer tail or as a first-choice material in themselves. In addition to natural animal hairs, a number of synthetics have come onto the scene, several of which show promise. It is good that development of synthetics is in progress, for the day will eventually come when most if not all of our natural hairs will no longer be available. Hence, it is appropriate that we examine the most popular of both types.

First, let's discuss the natural hairs. Some of the leading ones are calf tail, sometimes called kip or impala tail; Arctic fox tail; bear hair, excluding polar bear; skunk tail; and squirrel tail of various kinds. Presently all of these materials are reasonably easy to obtain and are within the budgetary limits of most of us. Some of the exotic fox tails are a bit costly—a Norwegian white fox tail currently sells for around $6.00—but there is so much material on one tail that it's a bargain in the long run.

Calf tail is very widely used as a streamer material, and serves double duty as wing material for dry flies. Its positive attributes:

1. Quite inexpensive
2. Very plentiful
3. A byproduct of a domestic food animal
4. Nice transluscency
5. Easy to dye
6. Multiple uses
7. Three valuable natural colors: black, white, and brown

And on the flip side of the coin:

1. Hard to find hair long enough for streamer work
2. Too krinkly for tying flies with eye-appeal
3. Doesn't tamp worth a damn
4. Slippery and hard to handle
5. The longer hair often contains curls so severe as to render the material useless

The negative aspects of calf tail are sufficient to sour me on its use as a deer tail substitute. On single-layer bucktails, such as the hair-winged Black Ghost, it is acceptible; however, for multilayer patterns, I find it less than satisfactory.

Anyone who elects to use calf tail for streamers would be well-advised to shop in person. In lieu of this, one should be very explicit with the vendor as to the intended application. Calf tail is used primarily for hair wings on Wulff-type dry flies, where the shorter hair is an advantage. A tail which will produce great Royal Wulffs may contain no streamer material whatsoever. So let the dealer know what you're trying to do, and allow him the option of a back-order or refund in the event that suitable tails are not in stock, which is frequently the case.

Artic fox tails contain beautiful, soft, white hair of sufficient length to dress streamers as large as the one in the exercise, and with prime tails, a size or two larger. The underfur, which is also snow white, makes great dubbing. The hair evens up very well when tamped, and makes superb wings on miniature Wulff patterns. It is easily dyed, though this is somewhat of a sacrilege. The handling qualities are superb. All things considered, it is just about the nicest hair for small- to medium-sized streamers one could ask for. If it has faults, they are being perhaps too soft and not flaring well. Adroit handling compensates for this quite adequately.

Artic fox tails are still in the catalogs at this time, and probably will be around for awhile. If you desire one, do not hesitate in making a purchase. Common sense and a marginal awareness of current trends indicate this animal will soon be added to the growing list of protected species, we hope before the point of endangerment is reached.

Bear hair is available through the catalogs, and while its primary use is for winging dry flies, some swatches contain hair long enough for streamer work. The species from which this hair comes is invariably the black bear. I don't recall ever having seen grizzly bear hair advertised, and hope I never do.

The odd thing about black bear hair is that it is seldom really black. The eastern black bear is quite dark, and certainly looks black when encountered in the wild, but usually the fur is a rich, dark brown. Western black bears, such as those that used to beg along the roads in Yellowstone Park, vary considerably in coloration, usually to medium brown or even cinnamon. In order for this hair to be truly black, dyeing is necessary.

In its natural shades, bear hair has a nice sheen and is both attractive and effective as a streamer material. It tends to disarray when tied onto the hook, but straightens out and looks good in the water. It responds well to tamping, and is a generally pleasing material to work with. Again, the tier must stipulate intent when ordering, for most swatches of bear hair are a bit too short for all save the smallest streamers.

Skunk tail is beautiful stuff. It is a shiny natural black, sometimes with a hint of dirty white at the base. This isn't a problem, as the hair is usually of sufficient length that the base is cut off as excess. I have never tried dying a skunk tail, because the natural color and texture are so lovely. I suppose it could be done, but the only object would be to get a true black throughout the entire length, and as indicated, this usually isn't necessary.

The hair is very straight and quite stiff, which is ideal for creating the median stripe on a Blacknosed Dace. The material responds extremely well to tamping, which usually isn't necessary, as the hairs are quite uniform in length as they come from the tail. While rather limited in application due to its uniform color, a skunk tail is worth having, if only for the one purpose just mentioned.

Skunk tails are advertised in the catalogs from time to time. Sources of supply are not dependable, even though it is such a common animal in most areas. I frequently encounter enough road-killed skunks in a weekend sortie into trout country for a lifetime supply. I have never taken advantage of this bonanza, however, because I simply don't know how to avoid the ever-present musk.

Squirrel tails contain a lot of very nice hair which is suitable for many applications. Several varieties may be purchased through the catalogs; the two most common are the gray squirrel and the red fox squirrel. The latter species is not to be confused with the small red squirrel. The red fox squirrel is a much larger animal, with tail hair which ranges up to 2½ inches, or approximately 63 mm, in length. The predominant color is reddish tan, with a lot of dark mottling on the top side. The underside contains hairs which

Blacknosed Dace

are much less mottled, sometimes being almost pure reddish tan.

Occasionally, natural black squirrel tails are advertised for sale. One shouldn't pass these up, as they are superb for the stripe on the Blacknosed Dace and similar applications. Squirrel tails also take black dye well, and are entirely satisfactory in all respects. Now and then some exotic squirrel tails come on the market for a brief period. These generally are some shade of brown, and are not easily described. If the tier happens onto such tails, and can visualize an application, he may wish to avail himself of a specimen or two. I have some beauties which I use on hair-winged Atlantic salmon fly patterns.

The common gray squirrel is one of our most ubiquitous animals. Even the urban fly-dresser should be able to keep himself supplied from road kills. A pocket knife is adequate for cutting off the tail, and no further treatment is required. Try to select only fresh carcasses which have not begun to decompose. If the reader is repulsed by the thought of carving the tail from a dead squirrel, the vendors seem to have a constant supply at modest prices.

Squirrel tail hair is fairly easy to handle, except that it is a bit slippery. Compensate for this by using very small quantities, building up the wing with supplementary bunches as required. The hair tamps well, but does not readily lend itself to hair-winged dry-fly work.

There are other hairs which are of varying appropriateness for streamer wings. One which I used for years on small streamers is known as monga ring-tail, and features alternate bands of white and very dark brown. The hair seldom reaches 2 inches in length, with 1¼ inches (38 mm) being about average, so it is only suitable for mini-streamers. When dyed, the white portions take the color very well;

18-25 Hair: artificial polar bear.

one then works around the dark hairs. Alternately, the entire tail may be dyed black.

Great as this material is for creating delicate miniatures,
I can no longer bring myself to use it since seeing the
animal starred in a Disney melodrama. Turns out the little
beast is actually a cacomistle, a sort of streamlined racoon
which inhabits Mexico and the southwestern United States.
It tames easily and makes a great pet. After watching a
cacomistle save the life of an old prospector trapped in a
mine, there's no way I can encourage the hunting or trap-
ping of this species by using its tail for fly-dressing. In fact,
I can hardly bring myself to use up my remaining supply,
which may sound ridiculous, but I guess I'm entitled to a
measure of sentimentality.

My experience with synthetic hair substitutes has been
rather limited, but revealing. A number of types are now
available, with considerable variation in appearance and
handling properties. Some are marketed under a trade
name, such as Dynel or Luron, which tells nothing about
the nature of the material. Most catalogs supplement the
name with some descriptive information, which is helpful,
but hardly conclusive. The only way to become familiar
with synthetic hairs is through actual use.

A pressing need for one type of artificial hair has been
created by the stringent restrictions most governments
have placed on the hunting of polar bears, which was long
overdue. Younger tiers may never dress a lure with polar
bear; no great tragedy, for with all of its natural beauty,
polar bear is miserable to handle.

The first artificial polar bear I used was packaged under
the name of a major distributor of fly-tying materials. It
consisted of a patch of cloth to which was affixed a bunch
of hairlike material. (photo 18-25) The fibers were very
fine, somewhat crinkly, and soft. Length varied widely,
the longest hairs being about 3 ½ inches (85–90 mm). This
posed a problem, since the material does not respond to
tamping at all. A fair amount of manipulation was required to even up the tips enough to permit the dressing

of a reasonably neat streamer. There was a great deal of underfur and short fibers which had to be discarded, creating a high percentage of waste. The synthetic underfur was marginally suitable for dubbing, a valuable by-product of the natural material. Also, there were quite a few short, kinky hairs which had to be culled out before the final evening-up process was undertaken. As one might gather, the preparatory process was tedious.

Having fought the battle of preparation, I proceeded to dress a very attractive Mickey Finn, whose photograph appears in the color section. The synthetic hair proved to be very easy to work with on the hook, because it compressed nicely, minimizing bulk. Using small bunches helped offset the evening-up problems. For a size 6, 6X-long Mickey, I used two bunches for each layer of wing, a total of six bunches in all. It was agreeably surprising to discover that despite its high luster, the material was not at all slippery, and the thread gripped it securely.

While leafing through the catalog of E. Hille, an anglers supply house in Williamsport, Pennsylvania, I noticed that several types of artificial hair were listed, and I ordered samples of each. One was described as ''Artificial Hair On Artificial Skin,'' and turned out to be the product just described. Another, using the Dynel trade name, is similar but much easier to use. It comes mounted on plastic strips and has no underfur. The tips are much more even than in the other type, and the hair is considerably longer, coming in either 4- or 6-inch lengths. A variety of colors is available, including several fluorescents. (photo 18-26)

The Artificial Hair is superior to the Dynel in a most important respect: it is much finer and softer, and therefore has excellent action in the water. So, despite Dynel's better packaging and handling qualities, I would opt for the finer material for stream-size bucktails.

Another brand name which the Hille catalog lists is Luron. Five colors are presently available: white, yellow, red, black, and blue. The material can be purchased in various lengths or in bulk skeins. It is slightly thicker and

18-26 Dynel.

Blacknosed Daces

stiffer than Dynel, and has the consistency of bundled leader material. I wouldn't consider it particularly appropriate for stream-sized bucktails. It makes good-looking saltwater patterns, but experienced anglers tell me the action and visibility do not compare to natural deer tail. Some lead-headed jigs tied out of Luron worked okay on blues, stripers, and weakfish.

Yet another variety of artificial hair is crimped nylon. This material comes in a continuous tow, sold in 1-yard lengths or on 1-pound spools, which contain approximately 17 yards. It is slightly thicker than Luron, and, as the name implies, is not perfectly straight. This material is suitable for the same purposes as Luron. A wide range of colors is currently available.

Let's take a brief look at these materials from a statistical standpoint. Here are the typical diameters of individual strands.

Artificial Hair: .0015 inch
Dynel: .003 inch

Luron: .004–.005 inch
Crimped Nylon: .005–.006 inch
Natural Deer Tail: .005–.007 inch

These seemingly minute differences are meaningful, especially when coupled with the variances in consistency between the materials. There is a night-and-day difference between an average-sized bucktail tied with Luron and with Artificial Hair. After all, a typical human hair measures around .003 inch, so the Artificial Hair is really getting down there. Incidentally, while natural deer tail may seem rather coarse, keep in mind the fact that it compresses much better than most synthetics.

This book is not a materials catalog—after all, who knows what will be available next year, or in 1984. It is hoped the fly-dresser has gained an awareness of the sometimes subtle possible differences between these similar materials. Then as new products appear in the marketplace, he will be in a better position to choose the one which best suits the particular application.

19

The Hornberg Streamer

TECHNIQUES TO BE LEARNED

1. Mallard flank streamer wings
2. Imitation jungle cock eyes
3. The unique Hornberg style

This fly, which is of rather unusual construction, is one of those "savior" patterns I never want to be without. I don't carry a large variety of streamers, except when heading into some specialized situation where probing the water with an array of streamers is the most productive angling method. The Hornberg is one of a small selection which is effective in widely ranging circumstances, and where I go, it goes.

The Hornberg was developed by Frank Hornberg, a Wisconsin game protector, with assistance of some kind by the Weber Tackle Company. Joseph D. Bates, Jr., in his notable work of 1950, *Streamer Fly Tying and Fishing,* tells us that in the East the Hornberg was considered "a great new fly." This supports my guess that it was created shortly after World War II.

In June of 1976, Dave Male, Colby Hansen and I took a vacation in the Rockies. We used West Yellowstone, Montana, as a base of operations and fished the surrounding areas, including, of course, Yellowstone National Park. The Saturday of July Fourth weekend found us on the fast water of the Firehole, where the river parallels the road. The fish are not large in this section—a fourteen-incher is a trophy—but they are hungry and plentiful.

The three of us were spread out over a half-mile section,

out of sight of one another but highly visible from the adjacent highway. After some moderately successful experiments with soft-hackled wet flies, I switched to the Hornberg and began to probe the pockets under the steep bank against the far shore. The little streamer drove those trout absolutely mad, and I seldom made three casts in a row without a slashing strike. Some of the trout were rainbows, and they performed with typical aerodynamic verve. The light rod spent much of the morning bowed in that classic arc which delights angler and spectator alike.

I noticed that many cars and even a few buses were stopping to watch the action, sometimes to the accompaniment of angry honks from impatient motorists to the rear. At length, I was hailed from the bank by a park ranger.

"Would you mind fishing somewhere else? It's the Fourth of July and you're causing a traffic jam," he pleaded. I agreed reluctantly, and waded ashore.

"What in the name of God are you using?" the ranger asked. "I thought this water near the road was fished out." I showed him the Hornberg.

"Beautiful fly!" he exclaimed. "Hope I can find some in West Yellowstone."

"Here's a start," I said, handing him a matched pair.

"Hey, that's awfully generous of you, and I'm sure grateful. I don't want to be a spoil-sport, but we have a real problem here. You were drawing more attention than a damn bear. Do you suppose you could find a piece of water away from the road?"

I assured him I understood, and wandered off downstream to a less conspicuous section.

At lunchtime I reconvened with my partners, who were beaming and quite smug.

"Guess what happened to us!" said Colby, "The ranger came along and asked us to move. We were stopping traffic."

"Hornbergs, right?" I said.

"Right. The ranger had never seen one before. We each gave him a couple."

"Is that so," I smiled.

The Hornberg is one of those patterns which has inspired a fair number of local innovations. One version is tied tent-wing in caddis dry-fly style. One has a single mallard flank feather tied flat on top of the hook. There are endless debates over how broad the flanks should be and whether or not they should cover the hook point, and arguments pro and con for the advisibility of bringing the tips together in a point with a dab of cement, as called for in the original dressing. A most attractive brown version employs bronze mallard flanks and brownish grizzly hackle from a crossbreed bird.

My favorite version conforms with the original as described in Bates. The sizes which work best for me are dressed on number 8 and 10 hooks, 4X long. We will use the larger of these two in our exercise.

COMPONENTS

Hook: Size 8, 4X long, medium or heavy wire
Thread: Black 6/0 prewaxed
Body: Silver mylar tinsel, 1/32 inch (1 mm) in width
Underwings: Yellow hackle feathers
Overwings: Mallard or teal flank feathers (see notes)
Eyes: Imitation jungle cock, large or extralarge (see notes)
Hackle: Grizzly, very soft rooster or hen

TYING STEPS

1. Tie on 1/8 inch (4 mm) back from the eye, cover the hook smoothly with thread, return to a few turns short of the tie-in point.

2. Tie in the mylar tinsel and create a tinsel body in the usual manner. (photo 19-1) Be careful not to leave a bump on top of the hook where the final turn of tinsel passes over, as this will cock the underwing.

3. If necessary, use some wraps of thread to create a smooth base for the underwing. Then tie in the two matched hackle feathers streamer-wing style. For this hook

size, the underwing should be 1 inch (25 mm) long from tip to tie-in point. (photo 19-2)

4. Select two matched mallard or teal flank feathers. Strip away excess fibers until you have 1 3/16 inches (30 mm) left of each feather, measured from its tip. (photo 19-3) The selection, matching, and preparation of these feathers are the most important ingredients in successful Hornberg tying. You may wish to read the notes before proceeding.

5. Prepare the flank feathers for tying-in by flattening the center stems at the point where the thread will intersect them. Use any implement which will not cut the stem. My choice is the closed tips of a pair of scissors. Simply lay the feathers on a hard surface and rub the target area flat without weakening the stem. (photo 19-4)

6. The flank feathers may be tied on individually or together. (photo 19-5) They should be absolutely perpendicular and should match perfectly at the rear. The tie-in point is very slightly ahead of the front extremity of the underwing, which is completely enveloped by the flank feathers.

7. Take one of the imitation jungle cock eyes and put a smear of glue on the back side. Refer to the note and photograph 19-6.

8. Position the jungle cock eye so that it lies centered on the near-side flank feather. It should be nearly half the length of the flank feather. (photo 19-7)

9. Press the jungle cock eye onto the flank feather so the glue takes hold, then secure in position with a few turns of thread.

10. Repeat the procedure for the far side. Use any method you find convenient to insure proper positioning, such as holding a small pocketbook-type mirror behind the fly.

11. Select a soft grizzly hackle feather with a fiber spread of 1/2 inch (12 mm) or slightly greater. (This is the size used for a size 10 dry fly.) Hen hackle is great if you can find any which is long enough to be wound and has pretty, contrasting markings. Body plumage is also excellent. And there's nothing wrong with soft rooster hackle, which, sad to say, most barred Rock capes have in abundance. Tie in at the forward extremity of the wings.

12. The hackle may be wound dry-fly style or folded, as in photograph 19-8. For those who want to fish the Hornberg as a double-duty dry-fly/streamer, use rooster hackle and do not fold.

13. Whip finish, two coats of black cement or laquer on the head. The completed fly should resemble photograph 19-9.

14. Option: take a small dab of high-viscosity cement between the left thumb and forefinger and preen the tips of the flank feathers to a point. My choice for cement: silicone glue if longer drying time can be allowed, Duco household cement if not.

19-1 Hornberg Streamer: tinsel wound.
Note position of thread.

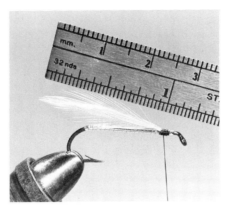

19-2 Underwing in place.

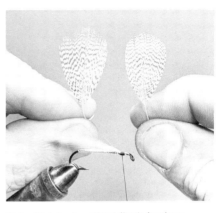

19-3 Matched mallard flank feathers.

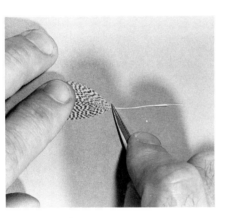

19-4 Flattening stem.

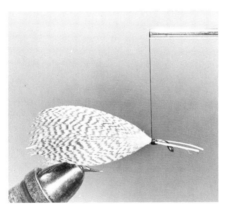

19-5 Tying in flank feathers.

19-6 Applying silicone glue to imitation
jungle cock eye.

19-7 Mounting the eye.

19-8 Folded hackle feather ready to be
wound.

19-9 The completed fly.

19-10   Mallard and Teal Flank Feathers: Feather on left is properly shaped for Hornberg.

19-11   Stripping off lower fibers will reduce curvature.

19-12   Curvature can be reduced here by crimping the stem.

MALLARD AND TEAL FLANK FEATHERS

Mallard flank feathers were discussed in connection with the Dark Cahill Wet Fly, but with a different application in mind. In the case of the Hornberg, we are using a whole —if somewhat reduced—flank feather to create the silhouette of a small minnow or bait fish. Naturally, the shape of the feathers when wet is what is important, as they tend to streamline when being fished. Select feathers of a shape similar to those in the photographs. A 1³⁄₁₆ inch (30 mm) feather should have a breadth of approximately ³⁄₈ inch (9–10 mm).

To aid the tying process and achieve the most beautiful fly it is important to select feathers which are the desired shape; matched closely in size, shape, shade, and markings; and not overly curved or cupped.

Optimum feathers are uniform in shape on either side of the center stem, rather than curved in either direction. (photo 19-10) This eliminates several problems, such as matching the two sides, obtaining proper shape, and getting the feathers tied onto the hook in the desired attitude. They also respond nicely to having the tips pointed with glue, if one chooses to do so.

Extreme cupping or curvature of the center stem is a problem, a fact no fly-dresser would deny. Feathers thus conformed can be separated in the sorting process; they may be perfectly suitable for imitation wood duck wings or some other application where the center stem isn't so critical. But not every flank feather which appears to be excessively cupped is unsuitable for the Hornberg. The important factor is the condition of the *usable* portion of the feather, that is, the part which is left after the excess is stripped away. Often curvature in the lower portion of the stem makes a feather appear to be much more cupped than it actually is. And the flattening of the stem just prior to tie-in may compensate for whatever curvature remains. (photos 19-11, 19-12)

The least expensive way to buy mallard and teal flanks is in bulk. The average fly-dresser will usually purchase ounce lots and obtain a year or two's supply from one bag. I bought a pound a few years ago, and am still rather awed by the amount of plumage it contains. Given normal life expectancy, I would say I have a terminal supply.

In a bag of feathers one usually finds a complete range of sizes, shapes, and markings. If it is a fair lot, an ounce bag will include feathers of the very finest quality, some that are useless, and everything in between. Sorting is a painstaking task which shouldn't be rushed, and the moment of need is not the time for it. The fly-dresser will profit greatly if he devotes a winter afternoon to sorting an ounce or two of mallard flanks.

I try to make this as painless as possible. I get a bottle of scotch and turn on the stereo. I dump the feathers into a shoe-box. Before me I have four soup dishes, one each for sizes 6, 8, 10 and 12. To one side I have another box into which will go feathers for dying imitation wood duck. I also have a paper bag for junk. On the table is my office stapler.

First I make a general sort in which I group the Hornberg-type feathers by size, depositing those which don't qualify in the box earmarked for dying and throwing out the unusables. Then I go back and begin pairing up the Hornberg feathers in each size grouping. When I get a match, I staple the two stems together and put the pair into the appropriate soup dish. When all feathers have been sorted, the batches are put into zip-lock bags with a moth-ball or two. By this time, I'm usually down four scotches. If I still feel competent, I might boil up a batch of dye and perform the wood duck transformation.

When selecting for shade, I prefer defined but not zebra-like barring of gray and off-white. Teal is nice, but sometimes the markings are not subtle enough for my taste. Mallard is often more closely barred than I prefer, but these feathers are widely and successfully used, however, so I guess that's just my idiosyncrasy.

IMITATION JUNGLE COCK

It is a sad thing to note the drastic depletion of the magnificent Indian jungle cock. Of all the materials which are no longer available, I feel the loss of this most keenly, not because of its fish-taking properties but because of the beauty these distinctive feathers add to a well-dressed fly. On the bright side is the hope that the bird will repopulate, although this is doubtful in light of the way India is demolishing its natural environment.

So now we have the imitations. Actually, they've been with us for quite a while, in one form or another. I recall seeing a plastic version in the Herters catalog in the early 1960s, and it may have already been available for many years. I didn't think much of that imitation. Today's are far superior, so much so that several catalogs claim they can't be distinguished from the real thing, once on the fly. That little piece of automobile-ad rhetoric needs no comment beyond the observation that even the most naive beginning flytier probably isn't that gullible, and certainly isn't that blind.

Be that as it may, we do have imitations that do not desecrate any save the most sacred traditional salmon flies. On the Hornberg, they look very nice. Although usually angling considerations are secondary, the case of the Hornberg is an exception. The fly appears quite bland without the jungle cock eyes, and its effectiveness is definitely lessened.

Imitation jungle cock eyes come in four sizes: small, medium, large, and extralarge. For the Hornberg, where the eye is being mounted on a fairly large feather, the larger sizes produce the desired look. Match with hook sizes as follows:

Size 6: extralarge
Size 8: extralarge, or in a pinch, large
Size 10: large
Size 12: medium

These sizes assume 4X long hooks. Many fly-dressers use

3X long and seem quite satisfied with the results.

As to handling imitation jungle cock eyes, there is one major problem which must be dealt with, and it has to do with fly-casting. The plastic eyes are made out of sheet stock, and no air can pass through. As a result, the eyes have a marked tendency to catch the air currents, which forces them to protrude from the hook shank almost at right angles. When this occurs, it sounds like an attacking hornet. And indescribable things happen to the leader.

The solution is simple; merely apply a small dab of glue to the back of the eye, then mount it in the usual manner. Vinyl cement is not very effective (synthetic jungle cock apparently is not made of vinyl). Silicon rubber glue adheres most effectively and is highly viscose, so it doesn't run into the flank feather.

The latter point is important, from the standpoint of appearance, if not performance, as the permeation of an adhesive into a soft feather ruins the texture and may discolor it. The best glue for this application effects only the area to which it is applied. The only disadvantage to silicon is its long drying time—the flies really should be allowed to sit overnight before use. If one isn't in a hurry, no problem. If time is of the essence, use Duco cement or something similar—the flies may be used in a matter of minutes. Under no circumstances should low-viscosity or liquid adhesives be used; they are much too runny and will mess up the flank feather.

As indicated in the tying instructions, first the flank feathers are tied, then the jungle cock eyes are mounted. With the imitation type, this method works out better than preassembly. The flat plastic stubs by which the fake eyes are tied in are rather bulky, and when coupled with the center stem of the flank feather, create an unwieldy mass. By tying in the two components separately, two advantages are gained: the eyes are positioned exactly as desired; and the tie-in points may be slightly staggered, thereby minimizing bulk.

A natural jungle cock eye mounted on a small shoulder feather, such as silver pheasant, can be positioned with great precision. This and the lesser bulk of the natural, dictate preassembly. Not so with the synthetic. It is definitely to the fly-dresser's advantage to position and secure the flanks and imitation jungle cock eyes independently.

20

The Gray Ghost Streamer

TECHNIQUES TO BE LEARNED

1. Hackle-feather streamer wings
2. Golden pheasant crest
3. Silver pheasant and jungle cock shoulder-cheek assembly

Of all her creations, Carrie Stevens is best remembered for the Gray Ghost. She became inspired to create an effective imitation of a smelt, and on July 1, 1924, she left her housework unfinished to work on the project. The result was the first Gray Ghost, which Carrie described as being crude, compared to subsequent dressings. Apparently, her near-wilderness lifestyle had isolated her from the fly-tying fraternity, and she knew virtually nothing of materials and techniques. She used dyed chicken breast feathers for the shoulders and some nondescript dotted feather for the cheek, as silver pheasant and jungle cock were foreign to her.

The great speckled trout of Mooselookmeguntic Lake overruled Carrie's self-criticism. Extending her truancy from wifely tasks, she walked down to the Upper Dam pool, which was a paradise in those days, and began casting the fly into the fast water. Less than an hour later, she hooked a 6-pound, 13-ounce brookie, which took second prize in the *Field and Stream* contest. Even in those bountiful times, a trout of that size was not to be sneezed at, and the story of the conquest with the new pattern caused excitement far and wide. Thus did Carrie Stevens became known as one of America's premier fly-dressers.

The Gray Ghost must look like something that a large fish considers delectable, because I have taken trout on this fly where no smelt exist. I have also used it with great success on landlocked salmon, bass, and walleyes.

The Gray Ghost is a challenge to the fly-dresser: anyone can tie the components onto the hook, but ending up with a finished product which is near-perfect is something else again. I suggest a study of the notes following the tying instructions before attempting the pattern.

COMPONENTS

Hook: Size 4, 6X-long, medium or heavy wire
Thread: 6/0 prewaxed in two colors, yellow and black
Body: Yellow-orange, medium thickness floss
Tag and Ribbing: Flat silver tinsel, 1/32 inch diameter
Throat: Five strands of peacock herl, bunch of white deer tail or substitute, short golden pheasant crest feather
Wings: Four olive-gray hackle feathers, long golden pheasant crest feather
Shoulder-Cheek: Silver pheasant and jungle cock, pre-assembled according to the notes

168

TYING STEPS

1. Using yellow or pale orange thread, tie on 3/16 inch (5 mm) behind of the eye and wrap neatly to the bend, covering the hook shank.

2. Tie in a 5-inch (125 mm) length of silver tinsel. Do not position it for ribbing, as described in previous exercises, because it will be used to create a tag first.

3. Wind the thread neatly and smoothly back to the tie-on point, tie in an 18-inch piece of the floss. *Be sure your fingers are clean.*

4. Create a smooth floss body as described in previous exercises.

5. Create a tag by taking a few turns of tinsel back slightly around the bend, then forward over itself.

6. Create the ribbing as previously described, using a preliminary coat of cement. Then, tie off, let dry, recoat with cement and let dry again, thoroughly. At this point, the fly should resemble photograph 20-1.

7. Tie on again, this time with black thread, 1/8 inch (3 mm) behind the eye.

8. Select five strands of peacock herl, preferably from up near the eye of the plume where the uniformity is best. (photo 20-2)

9. Using the upside-down pinch, tie in the strands beneath the hook shank with the curvature pointing upwards. It is sometimes necessary to tie in the strands one or two at a time to obtain this effect. They are to be as long as the wing, meaning they should extend approximately 1/2 inch (12 mm) beyond the rear extremity of the hook. Refer to photographs 20-3 and 20-4.

10. Tie in a sparse bunch of white deer tail which has been prepared by tamping. This should be slightly shorter than the herl. (photo 20-5)

11. Prepare a short golden pheasant crest feather (photo 20-6) by stripping off the superfluous fibers, then crimping and flattening the stem at the tie-in point. The feather is to be as long as the shoulder, so use that as a measuring guide. Crimping and flattening may be accomplished by using the tips of a pair of scissors on a hard surface. (photo 20-7)

12. Using the upside-down pinch, tie in the crest feather with the curvature pointing upwards, as in photograph 20-8.

13. Directly atop the hook shank, tie in a long golden pheasant crest feather, the same length as the herl. (photos 20-9, 20-10) It may be necessary to remove some of the curvature, using the pretying preparatory process described in the notes following. It is also necessary to prepare the feather by stripping off the superfluous fibers and flattening the stem. Don't crimp the stem too much; this feather should lie fairly flat, with what curvature there is pointing downward.

14. Prepare four well-matched olive-gray feathers by stripping the fibers off the butts until the desired length is achieved. (photo 20-11) Remember, the wings should be the same length as the herl. The tips of the feathers should match up precisely.

15. Prepare the feathers for tie-in by forming them into two wings consisting of two feathers each. The two feathers in each wing should lie together spoon-fashion, but the two wing assemblies should be faced with the curvatures opposing. (photo 20-12)

16. Be sure the tie-in area is smooth. Then tie in the four-feather wing grouping, using a slack or semi-slack loop instead of a pinch. The feathers have less tendency to roll when the thread is looped gently over the stems and the pressure applied gradually. (photos 20-13, 20-14)

17. Secure the wings with a series of neat wraps. At the same time, prepare for the mounting of the shoulder-cheek assemblies. (photo 20-15) Do not wrap the thread any further to the rear than is absolutely necessary, as a small, neat head is a definite style point.

18. Place the near-side shoulder-cheek assembly exactly in the desired position—the center stem of the silver pheasant feather matching the center stem of the outside wing feather. (photo 20-16) If the assembly was properly prepared, the jungle cock will also be centered on the wing.

19. Tie in the assembly with the same technique as for the wings; that is, sneak a semi-slack loop over the center stem and build up tension gradually with succeeding wraps. (photo 20-17) Before completely securing the assembly, check to see that it is in exactly the desired position and adjust if required.

20. Repeat the process with the far-side assembly. A small hand mirror is helpful for checking position.

21. Trim off the stems; create a small, neat head; whip-finish; two coats black laquer. The completed fly should appear as in photograph 20-18.

HACKLE-FEATHER STREAMER WINGS

Selection is more than half the battle when it comes to feather-winged streamers. Some feathers seem to go on so easily that the entire procedure is child's play. Others will roll, twist, lean, and do everything except lie straight. This can be maddening.

About the only guideline is to look for feathers which have fine center stems. Saddle hackles frequently have this characteristic. Thick stems have a tendency to roll, and also occupy too much space on the hook. Not that fine-stemmed feathers always go on nicely. When a cape or saddle patch is identified as having excellent streamer-wing properties, label it as such, for it has special value.

Shape is a somewhat arbitrary matter. I like a fairly slim

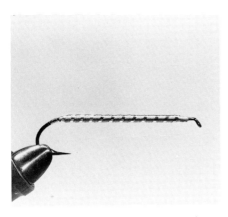

20-1 Gray Ghost Streamer: body and ribbing in place. Note slender shape.

20-2 Select herl from this part of feather.

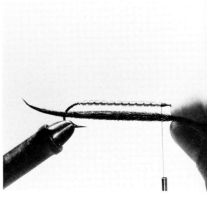

20-3 Position herl thus.

20-4 Herl in place.

20-5 Bucktail in place.

20-6 Short golden pheasant crest feather.

20-7 Crimping.

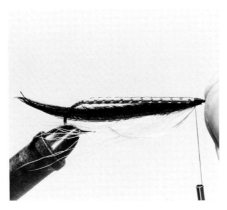

20-8 Crest feather tied in.

20-9 Long crest feather.

20-10 Crest feather tied in.

20-11 Stripping waste fibers from wing feathers.

20-12 Matching up the wing feathers.

20-13 Positioning wing feathers.

20-14 Tie in wings with slack loop.

20-15 Use thread to secure wings and create base for cheek-shoulder assembly.

20-16 Position shoulder-cheek assembly thus.

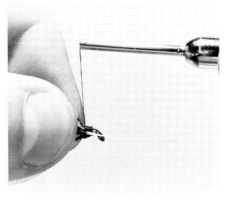

20-17 Use slack loop technique to tie in.

20-18 The completed fly.

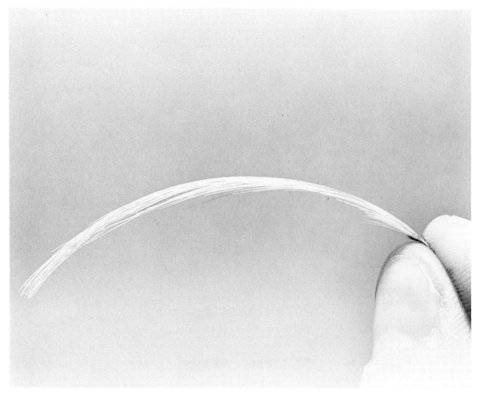

20-19 Reparation of crest feather: curvature reduced after molding.

silhouette, but I do not care for overly pointed or sharply tapered feathers. Styles vary considerably in streamer work, and many patterns take advantage of unique feather shapes to obtain special effects. However, for a conventional streamer such as the Gray Ghost, I prefer a feather which tapers gracefully to an elliptical tip.

GOLDEN PHEASANT CREST

These breathtakingly beautiful feathers are among the most difficult ones to handle in all of fly-tying. The way in which they are used on most patterns—as a decorative topping—adds greatly to the problems caused by the properties of the feathers. Very seldom does one encounter a golden pheasant crest feather which perfectly satisfies the application at hand in terms of size, shape, and tying qualities. Usually a fair amount of reshaping and adaptation is necessary.

One of the major difficulties involves the natural curvature of the feather, which is almost always different from that required for integration with the other components of the fly. This is particularly true in salmon fly patterns, where the crest feather is supposed to border the outer edge of the wings, with the end curving gracefully downward so that the tip meets with that of the tail to form a classic almond silhouette. Sometimes this effect can be

obtained by selection, but more often it is necessary to increase or decrease the curvature.

There is a very simple way to do this, the only condition being the foresight to do the process ahead of time. Simply take a few crest feathers, or as many as will be required, wet them thoroughly, and lay them around any object which has the desired amount of curvature. This could be anything from a water glass to a large bowl. When the feather has dried completely it will retain the shape of the mold. (photo 20-19) One can greatly accelerate the process by using a hair blow-dryer on low setting, but remember that the quill controls the curvature, and it remains damp long after the fibers are dry.

Some crests contain twists or compound curves. These should be avoided when selecting crests for purchase. However, other factors, such as pressing need or particularly brilliant coloration, might influence one to buy a twisted crest. I have found that all or most of the undesirable compound curvature can also be removed by the wetting-and-molding process. I recommend the feathers be soaked very thoroughly, so the stem is well-saturated, and allowed to dry naturally.

Selection for proper length has a great deal to do with one's success in handling crest feathers. A full, mature crest will carry feathers which vary considerably in size, which is most fortunate, as the patterns to which they are

20-20 Note thick stem and waste fibers.

20-21 When stripping waste, pay close attention to fiber conformity.

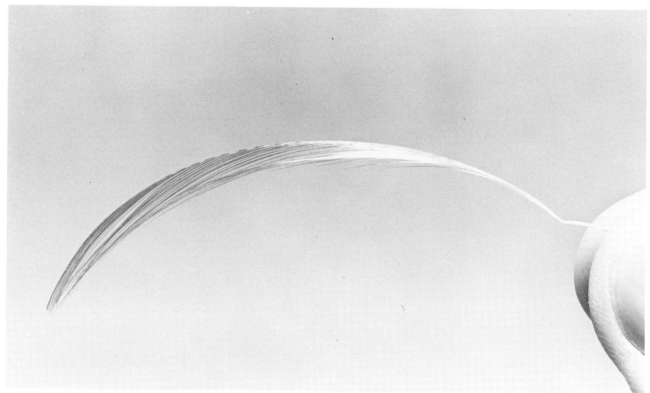

20-22 Crest feather stripped and crimped.

to be applied do likewise. The reason for care in choosing a feather of just the right length is the desirability of mounting the feather at its optimal tie-in point. Too short a feather will cause the unattractive butt portion to show. Too long a feather creates several serious problems in tying.

Remove a typical feather from a crest and examine it closely. Notice that the stem is quite thick at the butt, and tapers sharply as it approaches the beginning of the brightly colored fibers. (photo 20-20) Spread the barbules and you will also observe that they become longer and more colorful very suddenly as this point is approached. Because of this, one must be particularly careful to avoid stripping off too much material from the butt, which is certain to occur if the fibers are removed all the way up to where the bright gold meets the stem. *One must stop stripping when the fibers are of sufficient length and color to make a contribution to the fullness and luster of the crest feather.* (photo 20-21) The point at which this occurs is the optimal tie-in point.

Usually it is necessary to crimp the stem at the tie-in point, in order to cause the feather to assume the desired attitude. (photo 20-22) This may be done with the thumb nail or any implement the fly-dresser finds handy. Avoid an overly sharp edge, as this may damage the delicate stem. It is necessary only to dent and perhaps slightly flatten the

stem, so that the feather remains in position as the thread is applied. *Above all, be certain to crimp with the feather in precisely the attitude it must assume on the hook.* Otherwise, you will have created a problem.

SILVER PHEASANT-JUNGLE COCK ASSEMBLY

These two materials may be traced back into the majestic days of fly-dressing. Nearly all of the magnificent salmonfly patterns of the British Isles called for jungle cock eyes, while in this country some of the greatest streamer patterns called for the silver pheasant as well. The latter is still available at fairly reasonable prices. As for jungle cock, it will probably never again be marketed. The fly-dresser who wants a jungle cock cape will have to obtain it from a private collection at considerable cost. Its rarity and value are such that maximum utilization and protection are of great importance.

One must repair the splits which are almost always present in jungle cock eyes and at the same time protect the delicate little feather from the elements and the stresses of angling. (photo 20-23) Historically, this has been accomplished by using an adhesive of some sort and a piece of backing material. A common and reasonably effective traditional method was to trim a small hackle feather to the shape of the eye and cement it to the dull side. However, this is tedious and fraught with opportunity for catastrophies.

Silicone glue, a modern ''miracle'' adhesive which can be purchased in most hardware stores, renders the backing unnecessary. All one has to do is to smooth on the glue with the thumb and forefinger in a thin but thorough layer. Allow adequate drying time as specified on the tube, and you have an eye which is tough as surgical tubing, yet perfectly natural in appearance. Thus, with one quick and easy operation, the splits are healed and protection is assured. The results are so beautiful I am sure the bird himself would approve. (photos 20-24–20-26)

Silicone glue is also recommended for the joining of the shoulder-cheek assembly, as it bonds firmly without leeching into surrounding fibers. (photo 20-27) As an expedient, one may glue the eye in place on the silver pheasant feather while the protective coating is still wet. A better method is to treat the jungle cock eyes in advance and use a second dab for mounting. This produces a better bond and eliminates handling of a sticky feather.

As mentioned, silver pheasant feathers are still available. They are generally sold in packets of one dozen, or as a complete skin. The latter, while representing a significant initial investment, is in the long run far more practical for the fly-dresser who wishes to tie streamers or salmon patterns to any great extent. In addition to gaining the discount of a bulk purchase, one acquires a full range of sizes, shapes, and markings. This variation is important, for while these zebra-striped feathers may all look exactly alike at first glance, there are subtle variations which can have considerable effect on the appearance of the completed fly.

Carrie Stevens, who liked to use silver pheasant on her patterns, preferred a somewhat oversized feather with

20-23 Repairing and protecting jungle cock eye: typical split feather.

20-24 Apply silicone glue.

20-25 Preen.

20-26 The finished product.

20-27 Shoulder-cheek assembly.

plenty of barring. For illustrative reasons in the exercise, the Gray Ghost was dressed in this manner. What Carrie probably sought was the representation of the gill plates of a smelt or other bait fish, and the effect is quite convincing. The oversized feathers look slightly odd when dry, but wet they slim down and are most alluring. One could reduce the size of the silver pheasant shoulders a bit with no sacrifice in effectiveness or appearance. This helps stretch one's valuable feather supply.

A final note of caution. When selecting silver pheasant feathers and jungle cock eyes and matching them for gluing into assemblies, be sure the size relationship between the two is proper. I make up large numbers of assemblies in advance, and have learned that it is very easy to become disoriented. I now keep a few properly proportioned streamers in front of me as reminders.

21

The
Muddler Minnow

TECHNIQUES TO BE LEARNED

1. Trimmed deer hair
2. Muddle positioning and spacing

Of all the flies I tie and use regularly, the Muddler Minnow gives me the most trouble. In fact, the only flies which ever frustrated me more were a few of the really complex married-wing patterns.

The problems one encounters with the Muddler are insidious. No single operation is really that difficult; in fact, they are more or less simple. But to integrate them in perfect harmony on the same hook shank is a challenge. There are very few flies where lack of circumspection at each step can cause so many cumulative difficulties. I have seen good fly-dressers sit down at a vise and proceed to tie a Muddler they couldn't complete. Truly, it is a pattern where one can paint oneself into a corner.

I will confess without apology that I still don't particularly enjoy dressing a Muddler, and when I have to teach or demonstrate the pattern, I do so with sweaty palms. The problem is the amount of time involved. I'm a rather impatient sort of person, with a short concentration span, as any of my tennis partners will testify. A couple of volleys, and I want to put away the point, which more often than not causes an unforced error. The Muddler takes time, and the only short cut is the development of expertise in the particular techniques involved.

One of the most intimidating experiences of my life was my visit to Dan Bailey's shop in Livingston, Montana, back in 1968. In addition to his retail store, Dan runs a large commercial fly-tying operation. Nearly all of his tiers are women, or at least they were then. How it is today, with men's lib, I wouldn't know. Anyway, there were women there who actually specialized in the Muddler Minnow. They could turn one out in a few minutes, trimmed head and all, and damned nice ones, at that. I guess when one is on piece work, motivation runs high. This much I know: if I had to earn a living dressing Muddlers, I'd be on food stamps in no time flat.

Discouraged? Don't be, please. Not everyone harbors like feelings. Many tiers are perfectly content to dress these things one after another, and do so with relative ease. In my case, it's hard work—and it's worth it.

If I were allowed but one pattern, I would choose the Muddler Minnow. Already, I can hear the screams from those who believe the Muddler is a streamer—not that it isn't an incredibly effective one. It's also a hell of a wet fly and not a bad dry, in certain circumstances. It can be a nymph, a pupa, an emerging insect, a drowned terrestrial, a caddis in oviposit. Given a full range of sizes, weighted

Sculpin

and unweighted, the standard Muddler pattern is, in my opinion, the greatest all-around fly in existence. Throw in a few variations, such as the Yellow Muddler, the Spuddler, and the Missoulian Spook, and you have an inventory that will produce almost everywhere.

Colonel Bates's book informs us that the Muddler was originally dressed by Don Gapen of the Gapen Fly Company, Anoka, Minnesota. It was created to imitate the Cockatush minnow, which inhabits the Nipigon watershed in northern Ontario. From Bates's description, I must assume the Cockatush minnow is what we call a sculpin in these parts. The sculpin family is a large one, there being eighty-four known species in the United States and Canada, including saltwater varieties. The common trout-stream sculpin is a flattish, bottom-dwelling fish with excellent protective coloration and a habit for hiding under rocks. The species is nocturnal, which makes the Muddler an extremely effective night pattern.

The best brown I ever took in the Battenkill fell for a size 10 Muddler, greased and fished dry. It was late summer in the mid-sixties and the free-stone streams of the northeast were suffering through the worst drought in decades. The Battenkill, which depends more on cold spring waters than run-off from rains, was just about the only game in town.

It was fairly early in the morning. I was on the Vermont side, standing below a run of fast water, hoping for an assist from *Tricorythodes*. The diminutive mayflies hadn't yet shown, and I was passing the time fiddling with my leader. There was a deep-cut bank across from me, and a grassy meadow bordered the river.

I noticed that a few grasshoppers were becoming active as the sun began to dry the heavy dew. One of them decided to take wing prematurely, and ended up doing a splashdown a foot from the bank. I couldn't believe the rise which followed—it was one of the few times I had actually seen a trout take a hopper on the surface. I had to give the creature a shot, of course, but with what? A size 24 White-Winged Black hardly imitates a fair-sized grasshopper.

Then I remembered that in my streamer box, which was in the trunk of the car, there were a few Muddlers. I clumped the hundred yards in my Hodgmans, praying that no opportunist would pull up and grab my spot. None did, and I eased back into the stream with a Muddler dangling from freshly tied 4X monofilament. I rubbed the fly with Mucilin paste and cast it above the spot where I recalled the trout to have risen.

Faster than it can be told, the fish took, and was on. The rise was so aggressive I didn't even have time to overreact and jerk the fly out of the trout's mouth or snap the tippet. I merely held on while the creature surged downstream through a short stretch of pocket water and into the quiet pool below. It was a serious mistake, for were no opportunities for devilry there, and soon the fish was mine. It was a classic Battenkill brown, golden-flanked, orange-spotted, and well-formed. The tape read 18½ inches.

The *Tricorythodes* emergence began shortly and provided an hour of delightful sport. When it was done, I took my trophy to a local coffee-and-donut emporium, where the ever-present group of fly-fishers generously praised my feat, with a minimum of inferences about how easy it is to pick up a live grasshopper on such a dewy morning. It was one of those rare, perfect experiences which one stores in an imaginary silver box where it may be kept safe for future reliving.

A few years ago this magnificent fly could be constructed entirely of inexpensive, plentiful materials. Since then a problem has arisen with the mottled brown turkey feathers used for the wings and tail. Seems the American housewives insist on white turkeys (which explains their choice of marital partners). The bronze turkey's crime has to do with the tiny dark specks which are left on the skin when the bird is plucked. So even though it is a much better-tasting bird, it is now a country-fair conversation piece, along with the Plymouth Rock.

Turkey quills are still in the catalogs, at a price. Matched pairs now sell for around 75 cents, which not long ago bought a half-dozen pairs. It is a feather which has no acceptible substitutes, so you pay or do without. I sense the possibility of a manipulated market; bronze turkeys are still raised in great numbers overseas, and the feathers have little value other than to the fly-dresser.

COMPONENTS

Hook: Size 8, 4X long, medium or heavy wire
Thread: Brown 6/0, prewaxed, or brown monocord, prewaxed
Tail: Mottled turkey wing quill section
Body: Gold tinsel, 1/32 inch width
Underwing: Squirrel tail hair
Wing: Mottled turkey wing quill sections
Collar: Deer hair, untrimmed
Head: Deer hair, trimmed

TYING STEPS

1. Tie on ¼ inch (6 mm) back from eye, cover hook to bend.
2. Tie in a piece of turkey quill section for the tail. It should be approximately ⅜ inch (10 mm) long, measuring from the break of the bend. Tradition indicates the section should be tied in point down instead of up. Use the pinch,

but be careful not to cut the fibers, which are somewhat softer than those of a duck quill. (photo 21-1)

3. Wind down the excess, trim on the bias, save clipping for use as a nymph wing case, if you wish.

4. Tie in a 6-inch (150 mm) piece of gold tinsel and create a tinsel body. Do not crowd the head space, and be sure the tie-off is very smooth. Mylar is recommended. (photo 21-2)

5. Take a small bunch of hair from the base of a gray squirrel tail, where the whiteness of the tips is minimized. Even up the tips with a tamper, and preen out all short fibers.

6. Tie in the squirrel hair so that the tips extend not quite to the end of the quill tail-section. Use the pinch technique to keep the fibers on top of the hook.

7. Trim on the bias, intruding as little as possible into the head space area.

8. Secure with tight, neat wraps, creating a smooth base for the wing. Again, do not invade the head space area any more than is absolutely necessary, and be conservative with the number of wraps. (photo 21-3)

9. Cut two sections from mottled turkey quills with opposing curvature. (photo 21-4) Sometimes a single feather will furnish this. The section should be slightly wider than comparable duck or goose quill sections for a fly of this size.

10. Mount the sections on the hook with the tips downward. Allow the edges to slightly overlap the hook shank at the tie-in point, in order to create a tent effect. (photo 21-5)

11. Tie in the wings with a couple of pinches, taking care not to cut the fibers with the thread. Secure with a few tight wraps, avoiding the head space area.

12. Trim off the excess in close, wind down the butts with a few tight wraps. The fly should now appear as in photograph 21-6.

Grasshopper

Wild Bronze Turkeys

13. Now for the tricky part. Select a moderate-sized bunch of deer hair from a section of hide where the hair is fine and fairly short. Manicure the bunch, weeding out all underfur and excessively short hairs, then even up the tips, using the tamping technique. The hair should resemble photograph 21-7.

14. Using the slack loop, tie in the bunch so that the fibers are forced to deploy themselves around the hook shank. (photo 21-8) The tips should extend back only about ⅔ of the body length. The idea is that the pressure of the thread will cause the hair to flair, creating a collar which represents the prominent pectoral fins of the sculpin.

15. Supplement the initial bunch until a full collar is formed. Try to keep the butt ends from flairing back and mixing with the tip ends. The collar should now appear as in photograph 21-9.

16. Isolate the collar by encircling the tips with a narrow strip of masking tape, taking care not to disturb the wing. (photo 21-10)

17. Preen the butt ends so they flair out and slightly back, then lock them into position with a few wraps of thread tight to the base of the hairs. (photo 21-11)

18. Cut off another bunch of hair the size of the one shown in the illustration. Preen out the shorties, but don't bother to even up the tips, as they will be trimmed off later.

19. Tie in the bunch tight to that which is already on the hook, using the slack loop. Secure with a few tight wraps, but be careful not to use too many turns of thread, as this will produce unwanted bulk and make it difficult to pack the bunches on the hook shank. (photos 21-12, 21-13)

20. Snug up the hairs with your thumb nail, packing them as tightly as possible. (photo 21-14) If you prefer, use a piece of tubing of some sort. The empty barrel of a used-up ball-point pen works well.

21. Keep adding bunches and packing until the hair is a thread-width or two short of the eye (photo 21-15), then tie off with a whip finish. A hackle guard works wonders here. (photo 21-16)

22. Begin to trim and shape the head. (photo 21-17) *Take it slowly and carefully.* Hair which is cut off inadvertently cannot be replaced.

23. Form a sort of bullet-shaped head, slightly flattened on the top and more so on the bottom. This simulates the head silhouette of the sculpin bait fish. (photo 21-18)

TURKEY QUILL

Unfortunately, there is no really satisfactory substitute for mottled turkey, although the catalogs claim to offer a few. Since it is very much a case of waste not, want not, here are a number of ways to extend the use of turkey quills.

1. Don't use prime quill for the tail section. Practically any scraggly piece can be made to work okay. It is permis-

21-1 Muddler Minnow: tail in place. Note length.

21-2 Underbody in place. Note thread position.

21-3 Base for wing.

21-4 Matched turkey quill sections.

21-5 Edges overlap the hook slightly at the shoulders.

21-6 Wing in place.

21-7 Deer hair for collar.

21-8 Tie collar hair in with slack loop.

21-9 Note collar proportions.

21-10 Collar protector in place.

21-11 Standing up butts of collar hair.

21-12 Tying in hair for head.

21-13 Slack loop aids distribution and flairing.

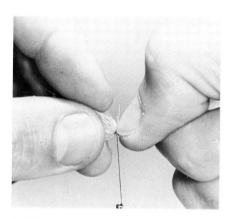

21-14 Packing.

21-15 Full complement prior to trimming.

21-16 Tying off, using hackle guard.

21-17 Trimming.

21-18 The completed fly.

sible to trim a section to shape with scissors, as little if any beauty is sacrificed.

2. Quills which have ragged edges or too much curvature can be rendered usable via the steam-iron process. Again, if the tips and edges need a bit of dressing up or shaping, it is allowable to do so with scissors.

3. Mottled turkey quill sections make attractive, realistic wing cases on certain mayfly and stonefly nymphs. Keep a small plastic box handy and save any clippings that are long enough to be utilized on a nymph.

As to noncommercial sources, check out any turkey-grower in the area to see whether he still raises some bronze birds. One pair of wings will provide a wealth of material. Also, if wild turkeys inhabit your region, and hunting is allowed, make some contacts within the hunting fraternity. The quills from a mature wild bird are the nicest of all.

HAIR

The various types of hair were covered in notes on the Blacknosed Dace. In the case of the Muddler, two criteria are of particular importance. The hair should be fine, so as to minimize bulk, maximize ease of handling, and produce the neatest, smoothest head possible. The hair should *not* be the hollow type, used for making bass bugs and other floating lures. The last thing an angler wants is a Muddler which drifts along with its head out of the water like a muskrat. Usually the finer hair floats poorly, so the one facet of the selection process takes care of the other.

As to the handling of this cumbersome material, here are a few tips which will supplement the descriptive material in the exercise:

1. Do not under any circumstances build up a thread base, as this adds bulk and inhibits packing. Actually, the best surface for working with deer hair is a bare hook shank. In the case of the Muddler, this simply isn't possible, because hair must be spun over the area where the wings and body were tied off. All one can do is use the least possible amount of thread in the tie-off procedures and avoid carrying the thread any further forward than is absolutely necessary, so the front part of the head area is left bare.

2. Don't try to tie in too large a bunch. This creates serious difficulties in handling, and often causes the hair to be spun on too loosely, resulting in a head which comes apart later on.

3. Conversely, don't tie in too small a bunch. This means more bunches will be required, which results in the use of excessive amounts of thread, causing bald patches and poor packing.

4. Make sure the entire head area is covered. If a bunch of hair proves insufficient to encircle the hook completely, use another bunch to fill in any sparse areas. Tie it in precisely where the bald spot appears and vary the thread handling technique so as to cause the hair to remain in place where it is needed.

5. Do a good packing job. Pack after each bunch is tied in, not all at the end.

6. Once again, be very conservative in the use of thread.

 # The Alternative

I want to introduce a fly which one might use in place of the Muddler Minnow. Not that I think it's a better fly; I've already expressed my sentiments regarding the Muddler. It is simply an alternative which circumvents two problems inherent in the Muddler: It does not require hard-to-get bronze turkey, and it does not employ the tedious clipped-hair technique.

I've spent almost six months trying to come up with a terrific name for my creation, with no results. I thought of naming it after myself—after all, I designed it. But the Talleur? The Dick? The RWT Special? Richard's Rat? My name was never meant to be on a marquee. I decided to simply call my fly the Alternative. As stated, it is an alternative to the Muddler, but a great many anglers won't know that.

I would have preferred more field testing, although I'm pleased with results to date. I absolutely murdered the bass in a local river with a size 6 Alternative, and took some nice browns in the Beaverkill and Battenkill. The trout liked smaller sizes—8's and 10's. I did best with a weighted fly, but the unweighted version produced also. I fished the fly slowly and tried to impart some subtle movement at all times.

As the dressing is quite simple by design, the instructions will touch only the major points.

COMPONENTS

Hook: Sizes 4 through 12, 4X long. A size 8, 4XL is used in this exercise.

Thread: Brown prewaxed, 6/0 for smaller sizes, monocord for larger

Tail: Two hen pheasant body or neck feathers

Underbody: Gold tinsel

Overbody: Brown mottled deer hair

Wings: Two hen pheasant body or neck feathers, prepared as described. Read step 4 before starting the fly.

Hackle: Grizzly dyed tan or light brown, or hen pheasant body feather, or grouse ruff feather

Head: Any soft brown dubbing, such as beaver

TYING STEPS

1. Tie on ¼ of the shank length back from the eye and wrap to the bend.

2. Prepare the two tail feathers by stripping off the lower barbules until only the tips remain. The portion remaining is now ½ inch (12 mm) long, or a hair less.

3. Match the feathers with the curvatures opposing and tie them onto the top of the hook at the bend. (photo 22-1)

4. Select two hen pheasant feathers which are similar in color to the tail feathers and prepare as follows:

   a. Strip off the lower barbules until ¾ inch (19 mm) of feather remains.

   b. Using thinned Pliobond, preen each feather into the shape of an almond. This is the same process as was used in the Perla Stonefly Nymph, except that the desired shape is slightly broader, or more ellipti-

22-1 Alternative: tying in tails.

22-2 Pheasant feather preened to shape.

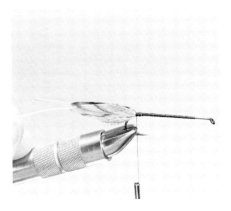

22-3 Tying in pheasant feathers.

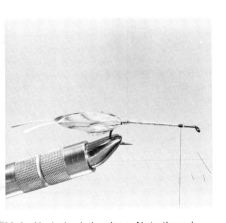

22-4 Underbody in place. Note thread position.

22-5 Overbody in place.

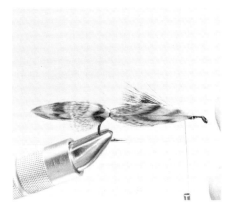

22-6 Fold pheasant feathers forward.

22-7 Pheasant feathers in place.

22-8 Tie in folded hackle.

22-9 Hackle in place.

22-10 The completed fly.

cal. Two or three strokes will do it. If the feathers are prepared before the fly is begun, they will be ready for use when that step is reached. (photo 22-2)

5. Tie in one of the prepared pheasant feathers by the tip on the near side of the hook, with the stem extending backwards beyond the tail. The outer, or convex, side of the feather must be to the inside against the tail, as the feather will be folded forward later. *Be sure to wrap right up to the bend, where the tail begins.*

6. Tie on the other pheasant feather on the far side of the hook, making it a mirror image of the one on the near side. (photo 22-3)

7. Wind forward to the tie-on point and create a gold tinsel body, exactly as with the Muddler (photo 22-4)

8. Cut off a modest-sized bunch of hair from the brown portion of a deer hide, cull out the extraneous fibers, tamp to even up the tips.

9. Tie in the deer hair, using the distribution-wrap technique, so the hair is deployed evenly around the circumference of the hook shank. This material's primary function is to fill out the body area, adding bulk and dimension. Keep it fairly short; do not allow the tips to extend back to where the pheasant feathers are tied in. (photo 22-5)

10. Either individually or both at once, fold the pheas-

ant feathers forward and tie them down, leaving about ¼ of the hook shank exposed to the front. (photos 22-6, 22-7)

11. Using a folded grizzly hackle feather dyed tan or light brown, create a narrow collar immediately ahead of the wing. Keep the turns tight together and closely packed, in order to leave space for the head. Or create a collar of hen pheasant or grouse hackle, using the technique described for the Grouse and Green Wet Fly. Refer to photographs 22-8 and 22-9.

12. Create a bullet-shaped head out of dubbing which generally matches the overall coloration of the fly. Whip finish, Ambroid. The finished product should resemble photograph 22-10.

VARIATIONS

If the Muddler-type collar and head present no difficulty, which is the case for some people, feel free to substitute for the grizzly-and-fur-collar-head described in the instructions. The effectiveness seems to be much the same.

There is a wide variety of shadings and markings on a hen pheasant skin, with feathers ranging from speckled beige to strongly marked dark brown. The fly-dresser can experiment and innovate to his heart's content. As a matter of fact, one shouldn't consider oneself limited to hen pheasant. Cock pheasants have some interesting body feathers, and so do grouse and various waterfowl. There is also wide latitude for experimentation with the collar, using the distribution-wrap technique as illustrated in the Grouse and Green pattern.

WEIGHTED VERSION

While weighted flies interfere with the pleasures of casting, they are extremely effective in certain circumstances. This pattern in particular benefits from an appropriate amount of ballast. This technique creates a keel-type effect which tends to stabilize the fly in the proper attitude, in addition to adding weight.

1. After tying in the prepared pheasant feathers, wind the thread back to a position just short of the original tie-on point.

2. Cut a piece of stout lead wire to a sharp point and secure it to the bottom of the hook shank, running the thread all the way down and back. The point of the wire should extend to the bend, or just short of it.

3. Bend the wire back over the first layer. Crimp it well, using pliers if necessary.

4. Wrap back about half-way with thread, then cut the wire on a bias so as to affect a continuation of the taper previously formed.

5. Cover the remainder with thread and wind back to the original tie-on point.

6. Coat the underbody with a generous amount of cement, preferably Ambroid. It should be sufficiently thinned to affect thorough permeation.

7. Cover with medium-wide gold mylar tinsel. Then proceed with the fly previously described.

23

The T-Bone

TECHNIQUE TO BE LEARNED

1. Deer-hair extended body

Extended body flies have always intrigued the angler, perhaps more so than they have the trout. Most look far better in the vise than on the water.

These deer-hair extended body dry flies have a startlingly realistic attitude on the water and are the most effective large flies I know of where slow, clear water mandates a clean image. Dressed generously and coated with a good floatant, they will also give a good account of themselves in rough currents.

Many methods have been employed in the construction of extended body flies. Such materials as stiff monofilament, fine steel wire, and quills of various types have been widely employed, all with a measure of success, but none without problems and complications. A fairly recent innovation, the Flybody hook, was introduced by the Leonard Company in 1975, and it also presented new difficulties to the angler and fly-dresser. Like any short-shanked model, the Flybody has inherently poor hooking qualities. It is also heavy, weighing more than twice as much as a Mustad 94840 of equal size. This problem is compounded by the fact that the metal extension shifts the balance to the rear, causing the fly to sit back on its tail. This defeats the intention of the extended body fly, which is to simulate the posture of the natural mayfly by suspending the abdomen and tail above the water in a gentle upward curve. If the tier happens to have some Flybody hooks, they can be used for constructing extended body nymphs, an application to which they are admirably suited. The hooking deficiency can be partially compensated for by bending the point inward slightly, which improves the angle of engagement.

In 1971 a book entitled *Selective Trout* was published which, to put it mildly, has become a landmark. The co-authors, Doug Swisher and Carl Richards, did a marvelous job with the entomology, the photography, and the fly patterns. Included is a unique and often overlooked method for using deer, elk, or similar animal hair to form the extended body. The technique was called to my attention by Jim Hopkins, a masterful angler and fly-dresser from Westchester County in New York state. Jim is a pilot by trade (he calls himself an ''airplane driver'') and has amassed considerable angling experience in his travels. A relentless pursuer of large trout, he is always looking for ways to dupe *Salmo gargantua,* and the deer-hair extended body is one of his favorites. I have added an optional innovation of my own, a thorax.

The deer-hair extended body technique, like other true advancements, opens up a new area to the fly-dresser. Entire families of extended body duns and spents can be created; in fact, this method is particularly suited to spent patterns. It is primarily intended for larger flies, although I have dressed lovely 18's with little difficulty. For this exercise, we will use a size 12 hook, with the resulting fly being a true size 8 or 10. We need better techniques for large flies, because the fish gets one hell of a good look at them, and even beautifully dressed patterns often fail under the quarry's baleful inspection.

For our basic deer-hair extended body, we will dress a Jim Hopkins pattern called the T-Bone. The aptness of the title will become apparent as the fly takes form.

COMPONENTS

Hook: Mustad 94840 or equivalent, size 12
Thread: Brown prewaxed
Body/Tail: Natural brown-gray mottled deer hair
Wings: Natural brown-gray mottled deer hair
Thorax (optional): Brownish-gray yarn or dubbing

TYING STEPS

1. Cover the middle portion of the hook shank, ending up with the thread in a position ⅓ shank length to the rear of the eye. Coat generously with cement, preferably Ambroid.

2. Cut off a bunch of hollow deer hair, cull out the underfur and short fibers, tamp to even up the tips. Refer to photograph 23-1.

3. Place the bunch of hair on the hook with the tips extending rearward the desired length of the tail, then tie in with the distribution-wrap technique, allowing the thread to carry the fibers around the shank. (photo 23-2)

4. Trim off the butts, secure with thread. (photo 23-3)

5. Take a few evenly spaced turns to the rear around hair and hook. (photo 23-4) Wraps should be firm but not overly tight.

6. When the point is reached where the under-thread stops (which should be well short of the bend), seize the bunch of hair with the left thumb and forefinger and lift it. Then take a turn around the hair alone, passing the bobbin under the left hand and above the vise. Take the bobbin as far as possible with the right hand, then hook it with the fourth finger of the left hand and swing it through to the front. (photos 23-5, 23-6)

7. Repeat until desired body length is obtained, then work back down to the hook shank (photo 23-7) using the same spacing. A diamond crisscross effect will result. Continue forward to the tie-in point of the hair body.

8. Create a thread base for the wings, apply a generous dab of cement. (photo 23-8)

9. Cut off another bunch of hair, manicure, and tamp.

10. Estimate the desired length of the wings, relative to the body-tail assembly, then tie in the bunch of hair, again allowing the thread to carry the material approximately half-way around the hook, creating roughly a 180-degree fan. (photo 23-9)

11. Secure with plenty of tight wraps, then trim off the butts and bind down the ends. (photo 23-10)

12. With the fingers, separate the fibers into two equal bunches, then construct the wings with a crisscross followed by a figure eight, as with the Quill Gordon. However, do not stand the wings up at a sharp angle. With this pattern, the wide semi-spent wings also act as hackle, stabilizing and floating the fly. (photo 23-11)

13. Optional: create the thorax, using either dubbing or a piece of yarn of appropriate shade, and crisscrossing the thorax area, as in the Hendrickson. (photo 23-12)

14. Whip finish. Then thin out the tail fibers with a sharp pair of scissors until the desired number remain. (photo 23-13)

15. Apply a generous smear of cement to the upper side of the body along its entire length and a drop to the head. (photo 23-14) The completed fly should appear as in photographs 23-15 and 23-16.

DEER-HAIR EXTENDED BODY FAMILY

While you may not think so the first time through, this is really an easy pattern to dress. The only real problem is handling the bulky, slippery deer hair. Two hints that will help in that area are to not use more hair than is absolutely required, and to use an effective cement when tying in the components, as per the instructions.

The odd technique used to pass the bobbin around the bunch of hair when creating the extended body is quite simple, and you will master it after a few tries. Just remember to maintain tension at all times and don't let your thumb and forefinger lose their grip on the hair.

For maximum floatation, use thick, hollow hair and don't compress the body by wrapping too tightly. The thickness of the hair is relative to the size of the fly you are tying, but use the thickest, most buoyant stuff you can get away with.

Once the deer-hair extended body technique is mastered, the fly-dresser can innovate to his heart's content. Just a few of the possible combinations:

1. Upright undivided clump-style hair wing with parachute hackle around the base, as shown in the color section.

2. Caucci-Nastasi Comparadun-style hair wing, a 180-degree fan.

23-1 Bunch of deer hair for extended body.

23-2 Tie in thus.

23-3 Trim, bind down butts.

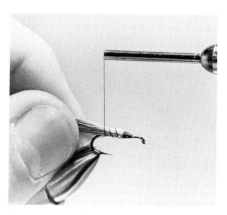

23-4 Take a few evenly spaced turns over hair and hook.

23-5 Lift hair, pass thread around it.

23-6 Technique for passing thread around hair.

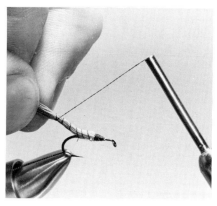

23-7 Work back to this point, then reverse.

23-8 Body completed, butts trimmed and bound.

23-9 Tie in wing hair thus.

23-10 Butts trimmed and bound down securely.

23-11 Wings divided and constructed with a figure eight.

23-12 Create thorax.

23-13 Thin out tail fibers.

23-14 Ambroid generously.

23-15 Completed fly.

23-16 Completed fly, front view.

3. Hackle-tip wings with either parachute hackle or upright **V** hackle dressed thorax-style.

4. Spent-style hackle wing, also shown in color.

A practically endless series of patterns can be produced simply by varying the size, shade, and silhouette of the components. For a sampler, try this Coffin Fly pattern when in green drake country:

MATERIALS AND COMPONENTS

Hook: Size 10–14 dry fly
Thread: White prewaxed
Body/Tail: White deer hair, tails darkened with black marking pen
Wings: Dark barred Rock hackle tied spent
Thorax: White polypropylene yarn

24

The Hendrickson Spent

TECHNIQUES TO BE LEARNED

1. Spent wing
2. Twisted feather chenille body

The importance of spent flies has become more or less common knowledge in the last decade, thanks to the angling information explosion. While not all aquatic insects are important in this regard, many are vitally so, especially certain mayflies. I have experienced fantastic action on spinner falls ranging in size from the giant *Hexagenias* to the tiny *Pseudocleous* and *Caenidae*. The procedure followed in this exercise will enable the fly-dresser to create whatever spents are required in his geographic area. Only the body need be varied, in order to accommodate diminutive hook sizes.

The *Ephemerella* mayflies produce some of the greatest spinner falls given anything approximating suitable weather and water conditions. Quite often the spinner fall provides much better fishing than the emergence. On pleasant May evenings the ovipositing phenomenon may go on from late afternoon until well after dark, making the relinquishment of a cocktail period and leisurely dinner no sacrifice at all.

Trout are generally selective to an extreme during the spinner fall of the *Ephemerellas* we call Hendricksons, particularly since there is very seldom any other insect activity at that time of day and year. The spread-eagle silhouette of the spent must be matched, or the angler is in for a maddening evening. This is no problem if one carries the easily tied spent patterns which simulate the expiring imagos.

The byword is translucency. The hyaline wings and ephemeral tails pass shimmering points of light to the expectant trout below. And the body, which has been reduced to a fragile tube by the extrusion of the eggs, transmits many of the light rays which strike it.

We can effectively simulate these sequins of the surface film by resorting to materials and techniques which produce translucency. I was fortunate enough to learn the Hendrickson spinner at the feet of Vincent C. Marinaro, perhaps the most circumspect of the breakthrough angling writers. Vince used seal hair for the body and dun hackle fibers for the tail and wings. It was—and is—a killing pattern. However, he has now come up with a fly he likes better, and it is this pattern we will tie.

I have deviated slightly from Vince's basic design in order to simplify the dressing, enhance durabilty, and adapt to readily available materials. This is to take nothing away from Vince—his pattern is fine just as it is. Those wishing to get aquainted with the original will find it described in the latest Marinaro book, *In the Ring of the Rise,* which incidentally is an extremely valuable and beautiful treatise on the more sophisticated aspects of the fly-rodding game.

My innovations have to do with the formation of the body, the technique for constructing a spent wing, and the creation of the thorax. Vince's dressing calls for a body of cock pheasant tail fibers wrapped around the hook shank. The result is most attractive, as the hundreds of tiny, protruding fibers produce a lovely transluscency. However, pheasant tail won't take much of a beating. I use the chenille-twist technique we examined in dressing the peacock herl body on the Leadwing Coachman. The fly is thus rendered much more durable with no sacrifice in appearance.

The wing and thorax innovations are related. I wind the hackle from which the wing will be formed after completing the tail and body. This brings the thread into ideal position for the construction of the dubbed thorax, which in turn separates and forms the spent wings. To abet this process, I cut a **V** from both the top and bottom hackles. The crisscrossing of the dubbing over the bottom and top of the thorax area flattens the wings into a spent attitude and locks them in place. The use of material with good floating properties also enhances the fly's performance.

COMPONENTS

Hook: Size 12 or 14 fine or extrafine wire, dry fly
Thread: Rusty brown prewaxed 6/0
Tail: A few dun hackle fibers
Body: Long, rusty fibers from a cock ring-neck pheasant tail
Wings/Hackle: Dun saddle or cape hackle
Thorax: Rusty brown poly dubbing

TYING STEPS

1. Create a sparse, well-spread tail, using just a few stiff barbules. Make it slightly longer than with a dun pattern of comparable size.

2. Set up the body by tying in three or four pheasant tail fibers by the tips along with the supplemental thread for twisting. Then advance the thread to where the body will terminate, approximately ⅓ of the shank length back from the eye. (photos 24-1, 24-2)

3. Follow the twist-wrap-twist-wrap procedure described in the Leadwing Coachman section. (photo 24-3)

4. Tie off, trim off the excess, advance the thread to a point half-way between the front extremity of the body and the eye. (photo 24-4)

5. Tie in the dun hackle, taking care to maintain the space between the tie-in point and the front of the body. (photo 24-5)

6. Wind the hackle back to the front of the body. (photo 24-6)

7. Wind the hackle forward through itself, to the tie-in point, tie off, and secure. (photo 24-7)

8. Cut a **V** out of both the top and bottom portions of the hackle. (photo 24-8)

9. Dub approximately 1¼ inches (33 mm) of material onto the thread. Be sure it is packed tightly and is not overly bulky. (photo 24-9)

10. Take a turn or two in front of the wings. Then form a crisscross underneath the thorax area by passing the dubbing back through the **V**, upward and across the top of the hook just behind the wings, then down and through the **V** again, ending up in front of the wings where you began. (photos 24-10, 24-11)

11. Execute a crisscross on the top side of the thorax area in exactly the same manner, but upside-down. Pass the dubbing through the top **V**, behind the far wing and down around the bottom of the hook just behind the wings, then upward and through the **V** again. (photo 24-12)

12. Finish off the forebody with another turn or two of dubbing, if it needs it. Then whip finish and cement. The completed fly should look like photograph 24-13.

SPENTS

As we have seen, the sequences, procedures and positional relationships are different with this style of spent fly. Winding the hackle back through itself is certainly a departure. The purpose is to obtain a well-flared wing silhouette and to accommodate the top and bottom crisscrosses of dubbing material.

I feel the hackle fiber spent wing is still the best. Experiments with everything from poly yarn to cellophane have produced nothing which holds its shape as well or creates as realistic an effect. Some of the synthetics look sexy in the air but are not very satisfactory astream. Vince Marinaro and his limestone cohorts hold the same opinion, and if they don't know, who does?

As to the construction of the wing, use plenty of hackle, so that when the top and bottom **V**'s are cut out, sufficient fibers remain. Saddle hackle—the long, skinny kind—works beautifully here, especially Buck Metz's dun saddles. Cape hackles will work, but it's not easy to find feathers which are long and skinny enough, so you will probably need two. Go for quality here; the stiffer the barbules, the better the appearance and performance of the fly.

The semi-spent silhouette, which is often so killing during the Hendrickson and other spinner falls, can be created by a simple variation in the procedure just described.

1. Cut only the bottom **V** and make it a bit wider than for the regular spent wings.

2. Execute two bottom crisscrosses instead of one. Apply a little more tension than usual. This will force the lower barbules into a semi-spent position.

3. Cut a very narrow **V** out of the top and make a sparse crisscross, using minimal dubbing material.

You might also find it helpful to make the dubbing slightly thicker. This will vary with the size of the fly and

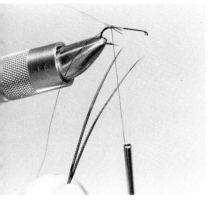

4-1 Hendrickson Spent: tail and twisting thread in place.

24-2 Fibers tied in, thread advanced.

24-3 Twist and wrap.

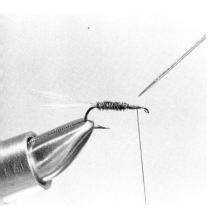

4-4 Completed body. Note thread position.

24-5 Begin hackle here.

24-6 Wind to front of body.

24-7 Wind hackle forward through itself.

24-8 Cutting a "V".

24-9 Dubbing for thorax.

24-10 Crisscrossing the bottom.

24-11 In position to crisscross the top.

24-12 Completing the top crisscross.

24-13 The completed fly.

the type of material used, so this isn't a firm prescription.

The object of using pheasant tail fibers for the body is to affect transluscency. Keep in mind that the material need not be pheasant tail; in fact, practically any feather of sufficient length will do. The fuzzy effect is caused by the little fibers along the edges of the feather section, which stand out when the material is wrapped around a hook. These interact with the surface film and the light from above to produce a diffused light pattern quite suggestive of a natural spent fly.

This type of body can be put to use on other types of flies, with spectacular results. The construction of nymph bodies is an excellent example, as the fibers look like gills. The more fibrous the feather, the better, especially on larger hook sizes. Turkey feathers work well and so do goose and swan cussettes.

Some anglers may prefer the more traditional dubbed-bodied spents, and with good reason, as they are easy to

dress and generally quite effective. The process is the same as for the fiber-bodied type, except that the body is made of a shiny, translucent dubbing material. Seal hair and polar bear underfur were the two great favorites, but these animals are protected now. Actually, this has worked to the fly-dressers' advantage by creating a need for a synthetic substitute. Several brands are now available which are easier to work with and produce better results than the coarse, slippery natural furs. I presently like Poul Jorgensen's Sealex best.

Sealex is different in texture than the soft synthetics we worked with earlier, and the spinning loop technique is a necessity. This is easy enough, except with smaller hook sizes, where bulk becomes a problem—a number 16 is just about the limit of practicality. To obtain a transluscent effect, fuzz up the body with a little brush, as described with the Hare's Ear Nymph, then trim the fibers so that the end result looks like a miniature bottle brush.

25

The Gangle-Legs Dry Fly

TECHNIQUES TO BE LEARNED

1. Hackle-stem parachute
2. Upright hackle-tip wings as final operation

Most people's lives are enhanced by characters who seem to assume bigger-than-life proportions. As an angler, Dud Soper is definitely one of these. Whether in a quiet pool or a spirited hot-stove session, Dud's presence is imposing. He is always in the foreground, radiating energy and making an impact on whatever is going on.

In *Fly-Fishing for Trout: A Guide for Adult Beginners,* I stated that Bill Dorato was the best all-around fly-fisherman I had ever known. Nothing has happened since to cause me to retract that statement, except that time never stands still, and the young guys keep coming on. Dave Male, a Battenkill postgraduate with whom I've cast a line on occasion certainly has all the tools necessary for superstardom, including tremendous motivation. Still, old Willie can hold his own in any company, for he possesses a great variety of uncanny skills with many types of flies and lures in widely diversified environments. On still water, however, Dud Soper is without peer. His forte is catching the smartest trout in the most difficult location in the most challenging pool, and the performances I have witnessed over the years have been truly awe-inspiring.

I once belonged to a private club on the Beaverkill which owned about a mile of water and had a lease on a mile more. The premier pool of the entire stretch was situated a scant quarter-mile from the club house, and a magnificent pool it was. The head portion was typically Catskill: rocks, pockets, and a deep-cut bank on the far side. The lower portion and tail were typically Soper: slick, slow, and clear. Many fine trout held there, and except when the water was high and off-color, it was the Devil's own task to catch them. I had scored well in this section at times, and had also walked back to the clubhouse talking to myself, with fly-rod and ego both at half-mast.

I invited Dudley to fish as my guest one beautiful evening in late spring, and by good fortune we found the house pool deserted. I naturally gravitated to the head waters, leaving Dud the expansive tail section. He proceeded to situate himself in a likely vantage point and began his vigil, looking for all the world like a great blue heron in search of dinner.

I began to probe the swirls and pockets with a Gray Fox Variant, dropping the large, high-floating fly onto the writhing currents with a slack leader. This is a devastating technique in the right situation, and I fared rather well. Meanwhile, Dud waited, fly in hand. At length, trout began rising sedately in the tail, making widening concentric rings on the glassy surface. Without changing position, Dud began laying his fly up and over these fish, showing them only the fly and the front portion of a very long leader. Action had slowed in my section, and I began to

197

Dud Soper

ease myself slowly in Dud's direction, being careful not to cause any disturbance of the flat pool.

I took perhaps thirty minutes to wade within a long cast of Dudley. During that period of time, he was into a trout almost constantly. His approach, presentation, and handling of hooked fish was so fastidious that the trout around him continued to rise steadily, unaware of his presence in their midst. One by one, Dud brought them to his little parachute pattern, releasing each fish with a fond caress save one magnificent eighteen-incher, which later served as the main course of a gourmet dinner for two. I have never seen a more impressive exhibition of effective angling on supertough water.

Most anglers who are acquainted with Dud think of him as a dry-fly purist, but that is not entirely accurate. It is a fact that Dud strongly prefers the floater, and I cannot recall many occasions where another type of fly was tied to his tippet. However, the various ways in which he presents these dry-fly patterns are something else again. A few refusals are often enough to influence Dudley to twitch his fly under the surface, thereby affecting an emerger type of presentation. The nontypical fly types which he generally uses lend themselves to this technique quite readily, more so than standard dry-fly patterns.

For many years, Dud has been a staunch advocate of the parachute style of fly, which he calls the flat-hackle. I'm not surprised that he was drawn to these odd-looking but murderously effective flies, for though Dudley is very much the dreamer and poet in some aspects of his life (his reputation as a composer of verse is borne out by the poem appearing at the end of this book), he is a pure pragmatist when it comes to deceiving trout. The parachute fly has a number of practical advantages over the conventional style, and if it wasn't for our cloying attachments to tradition and aesthetics, we'd all be tying and fishing the flat-hackles to a much greater extent than we are today.

Dud and I kicked the subject around one evening, and a few thoughts that fell out make a strong case for the flat-hackles. The parachute can be tied with mediocre hackle, with significant savings in both money and aggravation. The flat type of hackle doesn't hang down into the water in an unsightly mass upon becoming wet. Working like a snowshoe, flat-wound hackle can float a fly more effectively than conventional hackle with fewer barbules. The deployment of flat hackle is more suggestive of insect legs than conventional hackle. The parachute silhouette effectively imitates spent mayflies, and works quite well during spinner falls. The flat-hackled fly can be skipped and skidded along the surface in a manner reminiscent of the behavior of certain caddis flies. And finally, when twitched under the surface, the parachute makes a fair emerger. If further convincing is wanted, the tier might consider tagging along with Soper on a fishing excursion. He made a believer out of me, and I'm rather hide-bound. I carry more flats each season, and the results are most gratifying.

Now let us examine a rather special fly Dud developed a number of years ago, which he calls the Gangle-Legs, or Gangly for short. It is a most innovative flat-hackle. Dud says he was influenced by the creamish colored craneflies which are often present in considerable numbers in the shrubs and bushes which border many eastern streams. When disturbed, these spindly members of the order Diptera fly about erratically, looking for all the world like *Brobdingnagian* mosquitos off on a bender.

In order to imitate the cranefly, Dud created a pattern with a slender, synthetic yarn body and sparse, greatly oversized hackle. The pattern also features upright wings, which Dud says are more for him than for the fish. Dud is not an exponent of the pronounced-upright-wing school of fly dressing, and with all due respect to Vince Marinaro, Doug Swisher and Carl Richards, who can fault such angling success? The upright-wing-silhouette proposition is certainly valid, but the flush silhouette also has its points. I certainly agree with Dud as to the benefit of upright wings on the Gangly, or for that matter, any parachutes, as their low profile makes them tough to see on the water.

As is frequently the case with special purpose fly designs —Bill Dorato's Dry Hare's Ear is another example—the Gangly turned out to be effective in many angling situations, including those where no craneflies were in evidence. It even works during hatches of insects to which it bears virtually no resemblance. Perhaps its most valuable attribute is its effectiveness in pounding up nonrising fish in tough circumstances, as slow, clear water. Very few flies have this property. Of course, the terminal tackle has a profound effect on the success of such ventures, and the angler an even greater one.

Dud uses two basic Gangly patterns, a light and a dark. The light one is more or less the standard, and we will use it for the exercise. The dark is dressed in precisely the same manner, only the colors differ.

COMPONENTS: LIGHT GANGLY

Hook: Size 18 or 20 dry fly
Thread: Yellow, beige, or tan prewaxed 6/0
Tail: None
Body: Beige yarn, polypropylene or other synthetic
Hackle: Light to medium ginger throat or spade hackle, very much oversized. It may vary in spread from the diameter of a quarter to a silver dollar
Wings: Pale watery dun hackle points

COMPONENTS: DARK GANGLY

Hook: Same as above
Thread: Black prewaxed 6/0
Tail: None
Body: Black yarn as specified above
Hackle: Dark dun or natural black
Wings: Dark dun hackle tips

TYING STEPS

1. Tie on ¼ of the shank length back from the eye, wrap to the bend.

2. Tie in the yarn, wrap the thread back to the tie-on point.

3. Create a yarn body by wrapping the material forward to where the thread is and tying off. If using poly yarn, separate only enough strands to fill out the body, using the same method as for the poly yarn wing. Wrap the material very loosely, almost with no tension—this greatly enhances floatation. Refer to photographs 25-1, 25-2, and 25-3.

4. Select the hackle feather, and prepare it by stripping off most of the barbules below the tip area. Very few turns are required. (photo 25-4) *Be careful not to break the stem.*

5. Tie in the hackle feather with the shiny side down. (photo 25-5) Use four or five firm wraps, one atop the other, tight to where the body terminates.

6. Stand up the hackle stem by taking a few turns of

25-1 Gangle-Legs Dry Fly: separating strands of yarn.

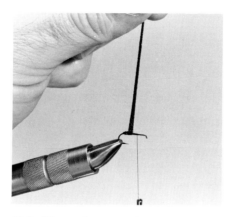

25-2 Wrap poly yarn under slight tension.

25-3 Completed body.

25-4 Prepared hackle.

25-5 Tie in hackle thus.

25-6 Standing up the stem.

25-7 Reinforcing the stem.

25-8 Winding the hackle.

25-9 Cutting a "V".

25-10 Tying down the stem.

25-11 Prepared wings.

25-12 Tie in wings thus.

25-13 Thread pressure against base causes wings to stand.

25-14 Apply cement here.

25-15 Thin out hackle, if you wish.

25-16 The completed fly, top view.

thread in front of it, as with a wood duck or hackle-tip wing. Reinforce with five or six wraps around the base of the stem. (photos 25-6, 25-7)

7. Wind the parachute hackle as described in the Dorthea Dun instructions, either with or without the gallows tool. (photo 25-8) The number of turns required will vary with hackle quality—seven or eight should do it. The idea is to create a sparse, evenly distributed hackle. The best method is to overdress, then thin out later.

8. Cut a **V** from the front of the hackle. (photo 25-9)

9. Lock in the hackle by bringing the stem forward over the tie-off point and binding it securely. (photo 25-10) Trim off the excess.

10. Prepare the hackle-tip wings by selecting a matched pair of pale watery dun feathers from a poor to mediocre quality cape and stripping off the unwanted barbules. Dud Soper recommends these wings be not quite as long and floppy as those of the natural—⅜ inch (12 mm) is about right. (photo 25-11)

11. To tie on the wings, simply grasp them with the left thumb and forefinger in a position which will allow the pinch to be used. The difference from the usual hackle-tip wing is that the position is reversed; that is, the hackles are pointing backward, the stems forward. (photo 25-12)

12. Tie on the wings with a pinch or two and secure with a couple of firm wraps. Then, before locking in place, stand the wings up and preen them a bit so they assume the desired attitude. This will not work if too many tight wraps have been taken, because the stems will have become fixed in position.

13. Lock in the wings with some very firm wraps. Use the thread to force them back against the base of the hackle stem. This will cause them to stand upright. (photo 25-13)

14. Whip finish. It is allowable to gently preen back the front hackles during this process, if they are stroked back into position afterwards.

15. Secure the wing-hackle assembly by placing one or two small drops of Ambroid at the spot where the base of the wings and hackle meet. (photo 25-14) Apply Ambroid to the head, also.

16. You may now thin out the hackle, if you wish. (photo 25-15) Dud's Ganglies are very sparse, containing only eight or ten barbules. I generally leave a dozen, but don't ask me why. The completed fly should resemble photograph 25-16.

All versions of the Gangly may also be tied spent-wing. To do this, tie on the wings in the very beginning, like the Adams. Then preen them into the spent position and secure with a couple of crisscrosses over the top. Later, you will tie in and wind the hackle over top of the wings, as though they weren't even there.

26

The Dry Hare's Ear

I know a great many people whose approach to fishing is basically technical and academic: read, listen, observe, practice. And, I know other people—more than a few, but not many—who seem to fish intuitively, almost without conscious effort or analysis. My long-time friend Bill Dorato is a fisherman of this ilk. Before the reader assigns a vaguely derogatory identity to these human pelicans who angle instinctively, let it be said that Bill Dorato is not out of touch with what's happening in the piscatorial arena, and is highly skilled and astute in a number of other fields, but he has never had to study in order to get dean's list grades from Brother Trout.

Before the fly-fishing renaissance of the 1960s, most trout fishermen started with organic baits. I was no exception, and neither was Bill. Accordingly to local legend, he was a great bait-man. What, then, is the motivation which compels people like Bill Dorato and myself to lay aside a successful, uncomplicated, inexpensive method and take up the Long Rod? I still wonder.

I am in total accord with Bill's approach to fly-fishing, in that he is basically a problem-solver, as he is in all things. This trait is strongly evident in his fly-dressing. Bill can tie classic patterns with the best—he cut his teeth on them—yet his fly-box contains a vast array of nondescript, subtly seductive creations, most of which have emananated from the man's mystical, infallible sense of what will work.

Bill Dorato is surely one of those unique persons who will spend his entire life identifying words and symbols for those things he has always known.

The Dry Hare's Ear was developed by Willie to cope with caddis imitation problems, particularly on the maddening Battenkill. I use it much of the time I'm on-stream, both as a caddis imitation and a general attractor. It is a terrific producer in any situation where the current is somewhat broken up or diffused, and will also take fish on quiet water under hatch conditions, given a modicum of adroit handling.

The fly was designed in such a manner that the overall effect is very buggy. The diffusion of light which the mottled coloration produces suggests movement, Willie feels, which typifies the behavior of many species of caddis. The abbreviated tail is another caddis attribute. The naturals have no tails at all, and only enough is used on the imitation to help support the rear of the hook.

The wood duck wings are optional. As most tiers know, caddis flies have tent-like wings, somewhat akin to those of a moth when at rest. But a caddis fly on the water is *almost never* at rest. For this reason, Bill opted for upright wood duck wings like the Quill Gordon, because the markings seem to suggest movement. Bill feels the wings also contribute to the overall image of the fly and make it more versatile.

Another significant design feature of the Dry Hare's Ear is its eminent twitchability; it can be subjected to a fair amount of manipulation before it begins to show signs of sinking. This may be attributed to several things: the fuzzy fur body, the short but well-fanned tail, and the flattened area where the bottom hackles are trimmed short (this is also an option; some people prefer the fly untrimmed).

The keys to dressing a really good Dry Hare's Ear are to

use top-quality hackle and to properly spread the tail fibers. This pattern works best when it floats high and lightly, so try to optimize the components which contribute to this. I carry a large supply of Dry Hare's Ears so as to avoid the necessity of using a water-logged fly, and I apply an effective floatant, such as Gink.

There are no new techniques to be learned in dressing this fly. Only the fly's assembly and architecture are unique. So, the instructions will simply list the materials for the three color phases, and will touch upon the main points of construction.

COMPONENTS: BROWN PHASE

Hook: Size 12 through 20 light wire, dry fly
Thread: Brown 6/0 prewaxed
Wings: Wood duck (optional)

Tail: Barred Rock or multivariant hackle fibers
Body: Shaggy grayish-brown mottled fur from a hare's mask, also any body fur which looks good. Leave in the guard hairs.
Hackle: Brown and grizzly mixed

COMPONENTS: CREAM PHASE

Hook: Same
Thread: Tan or beige 6/0 prewaxed
Wings: Wood duck (optional)
Tail: Barred Rock or light multivariant hackle fibers.
Body: Shaggy pale grayish cream fur dubbing. This may be obtained by lightening up the material for the brown version by blending in fitch underfur or any light cream fur
Hackle: Cream and grizzly mixed

26-1 Dry Hare's Ear: create a wood duck wing.

26-2 Tie in a well-spread, abbreviated tail.

26-3 Dub a rough body.

26-4 Hackle like the Adams.

26-5 Square off bottom of hackle.

26-6 The completed fly.

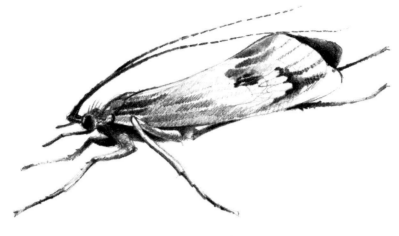

Caddis Adult

COMPONENTS: GRAY PHASE

Hook: Same
Thread: Black 6/0 prewaxed
Wings: Brown mallard (optional)
Tail: Barred Rock hackle fibers
Body: Same as brown version, but with more gray
Hackle: Slate dun and grizzly mixed

TYING STEPS

Here are the salient points of dressing the brown version. If the wings are not opted for, tie on near the bend and start with the tail.

1. Create a wood duck wing (photo 26-1), wind back to the bend and build up a significant bump with the thread.

2. Tie in a short tail, using a fair quantity of fibers, and cause them to fan out widely. (photo 26-2) The tail on a size 14 should be a scant 1/8 inch (3 mm) in length. It should vary slightly with larger and smaller hook sizes.

3. Using the spinning loop, create a fuzzy body. (photo 26-3) The effect may be accentuated by brushing the fur with a small steel brush. Any overly heavy or overly long guard hairs may be plucked out or cut off short.

4. Hackle the fly as you would an Adams (photo 26-4), whip finish, Ambroid.

5. Trim the bottom hackles so they are squared off approximately the same distance below the hook shank as the point. As mentioned, this is optional. (photo 26-6) The completed fly should resemble photograph 26-6.

27

The Haystack

TECHNIQUE TO BE LEARNED

1. Upright, undivided hair wing

In *Trout*, Ray Bergman wrote:

In northern New York, under the shadow of Whiteface Mountain, flows a river which has influenced the piscatorial thoughts of many Eastern anglers. Starting somewhere along the northern slope of MacIntyre, it gradually swells in volume as numerous tiny tributaries join it, and by the time it comes to an opening where the average fisherman sees it, the stream has become quite sizeable. It pauses a while, after decending from the really high places, and meanders lazily through wilderness meadows, gouging out deep holes close to grassy banks where large trout like to lurk, and presents problems that tax the anglers' utmost skill and ingenuity. Then it gathers together all its strength, and with a roar dashes and rages through the Wilmington Notch. It pauses momentarily here and there as obstructions or level spots slow its advance and provide ideal locations for fish, and then it tumbles wildly through the flume, where once during my time a man lost his life while fishing.

What I would have given to have fished the pre–World War II Ausable as a competent fly-rodder! Bergman reports that brown trout of a pound or slightly more were very common, with rainbows only slightly less so. His parties had personal minimum size limits of 2 pounds on browns and 1½ pounds on rainbows. Brookies ran smaller but

were quite plentiful in some sections, and were used for epicurean tablefare.

Around the time *Trout* made its appearance in 1938, an Adirondack youth named Francis Betters tied his first flies. A native of Wilmington, a small village on the Ausable's West Branch, Francis received early angling indoctrination from a fly-fishing father who tied rough but deadly bucktails out of gray and white deer hair and yellow yarn from Mrs. Betters's knitting stock. Young Francis was given a vise and fly-dressing materials at age nine, and learned most of his technique under the tutelage of the great Bergman himself.

Francis Betters became a virtual fanatic, fishing every day and working long hours at the vise trying to keep pace with the demand for flies, which he sold out of his parents' house by the banks of the West Branch. Aside from the fact that he now owns the Adirondack Sport Shop, a sizeable and flourishing establishment just outside of Wilmington, little has changed—Francis is *still* a fanatic. He dresses tremendous numbers of flies, sometimes approaching a thousand in a week, and while he no longer fishes every day, he doesn't pass up many opportunities, to the Ausable trout's unending regret.

Francis realized early that a rugged, high-floating dry fly was needed to effectively fish the surging pockets of his home river, a conclusion we all reached eventually. His two primary answers were the Ausable Wulff and the Haystack, a rather bizzare but simple and killing pattern. Francis recalls early prototypes tied by Eddie Lawrence, a renowned Adirondack hunter, trapper, and fisherman. The pattern which evolved is actually more of a type or family of flies, as they are dressed in a number of sizes and shades and employ a variety of materials.

The Haystack has attracted a virtual army of devotees who feel it is more effective than standard patterns in the type of environment one encounters on the West Branch. Francis feels this is mainly because the fly suggests three distinct phases of insect life. Tied sparse and twitched beneath the surface, it is an emerger. On the surface, it can present the upright silhouette of a dun as well as the spread-eagle appearance of a spent. Additionally—and this is the attribute I find most appealing of all—the design of the pattern and its superior floating qualities make it very twitchable, a tremendous asset during the heavy caddis emergences for which the Ausable is famous.

The Haystack offers several other benefits, all of which are consistent with the theme of this book: It is easy to construct; uses inexpensive, easily acquired materials; and can take a lot of punishment. Here are Betters's four basic Haystack patterns.

COMPONENTS: LIGHT

Tail: Small bunch of cream-dyed deer hair
Hackle/Wing: Larger bunch of cream-dyed deer hair tied fairly heavy and spread into a 180-degree fan
Body: Cream Australian possum, with a few turns in front of the wing thorax-style
Thread: Hot orange prewaxed

COMPONENTS: DARK

Tail: Natural deer body hair
Hackle/Wing: Same
Body: Darker brown Australian possum
Thread: Brown prewaxed

COMPONENTS: GRAY

Tail: Deer hair dyed blue dun
Hackle/Wing: Same
Body: Gray muskrat
Thread: Black prewaxed

COMPONENTS: BROWN

Tail: Deer hair dyed dark brown
Hackle/Wing: Same
Body: Muskrat dyed brown
Thread: Black or brown prewaxed

Francis advocates the Mustad 9671 hook—he is a hunter of large trout. For those of you who have a problem with this, the 94840 or equivalent is quite satisfactory. The patterns may be dressed in whatever size is required to suggest the prevalent insects one is tying to match. For example, a size 10 or 12 dark Haystack imitates the important mayfly, *Isonychia bicolor,* while a size 16 or 18 dark Haystack is very effective when certain small caddis are about. Francis Betters prefers 3/0 thread; I use the regular gauge. For our exercise, let's dress a size 14 dark Haystack.

TYING STEPS

1. Tie in near the front, coat the hook with thread, and tie in a tail ⅜ inch (9 mm) in length. (photo 27-1)

2. Wrap forward to mid-shank and trim off the butts. Then advance the thread to a point approximately ⅓ of the shank length back from the eye. (photo 27-2)

3. Select a bunch of deer hair for the wing and cull out the inner fibers. If the hair is coming off the hide with the tips reasonably even, it may be used as-is. If not, use a tamping tool. The bunch should have about three times the bulk of the tail after being manicured.

4. Position the deer hair slightly towards the near side of the hook and let the thread distribute the fibers across the top and around the far side to form a silhouette which is sort of semi-spent when viewed from the front. (photo 27-3) Don't be concerned if the effect isn't exactly what you want; we will adjust when dressing the body-thorax.

5. Secure the deer hair *thoroughly* with tight wraps at and just to the rear of the wing tie-in point. Then trim off the butts, smooth with thread and work back to the bend. (photo 27-4)

6. Apply the dubbing, using a slight amount of supplemental wax on the thread. Use the single-thread or spinning-loop method. Because of the substantial thorax and forebody, more dubbing is required than with a standard size 14 pattern, around 2½ to 3 inches (64–76 mm), depending on bulk and texture.

7. Wrap the dubbing to the rear base of the wing, creating a tapered body. (photo 27-5)

8. Cross over on the bottom and take a turn of dubbing tight to the front base of the wing. This will cause the deer hair fibers to stand nearly upright, but with a slight forward tilt. (photo 27-6)

9. Cross the dubbing back across the thorax, then around the top of the body behind the wing, then across the thorax again. By now, a nice thorax should have been formed and the wings should be secured in a semi-spent attitude. (photo 27-7)

10. Complete the forebody, whip finish.

11. With your fingers, adjust the wing to whatever degree of spentness or semi-spentness you wish. Secure

27-1 Haystack: tie in the tail.

27-2 Bind down the butts, position thread as shown.

27-3 Tie in wing material with partial distribution wrap.

27-4 Wing in place, thread positioned for body.

27-5 Wrap body to base of wing.

27-6 Cross over, stand the wing up.

27-7 Create the thorax.

27-8 The completed fly, side view.

27-9 The completed fly, front view.

with a generous drop of cement at the wing base. The completed fly should resemble photographs 27-8 and 27-9.

HAYSTACK VARIATIONS

As Francis Betters states, the Haystack is an extremely versatile fly, and it is hence appropriate that the fly-dresser feel free to innovate. For example, the forward tilt of the wing may be varied or eliminated entirely. I am partial to it when dressing Haystacks as caddis imitations because it increases twitchability. A turned-up-eye hook might enchance this property further—the tier may wish to experiment.

The texture of the deer hair is important. Ideally, the hair should be fairly stiff and thick out towards the tips. Francis has always preferred Key deer from Florida, but they are an endangered species now, and the hides are no longer commercially available. As a substitute, choose hair which is fairly short and stout, such as that found around the face and head and on the shanks.

Do not hesitate to experiment with synthetic body materials. My favorite is Andra, a good floater which is easy to work with and comes in many interesting colors and blends. The tier can also blend his own right on the thread.

AUSABLE WULFF

Another pattern originated by Francis Betters is the Ausable Wulff. This is also a tremendously productive fly on rougher currents.

COMPONENTS
Hook: Standard dry fly, size 10 to 18
Thread: Fluorescent orange prewaxed
Tail: Barred hairs from the tail of an old woodchuck
Body: Rusty-orange Australian possum, or a blend of furs to get the color
Wings: White calf tail
Hackle: Brown and barred Rock mixed

The use of fluorescent orange thread is a Francis Betters peculiarity which is found in some of his other dressings, including certain members of the Haystack family. Francis likes to dub sparsely so that the thread shows through the body. He is not sure why this coloration enhances fish appeal, but years of experience indicate that is the case. This tracks with something I was once told by Ray Smith, a legendary figure in Catskill angling circles. Smitty enjoyed more success with an orangypinkish cast in his flies. He used to dress a pattern he called the Red Fox, which was similar to a Light Cahill, except that the hackle and tail were fiery ginger and the body was bright rusty fox fur.

28

The Beady-Eye

TECHNIQUES TO BE LEARNED

1. Split bead head
2. Reversed marabou technique

The final pattern is a unique fly type from the vise of my creative photographer, Matt Vinciguerra. Matty calls his creation the Beady-Eye, a descriptive title by any measure. The version described here is the freshwater Beady-Eye. This should not be confused with Matty's saltwater variety, for while the two are similar in overall appearance, the tying methodology differs in several important areas.

I confess that I have not personally fished the Beady-Eye, although I've been aware of its existence for seven or eight years. I recall that shortly after showing me the fly for the first time, Matty brought home a large, toothy brown trout which he took in a tributary of the Housatonic. While impressed, I was too busy exploring other ideas to give the beady a whirl. However, several other members of the group stream-tested the pattern extensively, and waxed enthusiastic over the results.

The Beady-Eye looks like a difficult fly to dress, but in fact, it is next to impossible to louse up a Beady-Eye, providing a little care is taken with a few critical steps. It may be dressed regular or in a style Matty calls "sidewinder," which he feels has better action in the water. We will go sidewinder for this exercise. This merely means that the head of the vise is rotated ninety degrees and the fly sits on the hook shank flat instead of upright. If you have a true rotating vise, where the cylinder remains horizontal no

matter what the angle of the jaws, the tying experience will be the same as with the conventional method. If not, the hook will tilt at an upward angle. Don't be disconcerted; this presents no problem, as the illustrations clearly show.

Here again, we have a fly which is not pattern-limited. In fact, it probably has more potential for innovation than any other fly type in the book. The tier can dress both imitators and attractors, varying the size, color, and materials. We will use the Blacknosed Dace coloration for the exercise because it is the basic Beady-Eye that Matty originated, and also because it is the most instructive of the series.

COMPONENTS

Hook: 6/0 or 8/0 streamer, straight-eyed, size 4–10 (use a 6 for this exercise)

Thread: Black 6/0 prewaxed for basic working thread, red for supplementary work

Tail: White marabou

Body: Silver tubular mylar, narrow type

Head: A split bead about ⅛ inch (3 mm) in diameter

Eye: Black enamel or permanent felt pen

Protective Coating: 5-minute epoxy cement

Throat: White marabou

Back: Tan marabou

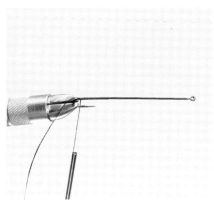

28-1 Beady-Eye: hook covered, supplemental thread in place.

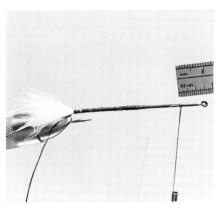

28-2 Tail and red thread in place.

28-3 Crimping on the bead.

28-4 Create bump behind bead.

28-5 Pass the thread through the split.

28-6 Create a bump ahead of the bead.

28-7 Tie off. Fly should now appear as shown.

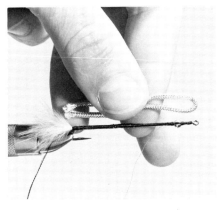

28-8 Double-length of tubular mylar.

28-9 Separate the strands

28-10   Pass opening over eye of hook.

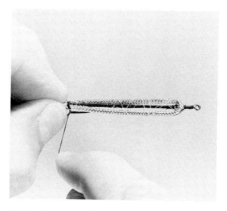

28-11   Secure with supplemental thread.

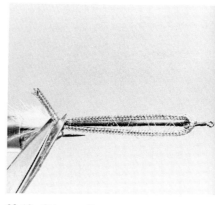

28-12   Trim neatly.

28-13   Tie on again at head.

28-14   Tie in white marabou for belly.

28-15   Proper amount of tan marabou.

28-16   Tie in tan marabou thus.

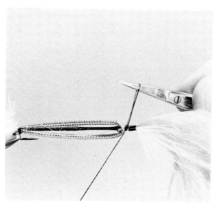

28-17   Tie off here with whip finish.

28-18   Secure tan marabou with red thread.

28-19 Secure white marabou, tie off.　　**28-20** Manicure head area for neatness.　　**28-21** The beady eye.

28-22 Apply epoxy.

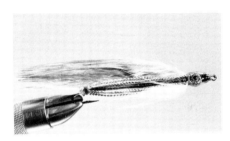

28-23 The completed fly.

TYING STEPS

1. Tie on ½ inch (13 mm) ahead of the bend, then cover hook back to the bend. Leave 10 inches (25 cm) of thread hanging loose for later use. (photo 28-1)

2. Tie in a 1-inch tail of white marabou, then bind down the excess with smooth wraps, working forward along the hook shank. Stop ¼ inch (6 mm) back from the eye.

3. Tie in an 8-inch (20 cm) piece of red thread. (photo 28-2)

4. Clamp on the split bead with the split facing you. The rear extremity of the bead should be flush to the front edge of the windings. *Important:* leave the bead open a crack so that the thread may be passed through the split. Refer to photograph 28-3.

5. Create a bump of thread behind the bead, then pass the thread through the split and create another bump in front. This locks the bead in position. Follow sequence in photographs 28-4, 28-5, and 28-6.

6. Wind forward to eye of hook and tie off. (photo 28-7)

7. Select a piece of narrow silver mylar tubing twice the length of the hook shank, plus a little extra for working space. (photo 28-8) Prepare the mylar by removing the core with tweezers. This is easy if you remember to hold the tubing by the front, so that the outer fibers don't close around the core like a Chinese finger trap.

8. Work a pointed object (fine scissors will do nicely) through the tubing at the center point, separating but not breaking the fibers. (photo 28-9)

9. Pass the opening thus created over the eye of the hook and down to the bead. (photo 28-10)

10. Pull the mylar loop tight from the rear. Wrap the red thread loosely around the tubing to get it out of the way. Then tie down the mylar tightly at the bend, executing

an extralarge-loop whip finish with the black thread retained from step 1. See photograph 28-11.

11. Trim off the excess mylar tight to the whip finish. (photo 28-12)

12. Tie on again just ahead of the bead. Turn the bead ninety degrees so that the mylar hides the split. You may wish to give the bead an additional squeeze with the pliers at this point, but be careful not to mash it or alter its shape. (photo 28-13)

13. Select a 1½-inch (38 mm) bunch of white marabou and tie it in with the tips pointing forward. Don't allow the butt ends to mess up or obscure the area around the bead. (photo 28-14)

14. Select a bunch of tan marabou 3–3½ inches (75–88 mm) long. (photo 28-15) The bunch should be full but not so bulky that it obscures the bead. Tie it in tips— forward, as with the white bunch, making sure to keep the two bunches separated. (photo 28-16) Moisten, if necessary.

15. Tie off with a whip finish and cement the windings. (photo 28-17)

16. Bring the tan marabou back over the top, taking care not to let it slip down over the bead. Secure with several turns of the red thread just behind the bead. (photo 28-18)

17. Bring the white marabou back beneath the bead, secure with red thread, and tie off. (photo 28-19)

18. Manicure the area around the bead, clearing out any excess material. Cement the red windings and also use a little cement to smooth down the marabou above and below the bead. At this point, the fly should appear as in photograph 28-20.

19. Create a distinct black pupil on each side of the bead using either an indelible felt-tip pen, or black enamel applied with a round tooth pick with the tip blunted. If a felt-tip pen is used, it must use a type of ink which will not be eradicated by the epoxy which will be applied subsequently. Let dry thoroughly. (photo 28-21)

20. Mix up a small batch of 5-minute epoxy and carefully coat the eye and head area, allowing the glue to saturate and fill in any small fissures. (photo 28-22) Coat the windings at the bend with epoxy also. The completed fly should resemble photograph 28-23.

I can envision a series of imitations of the common minnows and forage fish, and boxes of colorful attractors to entice less sophisticated quarry. I'm particularly interested in finding out how the Beady-Eye performs in other-than-trout-stream situations. I have a feeling it will be murder for pond brookies, bass, pickerel, Northern pike, and other game and pan-fish species. I have a vision of a large green, gold, and orange Beady undulating slowly over a Thousand Islands weed bed at gray dawn. A large Northern watches intently, its carnal instincts stimulated to the point of attack.

 # Thoughts on the Future of Fly-Tying

I feel that interest in fly-dressing is going to continue to grow, because it fills a human need for creativity and self-expression, yet is well within the innate capabilities of the average individual. Practically anyone who is motivated to devote a little time and energy to fly-dressing will know the gratification of rapid and dramatic progress. There are few pursuits indeed for which comparable claims can be made. And to top it all off, one can take his flies to the water and catch fish in the most exciting and pleasurable way man has yet devised.

Fly-dressing also satisfies another apparent human need, in that it provides an opportunity to learn about and relate to what has come before and then seek new directions. It is a good feeling to be able to dress the old patterns to perfection, and it prepares us for whatever creative challenges we wish to explore. Some of us are more adventuresome than others, and fly-dressing accommodates this; one can participate with whatever mixture of the traditional and advante garde one finds comfortable.

I see the avalanche of new fly-tying products subsiding in the future, in fact, there are signs this is already beginning to happen. In its place, I think we will see the continued refinement of various materials, tools and components, which will include the introduction of new technology *where it produces true value*. I expect the sort of proliferation we've experienced in recent years to subside somewhat, as the boomer growth market evolves into a quality growth market. Products will cost more, but value will be enhanced. The HMH vise and the premium-quality capes produced by Buck Metz, Bill Tobin, Henry Hoffman and others indicate this is already under way.

Two areas in which I expect marked advancement are synthetic materials and hooks for fly-tying. Certainly, technology can help us here, particularly in the replacement of materials which have disappeared from the market. For example, the imitation jungle cock eyes we worked with in the Hornberg chapter are good, but could be improved considerably, and I believe they will be. As to hooks, I am sure that advancements in metallurgy and the advent of computer controlled mass production will result in a line of products which will out-do even the old Ray Bergmans I covet so tenaciously.

Some traditional materials will, I think, be with us for many years to come. This should particularly apply to domestic animals which are used primarily for food production, with fly-dressing materials a byproduct. Chicken feathers, calf tails, duck and goose feathers, guinea hen plumage, and feathers from certain varieties of pheasant and turkey come readily to mind. Other commonly used materials which are a byproduct of hunting will probably be around for yet awhile, but I have a feeling that as personal and societal attitudes towards blood sports change, we will have to do without our deer, antelope, fox, moose, caribou, and bear hair, as well as the plumage of wild fowl.

Another critical factor which, in my opinion, will be of increasing importance is the position of the fly-dressing fraternity as regards the natural world and its denizens. We have become a major force in the environmental con-

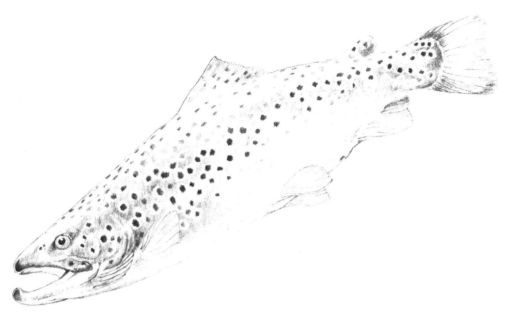

Brown Trout

servation movement, but we may eventually have to deal with the proposition that saving fish while killing, or supporting the killing of certain animals for the making of toys with which to play with these fish is rather contradictory. I am aware of the many points of view on this sensitive issue, nearly all of which have some degree of substantive rationale. It is a biological fact that many species of animals now suffer from the absence of natural predators, and need thinning out. There seems to be great controversy over man as a predator, perhaps because he shoots his prey rather than biting or clawing it to death. Also—and this tends to refute the population control argument advanced by the hunting contingent—man tries to knock off the strongest animals, rather than the weakest, as they look better on the wall.

Finally, my thoughts center on the potential fly-dressing offers for the enhancement of the quality of life. I *know* it has enormous therapeutic value. I have taught fly-dressing to several emotionally disturbed persons as part of a special program. None of them were fishermen, yet they all enjoyed learning to tie, and according to the therapist, bene-

fitted from the experience. And I can attest that a session at the vise usually calms my mind when the stresses of cultural shock become particularly intense. After World War II, the great Bill Blades taught fly-dressing at veterans hospitals to people with various levels of impairment. While the results of Bill's work were not very well-documented, I am told the program was highly successful and extremely popular. It is often possible for persons with serious disabilities to develop fly-dressing skills. I knew a man whose entire right side was totally paralyzed. He managed to tie excellent flies with his one good hand and some self-made tools he held in his mouth. I always tell this story to anglers I meet who don't think they could learn to tie.

For some time, I have been harboring a thought, and it's in my mind more frequently all the time: could a blind person be taught to tie flies? I have a feeling it can be done. Great patience and dedication would be required on the part of both teacher and student, but what a triumph if the project were successful! In this world, anything is possible, and I'd love to see it happen.

A MEETING ON THE BATTENKILL

A man met a man, and they talked:
Talked as men do who see and hear and feel
—as they walk.
            (and the Stream was there)
    Hours passed, from last light til the
sudden hush of moon revealed night,
and not all the moments were wordfilled,
but the talk was uninterrupted.
                (the Stream was there)
    No gamut was run of current things,
no feints were tried, no probes were thrust,
accord in all thoughts was no goal, neither's
ego was on trial.
                (the Stream was there)
    The day, the night, the ancient dam,
all drew comment, till the hour grew late;
    But it was the Stream and the men
that made a communicating triumverate.
        (—the Stream had always talked)
    —No need to say the Stream had trout,
or that talk started and ended with methods,
takes, and results of the Quest.
        —They were fly fishermen—did you
expect them home early?
Naturally not, and now, just as
inevitably—they are friends.
            (two more for the Stream)

DUDLEY SOPER

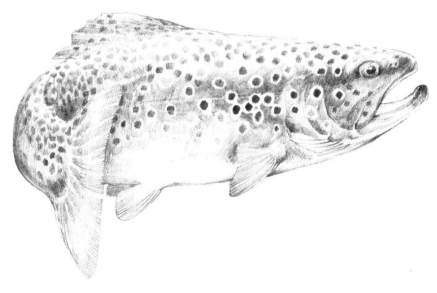

Brown Trout

Bibliography

Almy, Gerald. *Tying and Fishing Terrestrials*. Harrisburg, PA: Stackpole, 1978.

Bates, Joseph D. *Streamer Fly-Tying and Fishing*. Harrisburg, PA: Stackpole, 1966.

Bay, Kenneth E. and Vinciguerra, Matthew M. *How to Tie Freshwater Flies*. New York: Winchester Press, 1974.

Borger, Gary A. *Nymphing: A Basic Book*. Harrisburg, PA: Stackpole, 1979.

Boyle, Robert H. and Whitlock, Dave. *The Second Fly-Tyer's Almanac*. Philadelphia: Lippincott, 1978.

Caucci, Al and Natasi, Bob. *Hatches*. Comparahatch, Ltd., 1975.

Dubois, Donald, *The Fisherman's Handbook of Trout Flies*. Cranbury, NJ: A.S. Barnes, 1960.

Flick, Art. *Master Fly-Tying Guide*. New York: Crown, 1972.

———. *New Streamside Guide to Naturals and Their Imitations*. New York: Crown, 1969.

Fulsher, Keith. *Tying and Fishing the Thunder Creek Series*. Rockville Center, NY: Freshet, 1973.

Gordon, Sid. *How to Fish from Top to Bottom*. Harrisburg, PA: Stackpole, 1978.

Hellekson, Terry. *Popular Fly Patterns*. Layton, UT: Peregrine Smith, Ltd., 1976.

Jorgensen, Poul. *Dressing Flies for Fresh and Salt Water*. New York: Hawthorne, 1978.

———. *Salmon Flies: Their Character, Style and Dressing*. Harrisburg, PA: Stackpole, 1978.

Kaufmann, Randall. *American Nymph Fly-Tying Manual*. Portland, OR: Salmon-Trout-Steelheader, 1975.

Leisenring, James E. and Hidy, Vernon S. *The Art of Tying the Wet Fly and Fishing the Flymph*. New York: Crown, 1971.

Leiser, Eric. *Fly-Tying Materials: Their Procurement, Use and Protection*. New York: Crown, 1971.

Marinaro, Vincent C. *A Modern Dry Fly Code*. New York: Crown, 1970.

———. *In the Ring of the Rise*. New York: Crown, 1976.

Nemes, Sylvester. *The Soft-Hackled Fly*. Old Greenwich, CT: Chatham Press, 1975.

Pryce-Tannatt, T.E. *How to Dress Salmon Flies*. London: A.&C. Black, 1977.

Rosborough, E.H. "Polly." *Tying and Fishing the Fuzzy Nymphs*. Harrisburg, PA: Stackpole, 1978.

Schwiebert, Earnest. *Nymphs*. New York: Winchester Press, 1973.

———. *Trout*. New York: Dutton, 1979.

Solomon, Larry and Leiser, Eric. *The Caddis and the Angler*. Harrisburg, PA: Stackpole, 1977.

Surette, Dick. *Trout and Salmon Fly Index*. Harrisburg, PA: Stackpole, 1978.

Swisher, Doug and Richards, Carl. *Selective Trout*. New York: Crown, 1971.

Talleur, Richard W. *Fly Fishing for Trout: A Guide for Adult Beginners*. New York: Winchester Press, 1974.

INDEX

RICHARD W. TALLEUR is a technical systems analyst for AT&T and it is this professional background together with a natural love of fly-fishing and fly-tying which forms the foundation of *Mastering the Art of Fly-Tying*. He is the author of one previous book, *Fly Fishing: A Guide for the Adult Beginner,* and teaches fly-tying classes near his home in upstate New York as part of his active association with the local Trout Unlimited and other angling groups in the East.